Flowering Bulbs For Dummies®

by Judy Glattstein and the Editors of the National Gardening Association

Quick Reference Card

W9-AVN-813

Check Out Your Growth Zone

The U.S. Department of Agriculture has helpfully divided North America into plant hardiness zones based on average annual minimum temperatures. Planting instructions regarding depth and timing may change depending on what zone you're in. We refer to these hardiness zones throughout this book. You can find a map of these zones in *Gardening For Dummies*.

Zone	Minimum Temperature		Average fall-planting time for bulbs
	Fahrenheit	Celsius	
Zone 1	Below – 50°F	Below –46°C	by early September
Zone 2	– 50°F to –40°F	–46°C to –40°C	by early September
Zone 3	– 40°F to –30°F	–40°C to –34°F	by September
Zone 4	– 30°F to –20°F	–34°C to –29°C	by late September to early October
Zone 5	– 20°F to –10°F	–29°C to –23°C	by late September to early October
Zone 6	– 10°F to 0°F	–23°C to –18°C	by mid-October
Zone 7	0°F to 10°F	–18°C to –12°C	by early November
Zone 8	10°F	–12°C to –7°C	by early November
Zone 9	20°F	–7°C to –1°C	by early December (some chilling required)
Zone 10	30°F	–1°C to 4°C	by mid-December (some chilling required)
Zone 11	40°F	4°C and up	by late December (some chilling required)

Tips for Planting Spring-Flowering Bulbs

- Plant bulbs in groups. A cluster of flowers is more striking than a lone bloomer.

- Space large bulbs (2 inches or more) 3 to 10 inches apart; small bulbs 1 to 2 inches apart.

- Generally, plant large bulbs 8 inches deep; smaller bulbs, 5 inches deep; tiny bulbs like crocuses or snowdrops, 2 or 3 inches deep. The smaller the bulb, the closer to the surface you plant it.

- Cover the bulbs with soil and water generously. Mulch, while not required, is good for preserving soil moisture. Add 2 to 3 inches just before the ground freezes.

...For Dummies: Bestselling Book Series for Beginners

BUSINESS AND GENERAL REFERENCE BOOK SERIES FROM IDG

Flowering Bulbs For Dummies®

by Judy Glattstein and the Editors of the National Gardening Association

Approximate Guide to Bulb Flowering Times (Zones 5 and 6)

Early March	crocus, snowdrop, eranthis, *Iris reticulata*
mid-March to mid-April	glory of the snow, early daffodils, striped squill
April	early and species tulips, grape hyacinth, squill, hyacinths, *Fritillaria imperialis*, scilla
April to May	later daffodils, guinea hen flowers, later tulips
May	Dutch iris, spring snowflake, camassia, Darwin tulips, parrot tulips,
Early-to-late summer	caladium, oxalis, tuberous begonia
Early to midsummer	lily
Midsummer	gladiolus
Mid-to-late summer	canna, crocosmia, dahlia, tuberose
Fall	colchicum, crocus, cyclamen

These flowering times are approximate; add two weeks in Zone 4 and four weeks in Zone 3. In warmer zones, subtract two to four weeks.

How Many Bulbs to Plant

In general, you want to plant bulbs in groups, rather than singly.

Type of Bulb	Number per Square Foot (9.3 square centimeters)
Tulips	8–12
Hyacinths	5–7
Daffodils	5–7
Crocuses, miniature daffodils/tulips	10–15
Lilies	3–5
Caladiums	1–3
Canna	1
Crocosmias	3
Dahlia	1
Gladiolas	3–7

...For Dummies: Bestselling Book Series for Beginners

Praise for *Houseplants For Dummies*

"Indoor gardening, quite an intimidating prospect for the brown-thumbed novice, comes alive under the user-friendly guidance of *Houseplants For Dummies*. Larry Hodgson has succeeded in making interior plantscaping accessible for both the novice and the seasoned professional."

> Matthew Gardner
> President, California Interior Plantscape
> Association

Praise for *Lawn Care For Dummies*

"This book fulfills a real need for the do-it-yourselfer by providing the how-to's of lawn care in an easy-to-understand format. Unlike many other books, *Lawn Care For Dummies* covers the basics of grass establishment, growth, and care in an enjoyable, nontechnical fashion. I would recommend this book to anyone starting a new lawn or who is intending to improve an existing one."

> Kevin N. Morris
> Director, National Turfgrass Evaluation Program

"Sure to become many a homeowner's dog-eared favorite, *Lawn Care For Dummies* answers the common and not-so-common questions we all have from time to time about caring for grass. With its friend-talking-to-a-friend style of writing, the advice is easy to understand and put to use. If you don't have about 20 years to spend on lawn care guesswork or trials and errors, this is one book you should have, keep handy, and use often."

> Doug Fender
> Executive Director, Turf Resource Center, Rolling
> Meadows, IL

Praise For Container Gardening For Dummies

"If you're tired of the same old pot of red geraniums, be sure to check out *Container Gardening For Dummies*. This book is packed with planting and design ideas that will transform even the humblest of pots into a flower festival. Bill Marken's clear, concise, step-by-step instructions are worth the price of admission."

Doug Jimenson
Editor-in-Chief, *Garden Escape* www.garden.com

"Who better than to turn to for everything you need to know about container culture than a guy who has 'been there, done that' for a careerful of years? You meet that person in Bill Marken. Bill enjoys a remarkable ease of communication, which makes absorbing detailed information on his subject easy and as pleasant as chatting with a neighbor."

Joseph F. Williamson,
former Garden Editor and Managing Editor of
Sunset magazine

Praise For Gardening For Dummies

"This book has much to recommend it...a simple, well-laid-out introduction to basic gardening..."
Library Journal

"The beauty of *Gardening For Dummies*...is its clear, jargon-free text. This should be a great relief for you if you're truly interested in learning about the subject, but afraid to spend big bucks on a serious gardening book that will only amaze and confuse you."
Country Decorator magazine

FLOWERING BULBS FOR DUMMIES®

by Judy Glattstein
and the Editors of the
National Gardening Association

IDG Books Worldwide, Inc.
An International Data Group Company

Foster City, CA ♦ Chicago, IL ♦ Indianapolis, IN ♦ New York, NY

Flowering Bulbs For Dummies®

Published by
IDG Books Worldwide, Inc.
An International Data Group Company
919 E. Hillsdale Blvd.
Suite 400
Foster City, CA 94404
www.idgbooks.com (IDG Books Worldwide Web site)
www.dummies.com (Dummies Press Web site)

Library of Congress Catalog Card No.: 98-86176

ISBN: 0-7645-5103-5

Printed in the United States of America

10 9 8 7 6 5 4 3 2 1

1E/QV/QY/ZY/IN

Distributed in the United States by IDG Books Worldwide, Inc.

Distributed by Macmillan Canada for Canada; by Transworld Publishers Limited in the United Kingdom; by IDG Norge Books for Norway; by IDG Sweden Books for Sweden; by Woodslane Pty. Ltd. for Australia; by Woodslane (NZ) Ltd. for New Zealand; by Addison Wesley Longman Singapore Pte Ltd. for Singapore, Malaysia, Thailand, Indonesia and Korea; by Norma Comunicaciones S.A. for Colombia; by Intersoft for South Africa; by International Thomson Publishing for Germany, Austria and Switzerland; by Toppan Company Ltd. for Japan; by Distribuidora Cuspide for Argentina; by Livraria Cultura for Brazil; by Ediciencia S.A. for Ecuador; by Ediciones ZETA S.C.R. Ltda. for Peru; by WS Computer Publishing Corporation, Inc., for the Philippines; by Unalis Corporation for Taiwan; by Contemporanea de Ediciones for Venezuela; by Computer Book & Magazine Store for Puerto Rico; by Express Computer Distributors for the Caribbean and West Indies. Authorized Sales Agent: Anthony Rudkin Associates for the Middle East and North Africa.

For general information on IDG Books Worldwide's books in the U.S., please call our Consumer Customer Service department at 800-762-2974. For reseller information, including discounts and premium sales, please call our Reseller Customer Service department at 800-434-3422.

For information on where to purchase IDG Books Worldwide's books outside the U.S., please contact our International Sales department at 650-655-3200 or fax 650-655-3297.

For information on foreign language translations, please contact our Foreign & Subsidiary Rights department at 650-655-3021 or fax 650-655-3281.

For sales inquiries and special prices for bulk quantities, please contact our Sales department at 650-655-3200 or write to the address above.

For information on using IDG Books Worldwide's books in the classroom or for ordering examination copies, please contact our Educational Sales department at 800-434-2086 or fax 317-596-5499.

For press review copies, author interviews, or other publicity information, please contact our Public Relations department at 650-655-3000 or fax 650-655-3299.

For authorization to photocopy items for corporate, personal, or educational use, please contact Copyright Clearance Center, 222 Rosewood Drive, Danvers, MA 01923, or fax 978-750-4470.

About the Authors

Judy Glattstein is a garden consultant, an instructor of a required course in bulb identification for School of Professional Horticulture Students at the New York Botanical Gardens, a leader of tours and a horticultural expert for tours to Holland. The author of *Garden Design with Foliage, Waterscaping,* and *The American Gardener's World of Bulbs,* she lectures extensively across the United States and abroad, and has twice spoken for the Royal Horticultural Society at their Great Autumn Show in London. Ms. Glattstein lives in Frenchtown, New Jersey.

The **National Gardening Association** is the largest member-based, nonprofit organization of home gardeners in the United States. Founded in 1972 (as "Gardens for All") to spearhead the community garden movement, today's National Gardening Association is best known for its bimonthly publication, *National Gardening* magazine ($18 per year). Reporting on all aspects of home gardening, each issue is read by some half-million gardeners worldwide. These publishing activities are supplemented by online efforts, such as those on their World Wide Web site (www.garden.org) and on America Online (at keyword HouseNet). Other NGA activities include:

- ✔ **Growing Science Inquiry and GrowLab** (funded in part by the National Science Foundation) provides science-based curricula for students in kindergarten through Grade 8.
- ✔ 1972, the *National Gardening Survey* (conducted by the Gallup Company) collects the most detailed research about gardeners and gardening in North America.
- ✔ **Youth Garden Grants.** Every year the NGA awards grants, each of which includes more than $500 worth of gardening tools and seeds, to schools, youth groups, and community organizations.

For more information about the National Gardening Association, write to 180 Flynn Ave., Butlington, VT 05401 USA.

ABOUT IDG BOOKS WORLDWIDE

Welcome to the world of IDG Books Worldwide.

IDG Books Worldwide, Inc., is a subsidiary of International Data Group, the world's largest publisher of computer-related information and the leading global provider of information services on information technology. IDG was founded more than 25 years ago and now employs more than 8,500 people worldwide. IDG publishes more than 275 computer publications in over 75 countries (see listing below). More than 90 million people read one or more IDG publications each month.

Launched in 1990, IDG Books Worldwide is today the #1 publisher of best-selling computer books in the United States. We are proud to have received eight awards from the Computer Press Association in recognition of editorial excellence and three from *Computer Currents'* First Annual Readers' Choice Awards. Our best-selling *...For Dummies®* series has more than 50 million copies in print with translations in 38 languages. IDG Books Worldwide, through a joint venture with IDG's Hi-Tech Beijing, became the first U.S. publisher to publish a computer book in the People's Republic of China. In record time, IDG Books Worldwide has become the first choice for millions of readers around the world who want to learn how to better manage their businesses.

Our mission is simple: Every one of our books is designed to bring extra value and skill-building instructions to the reader. Our books are written by experts who understand and care about our readers. The knowledge base of our editorial staff comes from years of experience in publishing, education, and journalism — experience we use to produce books for the '90s. In short, we care about books, so we attract the best people. We devote special attention to details such as audience, interior design, use of icons, and illustrations. And because we use an efficient process of authoring, editing, and desktop publishing our books electronically, we can spend more time ensuring superior content and spend less time on the technicalities of making books.

You can count on our commitment to deliver high-quality books at competitive prices on topics you want to read about. At IDG Books Worldwide, we continue in the IDG tradition of delivering quality for more than 25 years. You'll find no better book on a subject than one from IDG Books Worldwide.

John Kilcullen
John Kilcullen
CEO
IDG Books Worldwide, Inc.

Steven Berkowitz
Steven Berkowitz
President and Publisher
IDG Books Worldwide, Inc.

WINNER

*Eighth Annual
Computer Press
Awards ≥1992*

WINNER

*Ninth Annual
Computer Press
Awards ≥1993*

*Tenth Annual
Computer Press
Awards ≥1994*

WINNER

WINNER

WINNER

*Eleventh Annual
Computer Press
Awards ≥1995*

Dedication

From Judy Glattstein: To my husband Paul who believes any day spent gardening is not a good day, but wholeheartedly encourages my belief in the exact opposite, and to all gardeners everywhere who share my belief, this book is respectfully dedicated.

Authors' Acknowledgments

From Judy Glattstein: Demented squirrels preparing for winter have nothing on gardeners planting bulbs in autumn. To all the students over the years who've taken my Bulb I.D. course at the New York Botanical Garden — thanks for your questions that keep me mindful of the down-to-earth basics. To Sally Ferguson and Judy Sloat at the Netherlands Flower Bulb Information Center — thanks for your assistance with sources and answers. To Leo Van Tol of Van Eeden Brothers — thanks for the thousands of bulbs I've bought that now bloom at BelleWood.

From the NGA: NGA thanks most of all author Judy Glattstein who brought prodigious knowledge and spirit to this project. Likewise, we thank Contributing Writer, Peggy Henry. At IDG Books, Chicago, we thank Sarah Kennedy, former Executive Editor, Holly McGuire, Acquisitions Editor, and Kathy Welton, Publisher, for their vision, energy, and support of these books. Also in Chicago, thanks to Maureen Kelly, Jonathan Malysiak, and Ann Miller. Project Editor Kathy Cox deserves major kudos for keeping the book organized and on track. Copy editors Kim Darosett and Diane Smith did a masterful job copy editing the book, and technical reviewer Dr. August De Hertogh was, as always, thorough and insightful. Thanks also are due to the NGA crew: Bill Marken, NGA's *...For Dummies* Series Editor; Charlie Nardozzi, Senior Horticulturist, Shila Patel, Assistant Editor, and Michael MacCaskey, Editor-in-Chief. We also thank David Els, NGA's President, and Larry Sommers, Associate Publisher.

Publisher's Acknowledgments

We're proud of this book; please register your comments through our IDG Books Worldwide Online Registration Form located at http://my2cents.dummies.com.

Some of the people who helped bring this book to market include the following:

Acquisitions, Editorial, and Media Development

Project Editor: Kathleen M. Cox

Acquisitions Editor: Holly McGuire

Copy Editors: Susan Diane Smith, Kim Darosett, Wendy Hatch

Technical Editors: Dr. August A. De Hertogh, Professor of Horticultural Science, North Carolina State University

Editorial Manager: Colleen Rainsberger

Media Development Manager: Heather Heath Dismore

Editorial Assistants: Maureen Kelly, Paul Kuzmic

Production

Project Coordinator: E. Shawn Aylsworth

Associate Project Coordinator: Tom Missler

Layout and Graphics: Lou Boudreau, Linda M. Boyer, J. Tyler Connor, Maridee V. Ennis, Angela F. Hunckler, Jane E. Martin, Drew R. Moore, Anna Rohrer, Brent Savage, Janet Seib, Kate Snell

Color Art: John Glover, England, supplemented by the Netherlands Bulb Association

Illustrations: Katherine Hanley

Proofreaders: Christine Berman, Michelle Croninger, Betty Kish, Nancy Price, Nancy Reinhardt, Rebecca Senninger, Janet M. Withers

Indexer: Ann Norcross

General and Administrative

IDG Books Worldwide, Inc.: John Kilcullen, CEO; Steven Berkowitz, President and Publisher

IDG Books Technology Publishing: Brenda McLaughlin, Senior Vice President and Group Publisher

Dummies Technology Press and Dummies Editorial: Diane Graves Steele, Vice President and Associate Publisher; Mary Bednarek, Director of Acquisitions and Product Development; Kristin A. Cocks, Editorial Director

Dummies Trade Press: Kathleen A. Welton, Vice President and Publisher; Kevin Thornton, Acquisitions Manager

IDG Books Production for Dummies Press: Michael R. Britton, Vice President of Production and Creative Services; Beth Jenkins Roberts, Production Director; Cindy L. Phipps, Manager of Project Coordination, Production Proofreading, and Indexing; Kathie S. Schutte, Supervisor of Page Layout; Shelley Lea, Supervisor of Graphics and Design; Debbie J. Gates, Production Systems Specialist; Robert Springer, Supervisor of Proofreading; Debbie Stailey, Special Projects Coordinator; Tony Augsburger, Supervisor of Reprints and Bluelines

Dummies Packaging and Book Design: Robin Seaman, Creative Director; Jocelyn Kelaita, Product Packaging Coordinator; Kavish + Kavish, Cover Design

◆

The publisher would like to give special thanks to Patrick J. McGovern, without whom this book would not have been possible.

◆

Contents at a Glance

Cartoons at a Glance

By Rich Tennant

"The next time you order flowering bulbs, I suggest you have them express mailed."

page 301

"Aside from a little beginner's confusion, I've done very well with my bulbs."

page 261

Talk about adding insult to injury—they planted lilies around me.

page 39

If it's all the same to you, I'd just as soon you'd hand me my bulbs for planting.

page 231

"Use less powder. You're planting them too deep."

page 7

"That's the last time I buy a flowering bulb from a circus clown."

page 195

page 129

Fax: 978-546-7747 • E-mail: the5wave@tiac.net

Table of Contents

Introduction

· ·

*E*veryone has had some experiences of the bulb kind. We hope that yours was positive. Perhaps years ago you bought some daffodils at the checkout counter, stuck them in the ground, and they've been flowering every spring since then. You're wondering if any other bulbs are as obliging.

Your bulb experiences may have been neutral. Perhaps you planted a tired pot of leftover Easter lilies in the garden, relieved that someone else had figured out which end was up.

Bulbs can be downright discouraging. Maybe you planted tulips and wondered why they weren't as good after the first year. Or you garden where the weather's warm in winter, and you have discovered that tulips and daffodils don't perform as expected.

This book's for all of you, and for every gardener and gardener-wannabe who's bemused by the magician's act of sticking those lumpy brown things in the ground and having them come up as flowers.

Everybody, gardener or not, knows about bulbs. Maybe you buy a bunch of daffodils to celebrate spring, or a pot of hyacinths for Easter. If you live where winter is one of the four seasons, you may see other houses in your neighborhood with gardens filled with crocuses in spring and lilies in summer. Perhaps you've wondered, "Could I do that?" The answer is "You bet you can!"

Or you've tried and failed to grow tulips in sunny, mild, dry California, but at the end of summer your neighbor manages to produce big pink lilies she calls "naked ladies." Your neighbor's success isn't due to some magical secret, it's just knowing which bulbs grow where and how to make them feel at home. Bulbs are beautiful growing in your garden, good for cut flowers, and useful in containers. Isn't it time you started right with bulbs?

Bulbs are easy to grow, if you plant the right kind in the right place at the right time. For many varieties, it doesn't even matter if you plant them right side up — the bulbs have that part figured out just fine! (And if you've gardened at all, you know that perennials would never accept being planted upside down.)

The spring blooming bulbs are like good house guests — they arrive in a timely manner, entertain you in the garden, and then depart as scheduled, returning the following year to do it all over again. You can find bulbs for sun or shade; spring, summer, or autumn interest; mild winter and warm summer or cold winter and moderate summer regions; and bulbs to plant in your garden, display in containers indoors or out, or for cut-flower use. Your residence doesn't matter. Whether you have an apartment with or without a balcony, a town house with a tiny patio to call your own, a city house with a handkerchief scrap of lawn and a flower bed, a suburban acre, or rural real estate with extensive grounds, bulbs are the happiest kind of plants.

About This Book

We've been gardening for a long time, as well as writing and lecturing about gardening, and designing gardens for others. We can't come to your house, but you can use this book in our place. Check up on bulbs before you buy or plant them — familiar or unfamiliar. Read the tips, techniques, and suggested plant combinations. Find out which bulbs grow well in your local climate.

It's easy to see that we really like bulbs. For the most part, they are very easy to grow. And they're beautiful. After all, that's what gardening is really about. We want flowers that look good as well as give us a feeling of satisfaction and achievement. Bulbs do that and more. Bulbs are fun. They're easy to plant, easy to grow, and rewarding. What more could a gardener ask for?

This book takes you down the garden path and gets you started gardening with bulbs. More than that, it will help you maintain the bulbs you plant, suggesting ways to keep them blooming beautifully year after year (and explaining why it's not your fault when some don't). Remember that every garden is different from the next, and so is each growing season. Work with what you have, and remember that there's always next year.

How to Use This Book

This book is practical and factual; it isn't fictional like a novel, which means that you don't need to read it from cover to cover. It provides lots of information about lots of bulbs, some background facts on growing bulbs (general information on planting, fertilization, and after-care), and some tidbits to liven things up. Use the Table of Contents or the Index to find information about some bulbs you bought on the spur of the moment and don't quite know what to do with, or bulbs you are seeking to fill a particular need.

How This Book Is Organized

We've arranged this book in several parts to make finding the information you need easier, even if you aren't sure just what you need to know. The parts are divided into chapters so that all the text doesn't run together in one large, incomprehensible, scary lump. Remember, the Table of Contents and the Index can help you get to where you need to be in the book, and headings within each chapter get you to the precise information.

Part I: Bulbs 101

This part has an overview and general information about bulbs. One chapter explains how easy and elegant they are, another suggests ways bulbs can be useful in your garden, and a third advises about selecting particular bulbs — which ones are good for which purpose.

Part II: Bulbs That Flower into Spring

In this part, you can find specific chapters about particular bulbs that flower in the spring. Some are familiar major league players: daffodils, tulips, and hyacinths, each with a chapter of its own. But wait, there's more: minor league team players with major impact, including little ones, blue ones, unusual ones, and bulbs to enchant you and enhance your garden.

Part III: Bulbs That Flower in Summer and Fall

Spring flowering bulbs aren't the only bulbs available; this part describes other bulbs, summer league players that keep the game going by flowering in summer. We include a chapter on lilies. Lilies, sure, you're familiar with lilies even if you've never grown them. Now you can, and they're easy. But how about ornamental onions — ever heard of them, or thought about growing them even if you are familiar with them? You should! And this part offers a chapter about tender bulbs for summer interest — snowbirds who don't like it cold even when they're hibernating — cannas, dahlias, glads, and more.

That's right, bulbs don't quit. Summer is over, but some bulbs push the envelope and keep flowering until the snow flies. We provide a chapter about southerners, bulbs from South America and South Africa. Another chapter deals with cold-hardy bulbs that bloom in September, October, and even November.

Part IV: Special Bulbs for Special Places

Here's where we put kitchen bulbs (mostly because we couldn't figure out a better place!), the lumpy things so vital to cooking: potatoes (sweet and white), onions, garlic, and shallots.

As a bonus, we even provide a chapter on growing bulbs in containers. Put those pots, flower boxes, and half-barrels to good use.

Part V: Getting Down to the Nitty-Gritty

Here's where we get down to the dirt. We provide information on buying bulbs: what to look for and where to buy them. We explain how to care for bulbs after you've bought them and before you plant. We tell you how to get them into the ground and what to do after that — both before they pop up and after they've flowered but haven't gone underground again. Even though, on the whole, bulbs are the least-troubled category of plants, we share some information on pests and diseases.

Part VI: The Part of Tens

In this part, you can find some bulbs grouped by a common characteristic, such as bulbs particularly useful for coaxing into early bloom so that you can have spring flowers indoors while winter rages outdoors. And we discuss antique bulbs that have been in cultivation for decades and, in some cases, quite literally for centuries. We offer a chapter on bulbs to grow for cut-flower use, so that your house can be decorated indoors as well as out with a lavish show of flowers.

Part VII: Appendixes

These days, more and more sources for bulbs are accessible. But the ones close to home usually have a limited selection available. We've prepared an extensive list of mail-order sources, not only for general bulbs, but also specialty growers with a wide assortment of lilies, dahlias, glads, and so on.

What's In a Name?

Like every living thing, bulbs have names and family histories that help you find the right plant for you. A tulip is not just a tulip. To get just the right tulip, you've got to get gossipy — checking out its family background and method of birth, which is all in the name.

Following naming conventions common in gardening, when we give a plant's common name, such as tulip, we list it in normal type with no capitalization. On those occasions where we need to mention its extended family, we use its Latin name, *Liliaceae,* and italicize. Members of the *Liliacea* family are more normally referred to by their genus name, such as *Tulipa* for tulips (or *Galanthus* for snowdrops). Genus and species names genus and species names are both italicized, but genus names begin with capital letters and species names do not — *Tulipa kaufmanniana* is a species name. (You may often see the genus name abbreviated, as in *T. kaufmanniana.*)

Finally, we have the cultivar name — the plant-equivalent of your first name. Cultivar names are surrounded by single quotation marks, as in *T. kaufmanniana* 'Stresa.' Sometimes, a name commonly used to represent a cultivar is inaccurate. In this case, you may see double quotation marks around the name.

The individual plants of a species may vary, just as people do. For example, *Fritillaria meleagris,* commonly called the guinea hen flower, can have nicely checkerboard-marked dark purple flowers or white flowers. These variations will appear when you plant the species — you won't know until the flowers grow. If, however, you plant the *Fritillaria meleagris* cultivar 'Alba,' every last one will have white flowers.

Cultivars are plants that are bred in the garden. In order to remain *true* (a term used by botanists and taxonomists) to the cultivar first given that particular name, plants must, in effect, be cloned. When you choose to plant bulbs of a single cultivar, you ensure that every flower that grows from those bulbs will look the same.

Don't be surprised to find regional variations to the common names in this book. Even the "official" names may change as botanists and taxonomists (naming specialists) debate each plant's true place in the world. Our *dog-tooth* violet may be your *dog's tooth* violet. That's why the species and genus names are important to know. You can find glory of the snow as *Chionodoxa* throughout the world.

Icons Used in This Book

We've added helpful little symbols called icons to highlight key bits of information that will make your bulb gardening even easier and less stressful. When you see the following icons beside a paragraph, here's what you can expect to find:

Keep your garden looking fresh by mixing your flowering bulbs with perennials that cover dying foliage as well as offer beautiful shape and color contrast. This icon points out plants that make good company for the bulbs you choose.

Sometimes it helps to speak the language. This icon points out terms you should know, if only to be clear about what you want at the local nursery.

How does your garden grow better? This icon highlights tips that expert gardeners have discovered. This information may save you some trial and error.

This icon highlights the stuff that's too important but all too easy to forget.

If you want a garden but your location lacks lots of sun, the bulbs flagged with this icon will really shine.

Sometimes you want to know why and how something happens. This icon highlights information you don't need to know but may want to know to enrich your gardening know-how.

This icon highlights information about potential dangers to you or your plants.

Where to Go from Here

Clearly, we think that you need to get out there in the garden and start digging, burying bulbs like a squirrel at the onset of winter. That intent is pretty clear all through this book. Whether you are one of those people who hop and skip through the text, or an orderly soul who begins at the beginning and straightforwardly continues through to the end, you'll get the idea. We hope that this book makes it easy for you to have a great time in the garden, beautifying your landscape with bulbs.

Part I
Bulbs 101

"Use less powder. You're planting them too deep."

In this part . . .

Hold up your right hand and take a close look at it. If you don't see a green thumb, don't worry! In this part, we give you all the basic information about bulbs.

You may not even know what a bulb really is. No problem, we explain what bulbs are and how they grow.

Then we help you plan your bulb garden. Don't fret if you don't have a garden; we also discuss growing bulbs in beds, borders, and containers (even inside the house).

Tulips, daffodils, hyacinths, or lilies? Grecian windflowers or Persian violets? Are you overwhelmed by the choices? We tell you how to choose bulbs that will grow in your location and suit your fancy.

Chapter 1

The Ease and Elegance of Bulbs

*B*ulbs are an easy gardening choice. Their flowers are beautiful, and you don't need special qualifications to grow them. Just think about it — bulbs are nice lumpy things that are easier to handle than tiny seeds. Because they're dormant (a fancy way of saying "sleeping") when you plant them, most tolerate small delays better than the actively growing perennials that have roots and leaves to maintain. And because bulbs come from many different places in the world, all gardeners, regardless of location, can find suitable bulbs. Bulbs grow in sunny or shady places; in average, moist, or dry sites; in regions with cold or mild winters; and in areas with arid or humid, rainy summers. And you can find bulbs for all seasons, summer, fall, and winter as well as spring.

Bulbs: Plants in a Package

By now you may be asking, "Just what are bulbs?" If you've ever grown a marigold, a tomato, or a houseplant, you know that these plants have stringy fibrous roots underground. The plants that grow from bulbs are different. These plants have lumpy underground things (see Figure 1-1). The bulb portion that lies underground is a plant in a package, protecting against difficult conditions of cold or drought, and using reserves of food and moisture to begin growing when conditions start to improve. Bulbs are plants that intend to come back year after year — that's why they store food.

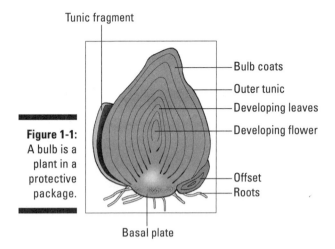

Tunic fragment

Bulb coats

Outer tunic

Developing leaves

Developing flower

Offset

Roots

Basal plate

Figure 1-1:
A bulb is a
plant in a
protective
package.

Gardeners are probably most familiar with bulbs planted in fall, that "rest" through a cold winter, and begin rapid growth and flower early in spring. That's the scenario for tulips, daffodils, and lots more bulbs.

Some bulbs, such as "Hardy" gladiolus, come from places in the world where it doesn't get very cold. These bulbs don't hibernate through winter. Instead, in their climate of origin, they rest — go dormant — when it's dry. (Weather patterns may be different where you garden.)

All bulbs are not the same. If you asked a botanist, you'd find out that everything gardeners call a "bulb" isn't necessarily a bulb. Why should you care? Because some of these differences have an effect on how you should grow the "bulbs" you plant. The following sections define some important terms.

Describing true bulbs

Everybody knows what an onion's like — a roundish, squat globe with a pointed top and a paper-like coat. Many true bulbs are like onions. True bulbs like daffodils and tulips, hyacinths and snowdrops, have a papery skin or tunic on the outside. Bulbs with a papery covering are called *tunicate* bulbs. The tunic helps protect the bulb from drying out when it's resting or waiting to be planted.

However, some true bulbs, such as lilies, don't have a tunic. As you'd expect, these bulbs dry out faster. They are more easily bruised, too. All true bulbs share the following characteristics:

- ✔ They are more or less rounded, sort of ball-like, and narrow to a point on the top. Leaves and flower stems appear from this point.

- ✔ With or without a tunic, true bulbs have a flat part, called a *basal plate,* at the bottom. That's where roots grow and also where shoots and scales are attached.

- ✔ True bulbs have new bulbs, called *offsets,* that form from the basal plate (see Figure 1-2). When they get big enough, these offsets, or daughter bulbs, produce flowers on their own.

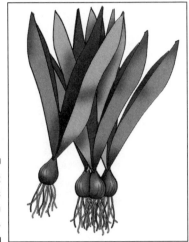

Figure 1-2:
True bulbs
form
offsets.

- ✔ If you cut a true bulb apart, you can see that it's made of rings, called *scales.* These are modified leaves that store food. Cut a true bulb, such as a hyacinth, apart at the right time of year, and you can find miniature flowers inside, just waiting to begin growing.

  Perennial true bulbs add new rings each year, from the inside. Old rings on the outside are used up, but the true bulb itself persists from year to year.

If even one of these characteristics is missing, the plant is not a true bulb. Instead, it's a corm, tuber, tuberous root, or rhizome, as described in the following sections.

Characterizing corms

Corms are like true bulbs in some respects, and different in others (see Figure 1-3). Corms have these traits:

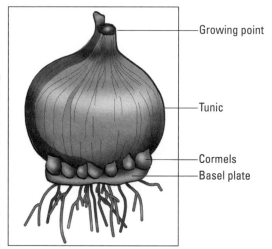

Figure 1-3:
Corms
resemble
true bulbs
in many
ways; this
corm has
little
cormels at
its base.

Growing point

Tunic

Cormels
Basel plate

✔ Corms have a tunic. It may be fibrous, what botanists call *netted* or *reticulate*. Or the tunic may be smoother, with distinct rings, what botanists call *annulate*. Some crocuses have reticulate tunics, others are annulate. That's one way scientists tell the crocus species apart.

✔ Corms have a basal plate at the bottom and one or more growing points at the top. So bulbs and corms both have a definite vertical orientation. They know which way is up.

✔ If you cut corms apart, you find that they are undifferentiated, uniform, and contain no rings. Corms are stem tissue, modified and developed to store food.

✔ Most important to gardeners, the corm you plant is used up growing the flower. Before it withers away at the end of the growing season, however, a brand new corm (sometimes several new corms) forms and replaces the mother corm. The new corm contains the food reserve for the dormant crocus or gladiolus until it's time to grow again.

Specifying tubers

Tubers are different from true bulbs and different from corms (see Figure 1-4).

Tubers have these features:

✔ They have no tunic.

✔ Tubers lack a basal plate. Most tubers root from the bottom.

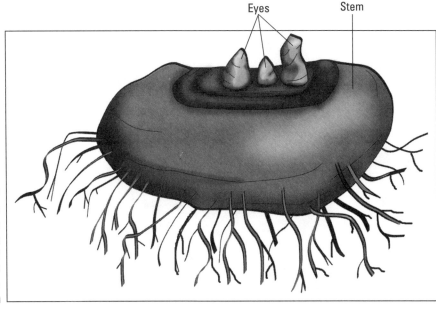

Eyes Stem

Figure 1-4:
Tubers
have
growing
points
called eyes.

✔ Tubers have several growing points, called *eyes*. More organized tubers, such as caladiums or tuberous begonias, have their eyes at the top. Some tubers, such as anemones, aren't so orderly. Distinguishing the top from the bottom of the tuber may be difficult. If you're not sure, plant it sideways and let the tuber figure out the direction in which to grow.

✔ Tubers are made of modified, undifferentiated stem or enlarged hypo-cotyl tissue, so they have no highly specific internal structure.

✔ Tubers don't make offsets like bulbs do; nor do they produce new tubers in the way that corms make new corms. Tubers usually just get bigger each year, making more growing points.

Identifying other lumpy things as bulbs

Most of the "bulbs" that gardeners plant are true bulbs and corms, and a few are tubers. You can find two other kinds of lumpy things at nurseries and garden centers along with the others that we discuss earlier in this chapter.

✔ **Tuberous roots** are modified, enlarged, specialized roots that store food (see Figure 1-5). Tuberous roots are used up during the growing season and replaced by new storage units. The tuberous roots cluster together, joined to the bottom of a stem. It's the stem that has the new growing point for the next year — a piece of root alone won't grow. To success-fully propagate dahlias, for example, you need to take a piece of stem along with each tuberous root that you separate from the original plant.

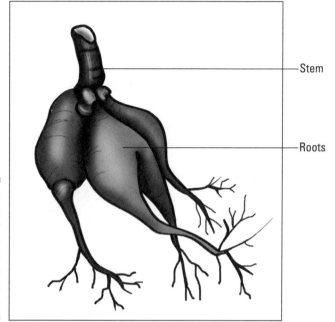

Stem

Roots

Figure 1-5:
You can
plant other
lumpy
things, like
this
tuberous
root.

🡲 **Rhizomes** are stems that grow sideways rather than up, running along the surface of the soil or just below it. Plants that use rhizomes for food storage have fatter, more bulblike rhizomes, covered with a dry base of leaves. Rhizomes branch out, and each new portion develops roots and a shoot of its own (see Figure 1-6). Cannas are popular plants that grow from rhizomes.

Unfortunately, nature isn't neat and tidy. Making gardening decisions would be easier if all true bulbs were hardy and able to survive cold winters, while other lumpy things were tender and could not. But there are tender as well as hardy bulbs, and hardy corms as well as tender ones.

Now that all the technical stuff is out of the way, we can generalize in the rest of Part I and just call all these lumpy things "bulbs." But in Part II, where we describe all the different lumpy-rooted plants, we will be more precise so you'll know how to manage the variations that distinguish each type in order to have them all flower beautifully.

Stem tissue

Leaf tissue

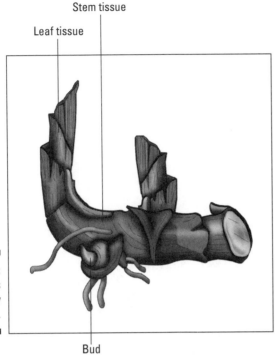

Figure 1-6:
Rhizomes
grow
sideways.

Bud

The Bulb Cycle: Growing and Resting

Most bulbs have a growing period and a resting time. That's kind of obvious — now you see them, and later you don't.

What all bulbs have in common is a stored food reserve underground that gets them through tough times. Bulbs draw on these reserves when they need them as growth begins, and they replenish the depleted reserves before the resting phase begins.

But a food reserve is the only similarity that all bulbs share. Bulbs don't *all* grow and rest simultaneously. Some bulbs grow for a short period of time, only a couple of months, before they go dormant. Others have a longer growing season. Some early spring bulbs — the familiar tulips, daffodils, hyacinths, and so on — grow early in the year when not much else is growing; then they rest while the majority of other plants are in bloom. Other bulbs — lilies, ornamental onions, and glads, for example — grow later in the spring and summer, when all sorts of plants are busy growing. Some bulbs — colchicums for one — even flower in autumn when just about everything else is going dormant.

What bulbs have going for the gardener is the certainty of good results the first time around.

Remember, bulbs are plants in a package. Start off with healthy bulbs, plant them in an appropriate place at the right time, and just stand back and enjoy the blooms. With little or no effort, many bulbs come back year after year. With a minimum of effort, results are even more assured. Sometimes, bulbs come back in increased numbers. Again, a little knowledge and effort on your part can help them along.

The diversity of bulbs is remarkable, matched only by the pleasure they provide the gardener who grows them.

Growing Conditions: Choosing the Right Bulbs for Your Climate

As you may expect from their protective layering, bulbs originate more frequently in places around the world with relatively harsh climates and conditions. But that doesn't mean that every bulb will grow in every place. They'll relocate, but they grow best in conditions similar to where they started. Gardeners, being brighter than their bulbs, can figure out how to get around potential limitations.

The bulbs you're probably most familiar with — tulips, daffodils, crocuses, and so on — are winter-hardy plants that thrive in temperate regions of the world. They accept cold winter conditions and a milder growing season. Hyacinths and snowdrops are native to Europe. Both China and North America are the source for some great lilies. The cold, dry steppes of Central Asia are home to wild tulips and crocuses.

Other bulbs — caladiums, cannas, and glads — come from places where winters stay on the mild side, and a regular extended dry period occurs. The Cape region of South Africa is one place where glads grow wild. Dahlias originated in Mexico and Guatemala.

Fortunately for us gardeners, lots of bulbs are willing and able travelers, adapting to new places far away from where they originated. But if you know where various bulbs came from in the first place, you'll have a better idea about which ones will grow best for you. Or, if you *really* want to grow a certain bulb, you'll know what you have to try and do to satisfy it.

GARDENING TIP

A case history: Wet growing season and dry resting period

Cannas are great summer bedding plants that give a lush, luxuriant, tropical look to any garden. Cannas originated in the tropics, places with hot summers and lots of rain. When the rain stops, plants rest. Although the air may cool off a bit, it doesn't get cold.

If you live in a region with hot, humid, rainy summers and mild winters, that's fine. Cannas naturally get what they need.

If you live in a mild but arid region with little rain and low humidity, you must supply what's lacking: You need to provide water and also figure out how to raise the humidity around your cannas so that their lush leaves don't dry up.

Compensating is easy if you live in a place with enough rain and warm to hot summers,

but cold winters. Just follow these steps:

1. **Wait until the first really cold frost turns the canna leaves to limp, black mush, and then carefully dig the rhizomes and trim away the now-dead leafy growth.**

2. **Pack the rhizomes in dry peat moss or some other storage material and keep them cool (40 to 50 degrees Fahrenheit) but not cold, until spring.**

3. **In the spring, replant the rhizomes in the garden or start them indoors in pots.**

As you can see, knowing the natural cycle that the bulbs expect helps you get along with the plants you want to grow.

Chapter 2

Using Bulbs in Your Garden

*B*y far, the majority of bulbs are grown for their lovely flowers. A few have attractive foliage — leaves that add interest to the garden because of their shape and/or color. Whether for flowers or foliage, bulbs are great for garden use. But don't stop there. Bulbs are good for cut-flower use. Just think of the daffodils, tulips, and lilies you buy at the florist. Growing these flowers yourself is cheaper. Did you ever buy a pot of hyacinths to cure yourself of the winter blahs? Coaxing the bulbs into early bloom yourself is simple. And you can keep some bulbs in pots as houseplants (amaryllis is one that works well in a pot). Think of bulbs as multipurpose plants, easy to plant, easy to grow, attractive, and useful in all sorts of ways.

Planning a Garden

Buying some bulbs helter-skelter and planting them any old way in whatever spot you're standing on doesn't do much to satisfy your longing for a beautiful garden. Beauty takes planning.

Think of yourself as an artist who just happens to be working with plants rather than paint. Do you want a vivid picture with bright colors (like a Mondrian painting, perhaps), or something softer and romantic (like the work of the artist Monet)? If you can't visualize just what you want, no problem. Visit a nearby botanical garden or public park and see what they're doing with bulbs. Get ideas from this book — after all, that's what it's here for!

Gardens *are* different from paintings because gardens are not static. Seasonal changes occur.

- Bulbs grow, flower, and go dormant. You need to think about what happens before and after the bulbs are in bloom, so you can team them up (called *companion planting*) with other kinds of plants to create the best effect.

- Some bulbs increase and multiply over time. That expansion is fine if space is available and you want an informal, cottage garden, or naturalistic look. In limited space or in a precise, formal kind of garden, a problem results if the bulbs crowd their neighbors and blur your design.

- You can use some bulbs on a "here and gone" basis. Treat them like annuals, enjoy them for one season's display, and then discard them.

After you decide what effect you'd like, sketch out the area you plan to use for your garden, indicating which flowers go where. You can find samples of such garden designs in many gardening books, including *Gardening For Dummies,* by Michael MacCaskey and the Editors of the National Gardening Association, published by IDG Books Worldwide, Inc.

Pay attention to flower heights so you can place the tallest flowers at the back. Also check out spreading tendencies, so you allow space for the spread. Having a rough idea of how much space you have for your garden and how you want to use that space will immeasurably improve its overall look.

The most common way of using bulbs is as garden plants in beds and borders (we talk more about beds and borders in Chapter 3). Think of flower beds and borders as organized spaces — designed places where plants are arranged in an orderly manner to create a deliberate effect. You've probably already planted bulbs for this purpose — "Heigh-ho, it's fall. I'll buy some tulip bulbs when I'm at the garden center getting lawn fertilizer." That afternoon, you spend some time planting the bulbs in a sunny place where the soil drains well. Next spring, you preen as friends and family admire the beautiful tulips you planted. That's one scenario.

The other scenario: You're busy, the bulbs sit around for a while (maybe a long while), and when you do plant them, the spot you choose has wet soil. Come spring, nothing happens. Depending on your personality you decide that "The bulbs were bad," or "I'm just not a gardener." This failure could be due to bad bulbs, just like the onions you bought at the supermarket that weren't sound. But, more likely, you used the wrong bulbs for that damp place. If you had chosen camassia, guinea hen flower, or summer snowflake, they'd have grown just fine. (Prompt planting also helps.)

Bulbs are not all the same in their likes and dislikes. Some like it sunny, others shady. Just because many prefer soil with good drainage doesn't mean that they all do. Many bulbs, like crocuses and daffodils, flower in the spring; lilies, glads, and others burst forth in summer. Nerines and colchicums are among bulbs that even flower in autumn. Lots of bulbs actually prefer winter — or at least its edge — while others get frostbite if they freeze. Whatever your conditions, you can find bulbs that will work for you. Chapter 3 offers suggestions for different situations, and we tell you each bulb's general likes and dislikes throughout this book.

How much space for your bulbs?

How much space do you provide for bulbs?

You've probably seen public displays where the bed is just filled with tulips. If you come by at the right time, the display is fabulous. Come back a month later and it's a different story. The tulips are finished (they've probably been yanked out), and the flower bed is full of annuals (flowers such as petunias that have a one-year growing cycle).

That approach is fine for a public garden, with deeper pockets than most homeowners and with groundskeepers to do the work. But it really isn't practical for homeowners to maintain that kind of labor-intensive, materially expensive type of garden. And what happens if the bulbs are daffodils, which you can't dig up and replant in the fall, as you can with tulips? Daffodils stay in place year-round, and you can't cut the leaves away until they turn yellow, so the space looks shabby and unattractive for the longest while.

In general, bulbs should occupy about 10 to 15 percent of the space in your flower beds and borders. That way, you won't break the bank when you buy them or wear yourself out planting them. If the bulbs are intended for seasonal color, you won't feel like a spendthrift when you discard them. And you can afford to replace them with annuals for another season's interest.

If the bulbs are permanent inhabitants of their piece of ground, you can plant perennials nearby that have spreading leaves — peonies, astilbes, hostas, or ferns, for example — to easily disguise the bulbs' aging foliage. Rather than the mainstay of the flower border, think of year-round bulbs as a permanent addition to the perennials you grow there, just as annuals and tender bulbs are temporary ones.

What should you use for a naturalistic garden?

A naturalistic garden is more casual, more laid-back, than flower beds and borders. As we discuss in Chapter 3, plants mingle together, giving the appearance of a setting that "just happened." The intention is to provide the look of a part of a meadow or forest. The design doesn't have to be grand and sweeping, either. Think about that tree in your backyard. That tree could be your own little woodland. Perhaps your foundation planting could include some bulbs and perennials to make the spot feel more like a woodland thicket.

A strip of lawn can be transformed from turfgrass to a grassland, with ornamental grasses, bulbs, and perennials. Remember that, just as with a more organized planting, you still need to choose the right bulbs for the proper place — sun or shade, moist or dry.

A naturalistic planting calls for bulbs that are especially good at taking care of themselves. Informal, naturalistic gardens are intended to be lower in maintenance — none of the staking, *dead-heading* (nipping off dead flowers), or other miscellaneous chores that occupy time in the bed or border. Single flowers look more natural than double ones and need less support, which means that you won't have to attach the plants to stakes so they won't keel over. Rather than removing the spent flowers, you leave the bulb flowers alone, which is a good way for bulb flowers that go to seed (such as winter aconites and siberian squills) to multiply themselves, too.

Bulbs that spread a little too well to be turned loose in a perennial border can be a good choice for naturalistic designs.

- ✔ Grape hyacinths can be a nuisance in more formal plantings where they spread far and wide, but the same characteristic can be excellent if they're growing around shrubs.
- ✔ Wood hyacinths multiply by seeds and offsets, which are aggravating in a designed, precise planting. However, they become wonderfully luxuriant in a casual woodland.

Rock gardens are a very special kind of naturalistic garden. Not a collection of rocks, this kind of garden uses low-growing plants, usually sun-loving, that flourish among rocks in well-drained soils. Dwarf tulips and crocuses fit right in with herbs (such as creeping thyme) and easy-to-grow carpeting perennial plants (such as moss pink, evergreen candytuft, or basket-of-gold alyssum).

How do you raise bulb flowers for cutting?

Cutting flowers from the garden is fun. But every flower you cut is one less on display in your flower bed. You spoil the show if you cut too many. A better approach is to buy extra bulbs in the fall and plant them somewhere out of view, where you can cut to your heart's content. If you look around, you can easily find an out-of-the-way corner where you can plant a handful of bulbs to use for cut flowers.

The best place to plant your extra bulbs is in the vegetable garden, if you have one. Rows of tulips or glads are just seasonal occupants, much like beets or carrots. Daffodils and lilies can be permanent plantings, just like the asparagus and rhubarb.

An established naturalistic planting can supply an occasional bouquet. Just make sure that you don't take all the flowers from one place. A dozen daffodils from a single clump is possible with an established planting, but you won't have anything left to look at. Rather, take a few flowers from every part of the planting. Taking one or two flowers from each of six or more clumps provides a dozen flowers, and this way no one will notice the loss.

Do what the florists do: Mix the bulb flowers with some filler flowers — an inexpensive bunch of baby's breath from the supermarket — or cut some greenery from your garden to make the flowers look more plentiful. Careful trimming of your shrubs — for example, rhododendron, yew, or azalea — not only provides more material for your bouquet, but helps keep your shrubs shapely.

Gardening in Containers

You can garden with bulbs even if you don't have a garden! Does that sound like a contradiction? It's true, because some bulbs are great when grown in pots. Pots of bulbs make ideal additions to your home's interior — and work well in the outdoor garden, too. Here are some tips:

- ✔ The bulbs you grow as "disposables" — seasonal signs of spring like hyacinths, tulips, and daffodils, or winter cheer in the form of florist's cyclamens and paperwhite narcissuses — all grow well in pots. If you keep pots of hyacinths and daffodils green and growing after they flower, you can plant them outdoors when spring arrives.

- ✔ Some bulbs don't like winter, so grow them as houseplants — amaryllis is a good example.

- ✔ As an accent, place a pot — or several pots — of seasonal flowering bulbs on a patio or terrace at the same time these plants are flowering in the garden. Think about how pretty a pot of grape hyacinths would be next to a bench or garden seat, or consider a window box of hyacinths.

- ✔ Summer containers in the shade can be kind of plain vanilla because most annuals are sun-lovers. Jazz up a shaded corner with caladiums, a bulb that thrives in low light.

- ✔ Lilies can add a rich romantic touch to a balcony or patio. Just remember to choose the lower-growing cultivars — a 7-foot-tall lily needs a big pot to anchor it!

Using Bulbs as Houseplants

You can convince hardy bulbs that winter has come and gone, so it must be time to flower. You can, therefore, grow spring flowers in the house in winter as one way to enjoy outdoor flowers indoors. But these are not houseplants.

Houseplants are plants with staying power — plants that you choose to share your home with as more than a passing fancy. Some bulb species are widely known as good houseplants, while others are less familiar. Some of the popular bulbs may seem a little tricky to grow indoors; others — just waiting for you to discover them — grow easily. Here are some bulbs that make great houseplants:

- ✔ Amaryllis *can* come back and flower year after year. Hints and tips on how to make it grow are in Chapter 15.

- ✔ Oxalis, the purple-leaved kind with a hot violet-pink flare at the base of each leaflet, grows from a small pink tuber. Keep this plant growing year-round if that's your fancy, or give it a dry winter resting period if you prefer.

- ✔ Veltheimia is a South African bulb that likes a mild winter and a summer drought. Reliably, it flowers in February with a spike of small, drooping, dusty pink flowers in a dense cluster.

And many more bulb types are available. We point them out as we describe specific bulbs throughout this book.

Finding a Bulb for Every Fancy

The neat thing about using bulbs is that, whatever your fancy, an aspect of bulb gardening can satisfy it. For example:

- Do you like to cook? You can find bulbs for your kitchen garden in Chapters 17 and 18.

- Do you want flowers for cutting? From anemones to daffodils, tulips to lilies, glads to dahlias, and more, bulbs can gladden a flower arranger's heart.

- Do you have a problem site that's soggy? Guinea hen flower, camassia, and summer snowflake are three that thrive with wet feet.

- Is your garden spot in the shade? Think about daffodils, snowdrops, or wood hyacinths.

- Do small children want to help, with little hands too small to handle seeds? Bulbs are nice big lumpy things, easy to grasp and forgiving of innocent mistakes (like planting upside down).

If you think about it, you can't really *avoid* gardening with bulbs.

Chapter 3

A Bulb Selection Guide

*Y*ou see bulbs and more bulbs. There are seemingly zillions of bulbs — each one as beautiful or more beautiful than the last. Clearly, bulbs aren't interchangeable. You can't quite mix and match them because not all bulbs grow in the same places. They all don't even flower at the same time, which is fortunate. (I mean, imagine this riotous explosion of flowers and then their absolute absence.) But visiting a garden center just to buy a few bulbs to beautify your garden can be intimidating if you don't know what to buy or where to plant them. Even if you're quietly opening a catalog in the privacy of your own home, you may feel overwhelmed by the number and variety of bulbs available.

In this chapter, we help you sort things out. We don't tell you about specific tulips (such as 'Prinses Irene' with orange and purple flowers that you meet in Chapter 6), but we do suggest that when selecting tulips as a cut flower, tulips in the Triumph or single early classes might work best. But that's already more information than you may feel ready to cope with.

Suppose that you want to grow some bulbs for cut flowers. Easy. Just turn to the section, "Bulbs as Cut Flowers," later in this chapter, and you'll find a listing of suitable bulbs. If something in this catalog of bulbs for cut-flower use intrigues you, you can find more detailed information in chapters specific to those bulbs, which tell you how to grow them and what specific cultivated varieties look like.

Remember: Bulbs are often multipurpose. Tulips are great cut flowers. Some are excellent for coaxing into early bloom while it's still winter outdoors. Some are super for the rock garden. Some make a stunning display when massed together for a colorful tapestry of flowers. They also combine beautifully with other plants in a perennial border. So don't be surprised if you see some bulbs listed in more than one category. Bulbs are wonderfully versatile.

About Bedding and Borders

Before we get into what bulbs go well where, we need to define some simple terms. *Bedding* is planting masses of whatever plant you're talking about for a really impressive display. It could be lots of an annual such as pansies, or heaps of a spring-blooming bulb such as hyacinths. The display is striking, no question about it. But then you need to think about what happens next. The hyacinth flowers fade, the leaves turn yellow, and you're left with a large expanse of bare dirt — except that the hyacinth bulbs are asleep underground, so you can't really dig and delve too much. Annuals are the answer, but they can get expensive.

Bedding out — planting lots of the same thing in tight groups — is usually accomplished in public settings such as parks or botanic gardens, but you also see it done in common areas of office buildings, condominium associations, and sometimes in your own backyard.

Borders are mixed plantings of perennials with some bulbs and annuals, maybe even a few shrubs and small trees. If you mix and match in this fashion, allowing maybe 15 percent of the space for bulbs, then the gaps when they go dormant aren't as obvious. And you'd probably want to plant some summer annuals anyhow. In addition, the leafy growth of perennials such as peonies and daylilies also helps conceal the yellowing, aging bulb leaves.

Bulbs for Spring Bedding

Hyacinths are ideal for bedding schemes. Their flowers are arranged in masses on stiff formal spikes that seem tailor-made for formal designs. With soft or deep blue, pale pink to deep red, cool white to creamy yellow to soft orange, there's a color for any pattern. You can create a design of geometric blocks, rhythmic curves, stripes or squares or circles. The bulbs remain year after year, and while the spike of bloom may be somewhat smaller after the first year, it's still enough to satisfy all except the most critical gardener. Hyacinths are discussed in detail in Chapter 7.

Daffodils are graceful enough for borders, emphatic enough for bedding. A host of golden daffodils is a sure sign of spring, even if you never memorized Wordsworth's poem in grade school! Be sensible about this: You'll want to choose larger, taller daffodils for bedding out; they'll make a more emphatic display than miniature daffodils. Although daffodils have a limited color range — yellow, white, bicolors of yellow and white, or yellow and orange, or white and orange — there is enough of a difference to be apparent.

A jumbled combination of several different kinds of bulbs is going to look muddy and have a weaker effect than if you plant blocks of a single kind.

We'd advise never buying mixtures, for any purpose. Sure, buy several different kinds of daffodils, but don't mix them within a single group. That way you'll control what's going where rather than leaving it to random chance. In a bedding scheme, it's important that the daffodils flower at the same time. You want to group early daffodils together, rather than having some early ones mixed with others that bloom later. If you mix them, some will be blooming while others are withering — not a pretty sight.

Daffodils stay in the ground year after year. Their bulbs generally increase into clumps. After several years, they need to be dug up, separated, and promptly replanted. You do this right after the flowers fade. You can read more about daffodils in Chapter 5.

Tulips are simply fabulous for bedding out. With their riotous range of colors from soft pastels to jewel-tone bright, you can create a carpet of color.

Tulips flower best the first year they are planted. If you are striving for a lavish display of bedding tulips, you'll need to be extravagant. You need to discard the bulbs that have finished flowering and plant new bulbs each and every year. Of course, there's an advantage to this, too: You can change the colors and design to suit your fancy.

Generally, you plant bedding tulips in blocks or groups of a single color. The adjacent group can be a related color for a subtle effect, or strongly contrasting for a more dynamic result. Trickier is interplanting two different tulips for a color-blending effect, say a purple with a softer pink, or a yellow with a peachy apricot. The tulips can be somewhat different in height, but it's critical that they flower simultaneously. You can bed out any of the cultivated varieties (cultivars) of tulips. Avoid the original wild types, however; they just don't work well in beds. If you use the early-flowering, low-growing kaufmanniana, greigii, or fostorianna cultivars discussed in Chapter 6, you can mix and match with some other early spring bulbs. Grecian windflower with daisy-like blue, pink, or white flowers are especially popular for such pairing, as are electric blue siberian squills.

Ornamental onions are not usually seen as bulbs for bedding out. The taller ones such as *Allium aflatunense* are really elegant for such use, however, with each bulb producing a soap bubble of purple flowers balanced on a slender stem. We saw them once in a public garden in England — the ornamental onions massed in a rectangular bed, with pink forget-me-nots carpeting the ground. The display was dynamite!

Because ornamental onions flower from May to July, they help fill the gap between the more familiar spring bulbs such as tulips, and summer bulbs like lilies. Ornamental onions are discussed in Chapter 13.

Bulbs for Spring Borders

Hyacinths, daffodils, and **tulips** are also excellent in spring flower borders. The difference between bedding out and borders is simple: Borders mix and match more kinds of plants.

Borders, no matter how formal, are less rigid than bedding out designs. In general, you plant a group of ten bulbs in a border rather than the many more used in a bedding scheme. You still keep to one kind within each group, say all white hyacinths rather than some pink, a couple of blue, one yellow, and the rest white. You could have several groups of hyacinths — all the same or a different color for each group — separated by other kinds of perennials such as peonies, daylilies, or astilbes. Or, you can combine a group of hyacinths with some perennials, next to a group of tulips or daffodils.

Crown imperial, *Fritillaria imperialis,* is a stunning addition to the perennial border. At about three feet tall, crown imperials really stand out, and the wreath of good-sized orange flowers, topped with a pineapple-like tuft of leaves, is unusual enough to really command attention.

Planted singly, crown imperial is like an exclamation point. Three to five of these big bulbs make a strong statement; more is really lavish.

Ornamental onions, *Allium* species and cultivars, make a great addition to the late spring border. Shorter ones such as *Allium christophii* or *Allium karataviense* are charming with hardy geraniums. Taller ones such as *Allium aflatunense* or the *Allium giganteum* cultivars are stately with larger perennials and/or ornamental grasses. Because their flowers make such a good show (and the bulbs cost a bit more than tulips and daffodils), I find that groups of three to five make quite a nice display. Ornamental onions are discussed in Chapter 13.

Bulbs for Summer Beds

Not as much bedding out is done with summer bulbs. Most are used in flower beds, combined with perennials and annuals.

Cannas are used for bedding, sometimes in those very Victorian bull's-eye schemes plopped into a lawn. You know, concentric rings of vivid yellow marigolds and bright red salvia with a canna, like a punctuation mark, in the center.

Public parks often feature bedding schemes with blocks of cannas, probably because they're tall enough to stand out in a summer garden. Modern canna cultivars have showy flowers — fat tropical blooms in vivid colors. Don't overlook cannas as foliage plants. Their varieties of bold leaves may be plain green, rich copper-bronze, and even variegated. Cannas are discussed in Chapter 14.

Dahlias work as bedding plants when you choose cultivars that are moderate in size. Dinner-plate dahlias with huge flowers on tall plants that practically need scaffolding for support are rather awkward _en masse_. Mid- to modest-size cultivars — for example, mignon type — are more suitable. Because dahlias bloom from late summer until frost, they really extend the display season. Dahlias are discussed in Chapter 14.

Caladiums are one of the major summer bulbs that work in the shade. Mass plantings create an attractive picture of tropical luxuriance, with large, broad, arrow-shaped leaves in various combinations of pink, red, or white with green. Caladiums are discussed in Chapter 14.

Bulbs for Summer Borders

Both **cannas** and **dahlias** are suitable for summer borders, where these tender bulbs mingle with perennials and annuals in a sunny place.

Think of cannas as foliage plants, and you'll find it easier to discover combinations that work. Cannas are sometimes awkward as flowering plants because they can grow 5, 6, or even 7 feet tall. Place them at the back of the border where the cannas and their tall companions can hang out without concealing shorter plants.

Try joe-pye weed, a lovely summer-blooming stately perennial with large flower heads of soft mauve. Dahlias continue flowering so late (right up to frost) that they team up well with other late season perennials. Consider fall asters, ornamental grasses, or shrubs.

You can even mix and match cannas with dahlias. Try a copper/bronze-leafed canna with orange or scarlet flowered dahlias. That's hot!

Lilies are bulbs with real stage presence. They hold their flowers at the top of the stem, making a noticeable display. Because they like to grow with their heads in the sun and their bulbs in the shade, lilies are ideally suited for a mix-and-match planting with perennials.

Bulbs for the Informal Shady Garden

Fly from coast to coast and you get the impression that some places still have lots of forest. Even where trees are individual specimens plunked in a lawn, they still provide some shade. And the north side of a building is not exactly sunny! What can you plant where the sun doesn't shine? Shade-loving bulbs, of course! And lots of 'em.

Spring bulbs

Many of these little bulbs flower so early in the year that, according to the calendar, it isn't even spring! Sensibly, they nestle close to the ground where they can find some protection from harsh winds. But size doesn't matter. Anything in bloom that early in the year is a welcome sight.

These bulbs are named in sequence by their Latin names, making it easier to look them up in a catalog index when you want to order some for your garden:

- **Grecian windflower,** *Anemone blanda,* has daisy-like flowers in blue, pink, or white. It blooms at the same time that you'd put pansies and primroses in the garden. Additionally, the lower-growing Grecian windflower pairs nicely with smaller daffodils and the earlier-flowering, lower-growing tulips, adding a soft accent. Look in Chapter 10 for more information.

- **Glory of the snow,** *Chionodoxa luciliae,* blooms while the weather is still a little nippy. It has charming blue flowers, several along a stem that's only a few inches high. It is obliging about increasing — happily seeding about — so give it room to romp. Try it under early-flowering shrubs or shrubs with long-lingering fruits from last autumn. Glory of the snow is discussed in Chapter 8.

- **Persian violet,** *Cyclamen coum,* is a treasure and well worth the search. It flowers so early that snow often covers it, only to emerge unscathed. The vivid magenta flowers make a bright display. Nestle the tuber at the base of an oak tree or in some choice location where the ground-hugging plant won't be overrun by vigorous neighbors while dormant. See Chapter 4 for more detail.

- **Winter aconite,** *Eranthis hyemalis,* is another harbinger of spring, also flowering before the snow is over. Yellow buttercup-like flowers on stems only a few inches high add early color to the woodland garden. Though sulky about having to be dried out for shipping and storage, those tubers that do survive the process are generous about seeding around and making more of themselves. This little treasure needs a place where it won't be disturbed when dormant. Special needs of this little tuber are discussed in Chapter 4.

❀ **Dogtooth violet,** *Erythronium* species, looks like a miniature lily, with a nodding flower or two in white, yellow, or pink. The upswept petals give a graceful look to a plant less than 1 foot tall. When planting, handle the dormant corms gently because they bruise easily. Give the dogtooth violet a special place to be admired, near a path where you can easily pause to appreciate it. Look in Chapter 10 for more information.

❀ **Guinea hen flower,** *Fritillaria meleagris,* is rather unusual. Each bulb has one or sometimes two nodding bell-like flowers clearly marked in purple and white, like a checker board. Either you like it or you don't, but no one's indifferent! Try this for something new and different because it is easier to grow than its uncommon appearance suggests. You can find information on how to plant it in Chapter 11.

❀ **Snowdrop,** *Galanthus nivalis,* is arguably the most popular of the little, early blooming bulbs for shady places. Its fresh white flowers are a sure sign of winter's end. Sturdy, easy to grow, every garden needs a patch to cheer housebound gardeners who know it's too soon to work outdoors. Snowdrops (and there are more kinds than you might have suspected) are mentioned in Chapter 4.

❀ **Wood hyacinth,** *Hyacinthoides hispanica,* is a vigorous plant best suited to casual places where it has space to spread, or paired with shrubs that will stand up to its habit of extending its territory. Spikes of blue, bell-like flowers make it all worthwhile. You'll find more information about wood hyacinth (no, it isn't as fragrant as its namesake) in Chapter 8.

❀ **Siberian squill,** *Scilla siberica,* is an excellent little bulb with electric-blue flowers that follow hot on the heels of glory of the snow. The few little flower bells face downward on each stem. As bulbs multiply by seed and offset, they spread into pools of blue, irresistible in woodland, delightful in a lawn too thin and patchy to pass as a putting green. If you want to add this beautiful blue to your garden's early display, look it up in Chapter 8.

❀ **Daffodils,** *Narcissus* species and cultivars, are a paradigm among bulbs. They're easy to grow, great in gardens and vases alike, and untouched by pests such as deer, rabbits, chipmunks, or voles. You have your choice of tall stately ones, small charming ones, singles or doubles, even a few that are fragrant. Daffodils and narcissuses are the same thing. Jonquil, what folks in the southeastern United States name every yellow narcissus, is more accurately used for a somewhat later-flowering group of usually fragrant daffodils that are mostly yellow (but earlier-flowering daffodils can also be yellow). Need to know more about this obliging bulb? Look in Chapter 5.

A shady summer bulb

Caladium is a real workhorse, accenting a shady place with colorful leaves. Caladium adds a special accent to a shady nook, perhaps in combination with annuals such as impatiens, or perennials like ferns and hostas.

Just remember that this tender tuber loathes frost and needs humid, hot weather and adequate moisture. Chapter 14 has more information to encourage your use of this foliage belle.

Bulbs for Rock and Herb Gardens

A *rock garden* is a great place for small treasures. Generally, plants grown here are less than 1 foot tall. Rock gardens are usually places with relatively infertile, well-drained soil. *Herb gardens* are not so different, because most herbs are sun-lovers that grow in well-drained sites and have the most intense flavor and fragrance when grown in infertile soil.

Crocus is one of the earliest, and best, little bulbs for these kinds of sites. Actually a toothsome corm popular for munchies with various pests, the gritty soil helps deter the underground vermin, and strong-scented herb foliage may provide a modicum of deer deterrence.

Growing crocuses under a ground cover of thyme is one combination that's not just pretty, it's practical. Different kinds of crocuses, and more detailed information, are in Chapter 4.

Tulips, not the big hybrids but the small species, are perfectly in scale for a rock garden and appreciate the sun and sharp drainage.

Dainty and colorful, their early flowers pair nicely with moss pink, *Phlox subulata,* or evergreen candytuft, *Iberis sempervirens.* Look for information on tulip options in Chapter 6.

Bulbs for Damp Places

In general, bulbs like good drainage, which is especially important when bulbs are resting. After all, a bulb is a plant's way of coping with stress, and stress often includes dry times. But every rule has exceptions, and there are a few bulbs that take constantly moist soil.

- ❀ **Guinea hen flowers,** *Fritillaria meleagris,* hate to dry out. A sunny moist meadow (= damp lawn) does just fine, and a damp woodland setting is even better. These smallish plants — flowering in early spring with unusual, purple-and-white checkered bell-like flowers, one or two to a stem — are ideally suited to your problem spot. Chapter 11 has more information.

- ❀ **Spring snowflakes,** *Leucojum vernum,* and their later-flowering cousin, the summer snowflake, *Leucojum aestivum,* both like moist soil in light shade. The spring version flowers as early as snowdrops do, with one or two green-tipped white bell-shaped flowers per stem. The summer version follows while weather is still in spring-time mode, with daffodils. Several somewhat larger flowers dangle jauntily from a taller stem. You can find spring snowflakes in Chapter 4 and summer snowflakes in Chapter 10.

- ❀ **Camassia,** *Camassia* species and cultivars, flower along with the taller tulips. In fact, they combine nicely — the tall spikes of nicely spaced, soft blue, starry flowers look charming with yellow, white, pink, or purple tulips. This obliging bulb even thrives in wet clay, a struggle for many plants. So for your problem site, or just a wet one, try this native American bulb.

- ❀ **Cannas** love water so much you can plant them in a pond! That's right, plunk their container right down in the water. Just remember that they don't like to freeze, so plan on storing the tubers indoors if winter is part of your yearly seasons. Think of cannas as foliage plants, bold and luxuriantly tropical, green, bronze, creamy yellow and green, blotched with white, or colored like a tropical sunset. Intrigued? Look in Chapter 14 to learn more.

In general, you shouldn't expect **lilies** to like soggy sites. But every rule is said to have its exception, and *Lilium superbum* is a lily for that sunny damp (no standing water, please) spot in your yard. Summer blooming, a generous number of showy orange flowers, whose curled back petals clearly reveal their black-speckled insides, adorn the tall and stately stems.

Mix and match lilies with other sun- and moisture-loving plants such as "joe-pye weed" or tall astilbes such as 'Ostrich Plume.' You can find more information on lilies in Chapter 12.

Bulbs for Summer Containers

Even though Judy has a garden, she still likes plants in pots. The plant seems more important when displayed in a container, and the containers really dress up a patio or terrace. Chapter 19 gives you all the details about growing bulbs in containers; the following bulbs are good ones to start with:

❦ **Cannas** are suitable for big containers, half-whiskey-barrel size. More exciting than geraniums, these bold beauties work well with some trailing plants — for example, variegated vinca vine — to soften the container's edge. Because they're such large, moisture-loving plants, they need lots of water.

❦ **Caladiums** are not only great in shady gardens where they grow in the ground, but super in containers on that shady patio or balcony. Their lush foliage adds a tropical look to your summer plantings. Look for general caladium information in Chapter 14.

❦ **Dahlias** make great container plants, if you chose the lower-growing kinds. In fact, some dahlias are dainty enough for a window box. Look for information about dahlias in general in Chapter 14.

❦ **Lilies,** especially the early summer-flowering mid-century hybrids, are nicely sized for container growing. And new, really dwarf lilies are just ideal for container use. Look in Chapter 12 for hints and tips on container growing these elegant bulbs.

Bulbs for Spring Flowers in the Winter House

You can fool Mother Nature! First, give potted spring-flowering bulbs several weeks at low temperature — a chilling period so they think it's winter. Then bring them inside where it is warmer, and they think it is spring. So they bloom. Early. It's easy to do and very rewarding. Specific information on potting for forcing can be found in Chapter 24. Following are some easy bulbs to force into bloom:

❦ **Tulips** are easy to coax into early bloom. The earlier they naturally flower in spring, the easier it is. Conveniently, the very early tulips are lower growing. It's easier to deal with a pot of foot-high flowers on your dinner table than something nearly 2 feet tall! We name specific cultivars and provide easy-to-follow instructions in Chapter 24.

❦ **Daffodils** naturally flower earlier in spring than do tulips, so they are even easier to force. You have the same consideration regarding height: Taller cultivars can be awkward to deal with.

❦ **Hyacinths** are not only easy to force, but smell good too. With their prepackaged flowers inside the bulb, you don't even need soil. Hyacinths will bloom if you just add water. Both methods are described in Chapter 24.

Bulbs as Cut Flowers

Even a visit to the supermarket in spring, with bunches of fresh-cut tulips and daffodils available in the produce section along with fruit and vegetables, tells you bulbs make great cut flowers. But you don't have to pay florist prices; growing bulbs for cut flowers is something you can do yourself. And you can grow and cut bulbs that aren't often available. You can find details about choosing and cutting bulb flowers in Chapter 23.

Among cut flowers for early spring, consider snowdrops, grape hyacinths, daffodils, early tulips, and hyacinths. For midspring try later blooming tulips and ornamental onions. Summer provides lilies, glads, and the lovely leaves of caladiums. Later in summer, use crocosmia and the first dahlias for arrangements, continuing with dahlias right up to frost. Gardeners in mild winter regions can raise enough amaryllis, naked ladies, and nerines to have some to cut.

A Bulb for Each Reason

Whatever your wants and needs (flowers for containers or cutting, early spring bedding or summer borders), wherever you garden (in regions with mild winters or those with snow) whatever conditions your garden provides (sun or shade, moist or average), bulbs are ready and willing to fulfill your wishes. You just need to know the which/where/what to do, and that's what this book is all about.

Part II
Bulbs That Flower into Spring

In this part . . .

*J*ust when you think that those bleak, dreary winter days will never end, up from the cold, barren ground emerge willowy white snowdrops, charming crocuses, gallant yellow daffodils, bold red tulips, daring blue hyacinths, and majestic orange crown imperials.

Check out this part to find out about growing these brave, early bulbs — and participate in the glory of spring.

Chapter 4

Swing into Spring with Snowdrops, Crocuses, and More!

. . . .

In This Chapter

▶ Enjoying frost-proof flowers that bloom through the snow

▶ Choosing and using snowdrops

▶ Challenging winter with crocuses

▶ Growing winter aconites, messengers of spring

▶ Losing the winter blues with spring snowflakes and cyclamens

. . . .

*W*e have an easy test for winter's end — if flowers are in the garden, winter's over. And, by planting snowdrops, winter crocuses, and Persian violets, we often have these special little bulbs in flower by Ground-hog Day. Not too bad in the tristate region of New York, New Jersey, and Connecticut!

You'd think that these little gems have antifreeze in their leaves and flowers — they freeze solid when the weather turns cold and thaw out just fine with the next sunny day. They get covered with snow, but when the snow melts, they reappear as crisp and pretty as before.

You don't need any special gardening skills either; just choose the right little bulbs and find them a suitable place to strut their stuff. Some bulbs are readily available and easy to find, and by choosing the right site you can give them a jump on the season. Others have fewer sources but are well worth a bit of a search. See Appendix A for a list of bulb suppliers.

In this chapter, we discuss the easy and not-so-easy bulbs for the winter garden, starting with the most familiar and finishing with some pretty special but uncommon kinds. You'll enjoy pushing back the edges of the season with flowers in the winter garden. It's easy, and it's fun.

Flowers at the Edge of Winter: Snowdrops

The name says it all — snowdrops *(Galanthus)*. Each little bulb sends up a few leaves and a single white flower, with three helicopter-like petals flaring out at the top of a green-tipped tube (see Figure 4-1). The common snowdrop has a price in line with its size — small. (Plants grow 4 to 5 inches high.)

Figure 4-1:
The common snowdrop.

Snowdrops are okay in cold winter regions and fine with moderate winters, but they dislike warm winters. You'll have to pass up snowdrops if you live in Southern California, Florida, or other hot climates.

Following are descriptions of three popular snowdrops:

✿ **The common snowdrop.** Common snowdrop, *Galanthus nivalis,* may seem like such a simple flower that ringing in any changes would be difficult. Two types that you're likely to come across are double snowdrops, with the inner tube replaced with lots and lots of ruffled petals, and the green-tipped snowdrop, whose three flared petals each have a green dot.

❀ **The giant snowdrop.** At 8 to 10 inches tall, the giant snowdrop, *Galanthus elwesii,* is hardly statuesque, but it is twice the size of the common snowdrop. And it flowers two weeks earlier! An easy way to tell the two snowdrops apart is to look inside the flower: The giant snowdrop has a second green band at the base of the tube; the common snowdrop has only one green band, at the opening.

❀ **'S. Arnott.'** Another super-size midget, 'S. Arnott' is also offered as 'Sam Arnott.' This large and pricey (about four times as much as the common snowdrop) snowdrop is quite robust and makes an attractive addition to a snowdrop collection. Even three of these bulbs make a nice display. Give them a choice site and provide a backdrop, perhaps nestle them against the roots of an oak tree.

Snowdrops have small bulbs that easily dry out, so they're not happy sitting around for several weeks waiting until you get around to planting them. Buy snowdrop bulbs and plant them immediately after you purchase them in autumn.

Planting snowdrops

Even though they are dormant — asleep underground — in summer, snowdrops like summer shade. Select a site with moist but well-drained soil under a tree or shrub, or on the shady side of your house. Because they flower so early in the year (when you may be disinclined to go for a stroll around the garden), plant snowdrops where you can easily see them — at the edge of a path or where they'll be visible from a window. Plant snowdrops in groups of 10 or 25 — or even more if you have the room — making a good display.

To plant snowdrops:

1. **Loosen the soil and add some organic matter in the form of compost or dried manure and 5-10-10 granular fertilizer.**

   (See Chapter 21 for more information on planting bulbs.)

2. **Mix until everything blends together, with no clumps of organic matter or concentrations of fertilizer.**

3. **Plant snowdrops with the skinny nose up and flat base down.**

   Set the bulbs 5 inches to base, which amounts to just a couple of inches of soil above the bulbs.

Snowdrops are pest free — deer and rabbits don't eat the plants, and chipmunks and mice leave the bulbs alone.

In summer, you may mistakenly think that bare ground means nothing is planted there and accidentally dig up your snowdrops while planting your annuals. Snowdrops are dormant by late spring, resting underground until next year. Avoid accidental disturbance by planting ferns or hosta next to the snowdrops in late spring — the perennials' summer growth conceals the space over the dormant bulbs.

Multiplying snowdrops

Snowdrops don't seem to multiply from seed in a garden, but they do multiply by *offsets,* which are new bulbs that grow attached to the mother bulb. Snowdrops make very dense clumps in a couple of years. You can easily increase your planting — wait until the flowers fade but the leaves are still green and vigorous. Dig up the clump, carefully separate the bulbs, and immediately replant them in the new place that you've prepared. If rainfall is lacking, be sure to water the bulbs until their leaves turn yellow and the snowdrops are dormant.

Remember, you can use snowdrops as cut flowers — just use a small vase. Place the vase on a small mirror, and you'll double the display.

Colorful Crocuses Challenge Winter

When you think about crocuses, you probably call to mind Dutch hybrid crocuses *(Crocus vernus)* — fat, cup-shaped purple, lavender, striped, white, or golden yellow flowers that bloom at the same time as the earliest daffodils, in April. These colorful early spring flowers have dainty, winter-blooming cousins: cultivars of *Crocus chrysanthus,* called snow crocuses for their habit of blooming so early that they often get covered with snow. (Some crocuses even flower in autumn; we write about them in Chapter 16.)

All crocuses are technically corms (see Figure 4-2). Like corms, they have a definite up end and down end, are solid inside like a potato if you cut them open, and have a papery outer covering called a *tunic.* The corm that you plant in autumn gets all used up in the process of growing and flowering the following spring; it dissolves and fades away. Before it goes dormant though, the crocus makes a new corm. In fact, each crocus usually makes several corms.

Crocuses like cold to moderate winter conditions — climate zones 5 to 7. They fail to grow in hot climates. Regions where folks go to escape winter are not suitable for crocuses.

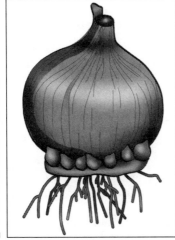

Figure 4-2: A crocus is a corm. Cormels (at the base) develop during the growing season.

Planting crocuses

Because crocuses are small, they dry out faster than large bulbs. So, plant them early in autumn, as soon as you can buy them. Plant them in the open rather than the shade (unless you live in the South) because crocuses like sun. You can plant them in the lawn, but you can't cut the grass until their leaves turn yellow and disappear. And weed killers will harm them, especially if applied while the crocuses are still green and actively growing.

Crocuses prefer a gritty, well-drained soil. A rock garden or herb garden is a good site, and small perennials that grow in such places make good crocus companions.

In the rock garden and herb garden, plant crocuses under creeping phlox or mat-forming thymes. The crocuses will come right through the ground-hugging plants. Using a ground cover of thyme or creeping phlox makes a better display, and keeps the crocuses' flowers from getting splashed with mud when it rains.

We really like crocuses' colorful flowers and think more is better. Ten of a kind is a minimum start.

To plant crocus corms:

1. **Dig the site and loosen the soil.**

2. **Add some coarse sand or fine gravel to improve the drainage.**

3. **Add 5-10-5 fertilizer, and mix well.**

4. **Set the crocuses 5 inches deep, more if your soil is sandy.**

   Crocuses have an up side, sometimes with the tip of the shoots showing. The bottom is flattened. Don't worry too much about which side is up; crocuses have contractile roots and will adjust their position downward if they feel the need.

Pests are a problem with crocuses — deer and rabbits eat the plants while mice and voles eat the corms. Planting in a gritty soil helps somewhat against tunneling pests.

If you have only a few corms, sink a plastic mesh cherry tomato or strawberry basket into the ground, fill it with gritty soil, and plant inside the basket.

Deer and rabbit repellents are available at garden centers. ***Remember:*** You need to reapply repellents after it rains.

Crocuses multiply by offsets. If you want to rearrange the extras, do so after the flowers fade but while the crocuses' leaves are still green. (Not only is the timing better for the crocus, but the leaves help you more easily find the underground corm!)

Adding early color with snow crocuses

To coax these little gems, *Crocus chrysanthus,* into the very earliest bloom, look for a warm, sheltered microclimate. A site against a building on the sunny side of the structure is just the thing: A little warmth leaks through the foundation, the sun warms a masonry wall during the day, and both provide moderate conditions at night. Such natural havens coax these little bulbs into bloom even earlier than in an open garden.

A *microclimate* is a small spot in your garden where conditions are different from overall conditions. This spot may be colder or warmer, exposed to more wind or better sheltered, or damper or drier than other parts of the garden. Seeking out suitable microclimates in your garden can be useful for all types of bulbs.

Growing Dutch crocus for larger, later blossoms

Vernus means "of spring" and is used for the second part of the Dutch crocus's Latin name — *Crocus vernus* — in reference to its time of flower.

If you've ever bought a bag of mixed Dutch crocuses and had the yellow ones flower earlier than the purples, lavenders, striped, and white ones, that's normal. Yellow Dutch crocuses have an early blooming species crocus as an ancestor. And, as well as their golden yellow color, Yellow Dutch crocuses inherited their early bloom time from *Crocus flavus*. So because they can flower at different times, buying different crocuses separately rather than as mixtures is better. You also get to decide for yourself which color goes where, instead of leaving the arrangement to random chance.

Woodland crocus: The exception to the rule

Attractive, easy, available, and tolerant of shady sites — what more could you want from this little treasure? Maybe a common name. *Crocus tommasinianus* is a darling, soft-lavender crocus that blooms in very early spring. You can see it pictured in the color section.

This crocus reseeds freely and soon makes large colonies — sometimes a problem in formal gardens with precise plantings. But this free increase helps keep the price of most cultivars way down. (The white-flowered one costs more.) This charming little crocus has been growing in gardens for more than 150 years, since 1847.

Try planting the woodland crocus with azaleas, under a dogwood tree, or just scattered and planted in a woodland garden.

Early Sunshine with the Golden Winter Aconite

The small golden flowers of the winter aconite, *Eranthis hyemalis,* make a bright cheery welcome to the garden (see Figure 4-3). *Hyemalis* (also spelled *hiemalis*) means "of winter" and was selected for the winter aconite's Latin name in reference to its very early flowers. Blooming from January in southeastern gardens and from March in the northeastern states, flowers appear when snow is still forecast.

Winter aconites grow only 3 or 4 inches tall, tiny enough to be covered with even a moderate snowfall. These durable messengers of spring reappear untouched as the snow melts, a frilly green leaf collar beneath their golden buttercup-like flowers. Sturdy and easy after they have begun growing, winter aconites can be tricky to establish at the start.

Figure 4-3:
The cheery
winter
aconite.

Winter aconites grow from tubers that look like wizened little sticks. Trying to get these tubers dry enough for storage and shipping to the store, but not letting them dry out too much so that they die, is tricky.

Buy tubers *early* — which is more important with aconites than with snow-drops and winter crocuses — and buy at least 25 tubers because most of them won't grow. Only about 20 to 25 percent will grow and flower next spring.

That low success rate sounds scary, hardly worth your time and effort. Don't worry — winter aconites grow very well, they just dislike drying out. Those tubers that *do* grow make lots of seed and offsets and start multiply-ing rapidly.

To plant winter aconite tubers:

1. **The night before you're going to plant, soak winter aconite tubers overnight in a container of damp peat moss.**

   The tubers take up the moisture, plump up, and are ready to start rooting right away when you get them in the ground.

   Remember: Only soak the tubers the night before you plant. If they sit around for a day or two after soaking, tubers become moldy.

2. **Choose a shady, woodland setting with lots of organic matter in the soil, and one that won't dry out in summer.**

3. **Loosen the soil and plant tubers an inch or two deep.**

   Don't worry about which side is up — the plant knows and sends shoots up and roots down.

4. **Water first, and then mulch with chopped leaves or shredded bark.**

5. **When flowers come up in spring, enjoy.**

You can easily increase existing plantings of winter aconites two ways:

✔ Watch for the seed, looking like small tan BB pellets when ripe. Just scratch the soil and scatter the seed, covering lightly, which helps new plants get started.

✔ In three or four years, after winter aconite is established in your garden, you can start moving plants around in spring. Wait for the flowers to fade but before the leaves turn yellow; then dig the tubers and replant them right away. Unlike fall planting with dormant tubers, spring planting while plants are still green and growing is almost 100 percent successful.

The English call this planting *in the green,* meaning while bulbs still have their leaves. Planting in the green works very well with snowdrops, daffodils, and lots of other bulbs besides winter aconites.

There's no trick to growing a nice patch of winter aconites — it just takes time, and not everyone is patient enough. The reward of cheerful flowers so early in the year makes all the effort worthwhile.

Not Quite a Snowdrop, a Spring Snowflake for Winter Flowers

The spring snowflake, *Leucojum vernum,* flowers as early as the common snowdrop. (*Vernum* is just a variation of *vernus,* and also means "of spring.") It has richer green leaves, and the charming flowers, one or sometimes two to a stem, look like fat little bells with green-tipped petals (see Figure 4-4). The spring snowflake is a small bulb, and plants grow only 6 inches tall.

Spring snowflakes do best in light to medium shade. They prefer a site that won't dry out in summer, with soil high in organic matter.

Plant spring snowflakes in regions where snowdrops thrive. Autumn planting is best. Ten is a good number of bulbs to begin with.

Figure 4-4:
Spring
snowflakes
like light
shade.

To plant spring snowflake bulbs:

1. **Loosen the soil.**

2. **Add organic matter and 5-10-5 fertilizer.**

3. **Combine all ingredients thoroughly.**

4. **Plant bulbs right side up about 5 inches to base.**

   The spring snowflake is a true bulb with a pointy tip, a flat bottom, and wrapped in a papery brown tunic.

Spring snowflakes make offsets at a modest rate. When the clumps become crowded, lift and separate them in spring (after flowering but before the leaves yellow and die back).

Pests leave spring snowflakes alone — deer and rabbits, voles and mice seem to find them uninteresting.

We like spring snowflakes because they flower so early, and they are a bit different from snowdrops. They're nice if you have a damp site where other bulbs rot in winter wet. *Damp* is the operative word, soggy or sodden is too wet even for spring snowflakes.

Plant spring snowflakes with a ground cover of myrtle, whose glossy evergreen leaves make a nice carpeting background and cover the dormant bulbs. (Pachysandra is too tall and vigorous.) Ferns are good companions to spring snowflake, also disguising the bare place when the bulbs are dormant.

Spring Cyclamens: Fabulous Foliage and Vivid Flowers

If you've ever had a cyclamen as a house plant and wished it was hardy enough to grow in the garden, then the spring cyclamen (also called Persian violet), *Cyclamen coum,* is the plant for you.

This sturdy little plant is astoundingly weatherproof — it sends its leaves up and makes flower buds in autumn, to sit right through the winter and flower before spring arrives. Spring cyclamens know what they like and, given the right conditions, will thrive for years and years, getting bigger and fatter with more flowers, and even seeding to make new plants.

If you live in the southeast or northeast, spring cyclamens make a charming, special addition to your garden.

Planting spring cyclamen

The spring cyclamen grows best in woodland shade, and, though it likes good drainage, it doesn't want drought. Dryness in summer when the plants are dormant is okay, but not when plants are growing in autumn and spring.

Low-growing, this choice plant needs a choice site — nestled against the roots of an oak or beech tree, or next to a rock on a slight slope to promote drainage. Only 3 or 4 inches tall, a prominent location for easy viewing is appropriate.

Plant them in autumn just before the fat cookie-like tuber-corms start into growth. A *tuber-corm* is a little like a tuber, with several growing points, no interior structure, and no papery covering or tunic. It is like a corm because it has a definite this-side-up orientation. Cyclamens have small growing points on the top.

Plant the tuber-corms just under the soil surface, and be sure to add organic matter — dried manure, compost, leaf mold — to the soil. Then add a mulch of shredded bark or chopped leaves.

Leaves grow in early autumn — handsome rounded dark green leaves laced and blotched with silver. Every plant seems to have different leaf patterns. The leaves of spring cyclamens last right through the winter, making an attractive display.

Flower buds form in autumn, tightly furled like a miniature umbrella, bright cerise pink in color. Winter comes, winter goes, and the spring cyclamen unfurls its flowers like a miniature badminton shuttlecock or some tiny butterfly (see Figure 4-5). Plants go dormant in June.

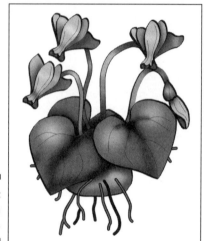

Figure 4-5:
Spring
cyclamen.

Choosing companion plants for this small charmer is a little tricky because of the cyclamen's small size and time of growth. Our favorite is Japanese painted fern, with silver fronds that accent the spring cyclamen's leaf markings.

Making more cyclamens

Unlike most other bulbs, corms, and tubers, the cyclamen never makes offsets. The tuber-corm just gets bigger and fatter and makes more flowers. If you want more cyclamens, seed is the only way. Seed is ripe when the capsule holding the seed opens and spills out the sticky brown BB-sized seed.

Ants like the seed and carry it away, so pay attention and collect seed before the ants do.

Soak the seed for a couple of hours or overnight in tepid water with a drop or two of dishwashing liquid. The detergent removes the sticky coat. Then sow the seed right away. Grow them in pots, and then after the second growing season, transfer them to the regular garden.

Fresh seed sprouts in about nine weeks; old seed can take nine months or longer, and fewer seeds will sprout. Mice like the tiny tubers and eat 'em up, so grow them in pots rather than the open ground. Or you can try planting seed in mesh, pint-sized cherry tomato baskets, sinking the baskets into the ground. Seedlings reach flowering size in their second or third year, and just get better and better after that.

For some reason spring cyclamens (and their autumn-flowering cousins we describe in Chapter 16) are not as popular in the United States as they are abroad. In England and Holland, for example, cyclamens are widely grown in gardens both public and private. True, they're not as forgiving as daffodils, but their lack of popularity may be more a matter of finding the tuber-corms to start with. After all, if you don't know about cyclamens, you're not likely to search for them and discover how wonderful they are for winter interest and extra early flowers in your garden.

You can occasionally obtain spring cyclamens from specialty mail-order catalogs (see Appendix A).

Treat Yourself to Winter-Spring Blooms

Having flowers in spring and summer is easy, but having flowers at the edge of winter is a special treat. As this chapter explains, you can easily achieve this delightful treat with some planning. Before other plants — perennials, trees, or shrubs — wake up, these little bulbs reward the thoughtful gardener with flowers. From familiar and easy to uncommon and somewhat demanding, these little bulbs merrily swing from winter into spring, carrying you along. Try growing these charming sprites and see what we mean.

Chapter 5

Daffodils, Harbingers of Spring

• •

• •

*I*f you're looking for a reliable spring bulb to add to a sunny perennial border, partially shaded woodland, or cutting garden, start right with daffodils.

Late in winter, these harbingers of spring show up as sunny yellow trumpets in florist shops and supermarkets; then they burst into bloom in your garden a couple of months later. But there's more. Daffodils also come in white and as bicolors — white and yellow, white and pink, or yellow and orange. You can plant dwarf daffodils that are under a foot tall as well as taller, more regal beauties. Some daffodils have several flowers to a stem, others are double, some are even fragrant.

The great thing about daffodils is their easygoing nature. Just plant them in autumn and watch them flower the next spring, and come back year after year with almost no care. In fact, a couple of antique daffodils have been grown since the 1600s. In this chapter, we tell you how to grow your own sunny daffodils, and how to select your favorites from the huge number of cultivars available.

Classifying Daffodils: An Even Dozen

Daffodils are classified in 12 different divisions, based on the number of flowers to a stem, details of the flower's shape, and the wild species that was the parent of the modern hybrids. (Division 12 holds all the daffodils that don't fit the classifications in the other 11 — a miscellaneous division, so to speak.)

All daffodils make great cut flowers, but some are better for one kind of garden use than another. As far as gardeners are concerned, Division 6, the cyclamineus hybrids of garden origin, and Division 9, poeticus hybrids of garden origin, are the absolutely most reliable about naturalizing and returning year after year (perennializing) with little care. Figure 5-1 shows representatives of daffodils from each division.

Figure 5-1: Daffodils are classified by their number of flowers, their shapes, and their parent species.

Trumpet

Large cupped

Short cupped

Double

Triandrus

Cyclamineus

Jonquilla

Tazetta

Poeticus

Species/wild

Split corona

The image of the daffodil: The trumpets of Division 1

Division 1, the trumpet daffodils of garden origin, are the traditional kind, "what everyone thinks of when they think of daffodils," and are really excellent in the perennial border.

Impressive single-stemmed flowers feature a prominent trumpet that's as long as or longer than the petals. These familiar and popular plants also work well in beds, planted in drifts or naturalized, or used as cut flowers. They bloom from early to late spring and grow 8 to 18 inches. Here are our recommendations:

- ❀ **'Arctic Gold':** These early to midseason bloomers produce show-quality, long-lasting gold flowers that grow to 16 inches. They display excellent form and bright color. Use them in beds, borders, and landscape settings.

- ❀ **'Beersheba':** This early to midseason radiant flower with pure, white blossoms has been grown and enjoyed for decades. With growth to 14 inches, it's great for bedding and landscape use.

- ❀ **'Dutch Master':** Early to midseason yellow flowers grow to 20 inches. These large, showy, golden yellow flowers similar to, and often used in place of, King Alfred make quite an impact in mass plantings.

- ❀ **'Holland Sensation':** With midseason blooms reaching 24 inches, this classic, showy, two-toned flower features white petals and a large, fringed, yellow trumpet. It's excellent for landscape use or arrangements.

- ❀ **"King Alfred" type:** This early yellow bloomer grows to 18 inches. Perhaps the best-known daffodil, its large, deep yellow flower has graced gardens for nearly a century. It's ideal in mass plantings, beds, and borders.

- ❀ **'Mount Hood':** Midseason white flowers grow on 17-inch stems. These excellent, long-lasting flowers feature a flanged yellow trumpet that fades to white. Vigorous plants are successful either naturalized or grouped in beds or borders.

- ❀ **'Primeur':** Richly colored golden-yellow flowers that grow to 20 inches bloom mid to late in the season, after almost all others. These long-lasting, abundant flowers add value to beds, borders, and landscapes.

- ❀ **'Rijnveld's Early Sensation':** This very early yellow bloomer grows to 14 inches. This trumpet offers a preview of spring, often blooming in January in many regions. It is suitable for naturalizing, beds, borders, and forcing.

❀ **'Spellbinder':** Early to midseason flowers fade from yellow to white on 1-inch stems. Unique, changing colors provide plenty of sparks in beds, borders, and mass plantings.

❀ **'Topolino':** This early to midseason bloomer has white/yellow blossoms on 8-inch stems. It's excellent in rock gardens and forced.

The cupped daffodils of Divisions 2 and 3, of garden origin, are great for the flower garden, too. We discuss those in the next two sections.

Division 2: Large-cupped daffodils

The large-cupped daffodil category includes popular bold flowers that have large central cups with ruffled edges, one blossom per stem. They're ideal for beds, borders, naturalizing, cutting, showing, and in some cases, forcing. Flowers bloom from early to midseason, ranging from 14 to 18 inches. Try these cultivars:

❀ **'Accent':** With mid- to late-season flowers that reach 16 inches, this cultivar offers an outstanding combination of white petals and a durable pink cup. It's a vigorous and versatile grower, good for naturalizing, showing, or featuring in the garden.

❀ **'Ambergate':** This midseason flower grows to 16 inches. A warm glow radiates from this unusual combination of a large red cup surrounded by petals in shades of orange. It makes an arresting display in beds, borders, and landscapes.

❀ **'Camelot':** This is a late bloomer with golden yellow flowers on 16-inch stems. For a long-lasting, late-season show, try this sturdy, prolific daffodil. Use it in beds, borders, mass plantings, or naturalized.

❀ **'Carlton':** This plant has early midseason flowers in yellow tones on 20-inch stems. A two-toned, vanilla-scented yellow, this plant is vigorous, adaptable, and one of the most widely grown of all daffodils. It naturalizes beautifully and is good forced or cut.

❀ **'Delibes':** This is an early midseason bloomer with flowers that grow to 18 inches. Gradually fading soft yellows and oranges set this cultivar apart. With long-lasting, showy flowers, it's ideal naturalized or massed in the garden.

❀ **'Flower Record':** This has midseason flowers and grows to 18 inches. One of the best for naturalizing, this flower has elegant good looks. White petals surround a yellow cup edged in red. This one shines in beds, borders, and arrangements.

❀ **'Ice Follies':** Early midseason flowers top 18-inch stems. Large flowers in creamy white and soft yellow highlight this ever-popular choice. It is perfect for naturalizing and combining with tulips and hyacinths or for forcing. This is the best large-cupped daffodil to start with!

❀ **'Salome':** Late midseason flowers reach 18 inches. Going from apricot-yellow to salmon pink, this flower is a frequent show winner and works well in beds, borders, or mass plantings.

Division 3: Short-cupped daffodils

These early-to-late flowers feature a cup that is one-third or less than the length of the petals, with blossoms one to a stem. They work well naturalized, in beds or borders, and as cut flowers, growing 14 to 18 inches. Here are a couple of seggestions:

❀ **'Barrett Browning':** Early flowers top 16-inch stems. The pure white petals and red-orange cup are striking up close or from a distance. Try them in beds, borders, or massed plantings. They're good naturalized and forced.

❀ **'Birma':** Early flowers reach 18 inches. A deep red cup, ringed with dark yellow petals make this bloom hard to resist. It adapts well to naturalize in the garden and offers show-quality flowers in beds and borders.

Division 4: Double daffodils, caring for twins

Division 4's double daffodils are really fun, but some need more care than other daffodils. They have so many petals that when it rains, they soak up water like blotting paper, get heavy, and fall over. So you may need to stake or protect them.

Showy, double, rose-like flowers in single and multiple blooms highlight this group. The award winners are striking choices for beds, borders, and as cut flowers because many are fragrant. Protect the 12- to 16-inch flowers in windy areas. Check out these cultivars:

❀ **'Bridal Crown':** Early midseason light yellow flowers bloom on 16-inch stems. Soft blooms in cream and pale yellow give this fragrant flower wide appeal. It is one of the earliest doubles and is excellent in beds, borders, containers, or forced.

❀ **'Cheerfulness':** Late, flowers top 16-inch stems. Striking multiple blooms have pale yellow petals with creamy yellow centers flecked with white. The small but prolific fragrant flower clusters are good forced, cut, in containers, and naturalized.

❀ **'Erlicheer':** Early midseason white and yellow florets reach 14 inches. Each stem produces 15 to 20 superb show-quality fragrant florets. It's an ideal choice for beds and borders.

❀ **'Ice King':** Early midseason flowers reach 18 inches. This ruffled delight sports pearly white petals with a fully double soft yellow cup. Use it for show and to brighten beds and borders.

❀ **'White Lion':** Midseason white and yellow flowers that grow to 18 inches. Delightful fragrance and large gardenia-shaped blossoms highlight this vigorous grower that adapts to tough conditions. Use it in beds, borders, and for cutting.

❀ **'Yellow Cheerfulness':** Late, multiple, yellow blossoms top 16-inch stems. The prized all-yellow flowers offer fragrance and abundant color. This bloom naturalizes well, is a winning cut flower, and looks good in beds, borders, and mass plantings.

Division 5: Triandrus daffodils

Small, nodding, fragrant flowers in this group offer an elegant display. Multiple flowers rise above slender foliage. Use them naturalized, in rock gardens, borders, containers, and as cut flowers. Bloom time is mid-to-late season, and the height range is 12 to 16 inches. Try these cultivars:

❀ **'Ice Wings':** Early midseason white flowers have two to three blooms per 14-inch stem. These absolutely pure white flowers are long-lasting with a sweet scent. They do well in beds, borders, rock gardens, and pots.

❀ **'Liberty Bells':** Late midseason golden-yellow flowers sprout up to five blooms per 14-inch stem. Expect an abundance of these nearly perfect, bell-like flowers. They make a memorable show in beds, borders, and arrangements.

❀ **'Thalia':** Late midseason multiple white flowers top 14-inch stems. Known as *Orchard Daffodil,* this popular heirloom flower offers fragrant blossoms on prolific plants. Use it in beds, borders, and landscape settings.

❀ **'Tresamble':** Late midseason white flowers grow one to three blooms per 16-inch stem. Graceful arching petals accent frilled cups on these large flowers. Another old-fashioned favorite, this selection is ideal for naturalizing, or planting in borders and beds.

Division 6: Cyclamineus daffodils

These flowers feature a trumpet cup set above flared-back petals, much like cyclamen. Expect early blooms and reliable performance in rock gardens, borders, cutting gardens, containers, or naturalized in the landscape. They grow 7 to14 inches. Check out these varieties:

❀ **'February Gold':** Early bright yellow blossoms grow to 14 inches. Choose this one when you want robust flowers for early forcing. They also do well in containers, including window boxes, and offer excellent long-term displays when naturalized.

❀ **'Foundling':** Early or midseason flowers top 12-inch stems. This small flower with a dainty apricot cup and graceful white petals is a true winner. It naturalizes well for good long-term use in beds, borders, and landscape settings.

❀ **'Jack Snipe':** Early to midseason flowers top 10-inch stems. Stunning white star-like petals surround a fringed yellow trumpet center. Use it in containers, beds, or for forcing and naturalizing.

❀ **'Jenny':** Midseason white flowers top 12-inch stems. Flowers change from creamy to pure white on this outstanding selection. Expect good results in rock gardens, beds, borders, or naturalized in small gardens.

❀ **'Jetfire':** Midseason red-orange and yellow flowers top 14-inch stems. This one offers abundant blooms in vivid, slightly varied colors. Plants naturalize well and work in beds, borders, containers, and forced.

❀ **'Jumblie':** Midseason deep yellow-gold flowers reach 7 inches. Expect plenty of success with this cultivar, featuring two to three flowers per stem. Try it in beds, borders, rock gardens, or naturalized in drifts.

❀ **'Peeping Tom':** Early midseason yellow flowers top 15-inch stems. Valued as a strong naturalizer with healthy, long-term garden performance, this selection is perfect in rock gardens, beds, borders, and early forcing.

Division 7, jonquilla daffodils of garden origin, and Division 8, tazetta daffodils of garden origin, are good choices for gardeners in milder climates (see the following two sections). Daffodils need a winter chilling to send the proper signals that "it's time to flower now"; where winter is uncertain at best, many daffodils flower poorly unless they're chilled in a refrigerator first. Jonquillas and tazettas happily accept less chilling before they'll perform. They're fragrant, too.

Division 7: Jonquilla

Jonquillas offer fragrant small flowers, several to a stem and small, dark green, slender foliage. Bulbs naturalize very well but also shine in beds, borders, rock gardens, and arrangements. They bloom mid to late season and reach 8 to 18 inches. Here are some suggestions:

- ❀ **'Bell Song':** This late bloomer has three to five cream and pink flowers per 14-inch stem. Sweet fragrance and classic good looks describe this cultivar. Include it in the rock garden, bed or border, or naturalize it in the landscape.

- ❀ **'Bunting':** This late bloomer has two to four yellow and orange flowers per 14-inch stem. This show flower adds impressive late color to your rock garden, bed, border, or indoor arrangement.

- ❀ **'Curlew':** These midseason flowers, two or three per 14-inch stem, have creamy petals with a longish white cup. These flowers offer classic beauty with subtle color changes. They work well in many garden settings and indoors.

- ❀ **'Dickcissel':** This is a mid- to late-season bloomer with two or three flowers per 12-inch stem. Shading from soft yellow to creamy white, this prolific plant makes a valuable addition to the rock garden, bed, border, or cutting garden.

- ❀ **'Pipit':** Midseason pale yellow multiple flowers top 8-inch stems. This charming, diminutive winner is ideal for rock gardens, naturalizing, or grouping in small gardens.

- ❀ **'Quail':** Midseason multiple yellow flowers top 18-inch stems. The abundant flowers in sunny yellow are long-lasting and fragrant. Use them in groups in the border or landscape.

- ❀ **'Suzy':** This is a midseason bloomer with several yellow and rust flowers per 17-inch stem. Striking color is the payoff with this sturdy, prolific daffodil. Use it in beds, borders, and naturalized where you want a strong accent.

Division 8: Tazetta

This group offers multiple, fragrant flowers of up to eight per stem from midseason to late spring. Useful in beds, borders, cutting gardens, or naturalized, these daffodils are successful in warmer regions with plants from 6 to18 inches tall. They are ideal for forcing. Try these cultivars:

❀ **'Cragford':** This early midseason bloomer provides three to five white and orange flower clusters on 14-inch stems. Popular for forcing, this daffodil has very fragrant, rounded flowers. It's also effective in beds, borders, or as a cut flower.

❀ **'Geranium':** Growing in midseason, three to five white and orange flowers top each 17-inch stem. The long-lasting fragrant flowers on this old-time favorite do well naturalized or very forced late in the season. *(You can see this one in all its glory in the color section.)*

❀ **'Minnow':** This midseason miniature has two to three white and yellow flowers per 8-inch stem. Delightful two-toned flowers on compact plants make this a very good choice for the rock garden or planted in groups in beds and borders. It naturalizes well, too.

❀ **'Scarlet Gem':** Late midseason flowers in yellow and orange bloom three to five per 16-inch stem. Put this heirloom daffodil in the show category, because the soft yellow and red-orange combination is striking in the garden or indoors.

Division 9: Poeticus

Dogwood-type flowers with white petals accented with yellow-orange cups have made these cultivars timeless treasures. The spicy fragrance adds a lovely touch indoors, and the flowers perform well in beds, borders, or naturalized. They are a good choice in cooler regions. Check out these cultivars:

❀ **'Actaea':** These late midseason bloomers top 17-inch stems. A strong yellow cup, banded in red, surrounded by perfect white petals gives this flower a classic look. Choose this when you want impressive naturalized flowers that perform well over time.

❀ **'Cantabile':** Late flowers bloom on 14-inch stems. The green and yellow, red-edged cup against the pure white petals make this fragrant flower a true showstopper. Use it for accent in beds and borders or in groups in the landscape.

❀ **'Felindre':** This late bloomer tops 18-inch stems. An heirloom plant, this daffodil has outstanding flowers in beautiful form highlighted by impressive green, yellow, and red cups. Use it as a versatile outdoor plant or cut flower.

❀ **'Milan':** Late flowers top 18-inch stems. Since the 1930s, this has been a popular choice in the garden grouping. Use this graceful flower in beds, borders, naturalized, or as a cut flower.

Division 10: Species and wild forms

For an unusual but charming touch in the garden, select from this group of species and wild plants and their hybrids. Plants vary in size and shape but offer excellent results when naturalized or planted in many garden settings, including restoration (18th-century) gardens.

Useful in woodland or rock gardens, these daffodils are often less available than the other kinds depending on which one(s) you choose. These are something you'll mail order rather than pick up at the garden center (see Appendix A for sources):

- ❀ **Hoop petticoat (*Narcissus bulbocodium*):** Midseason yellow flowers top 6-inch stems. Megaphone-shaped cups and reed-like leaves offer a striking look. These flowers show and force well; they also work in containers or naturalized.

- ❀ **Pheasant's eye (*Narcissus poeticus recurvus*):** This very late bloomer has white flowers with red/yellow cups atop 13-inch stems. This one gets high marks for a spicy fragrance, good cold tolerance, and overall use.

- ❀ **Tenby daffodil (*Narcissus obvallaris*):** Very early rich golden trumpets top 10-inch stems, making this outstanding for forcing or naturalizing.

- ❀ **Van Sion (*Narcissus telemonius plenus*):** This early bloomer with yellow flowers reaches 14 inches. Set apart by its double-flowered cup, this long-time favorite is good for naturalizing and forcing.

Division 11: Split corona

With the corona, or cup, split by at least a third, having a flatter, full face gives these flowers the distinction of being among the showiest of daffodils. Use them naturalized in mass plantings, or in arrangements, beds, and borders. Plants range from 14 to 18 inches.

- ❀ **'Cum Laude':** Midseason white and yellow flowers top 16-inch stems. A frilled flower, this one is ideal either for showing, or for showing off in beds, borders, and landscapes.

- ❀ **'Love Call':** Late midseason white, yellow, and orange flowers top 16-inch stems. Another showy flower with excellent coloration, it's great in arrangements, or for accent in beds, borders, and mass plantings.

- ❀ **'Papillon Blanc':** Late flowers reach 18 inches. The yellow and greenish center surrounded by white gives this flower plenty of charm whether you plant it outdoors or use it inside.

The funky split-corona daffodils of Division 11 look quite different from those traditional yellow trumpet daffodils. Try them if you're looking for something really different, but don't expect them to be as permanent as cyclamineus or poeticus daffodils.

Grading the Bulbs: Bigger Is Better

You can find size grades within each classification, and it is worth the money to buy bigger bulbs.

- ✔ **Number 1 grade double-nose,** sometimes called *exhibition size* or *mother bulbs,* have three "noses" or offsets, and you'll generally get a flower stem from each nose; pay for one bulb and get three flowers.

- ✔ **Number 2 double-nose,** also called *top size* or *bedding size,* have two noses, and produce two flowers stems.

- ✔ **Number 3 rounds,** also called *landscape* or *naturalizing* bulbs, have a single nose and produce a single flower stem.

Remember: Actual bulb sizes (circumferences) vary from one classification to another. Trumpet, long-cup, and split trumpet daffodils are larger within each grade than a similar grade of short cup, *triandrus, cyclamineus, jonquilla, tazetta,* and *poeticus* daffodils. For example *cyclamineus* daffodil 'Jack Snipe' bulbs are never as big as those of 'Dutch Master', a trumpet daffodil.

Be sure to buy healthy bulbs. If you are choosing your own bulbs at a garden center or nursery, select firm daffodil bulbs, plump and heavy for their size. Avoid any that feel squashy or have a soft basal plate.

Planting Daffodils

Daffodils grow best in sun or partial shade. They're great in the perennial border and equally useful in a shady garden. In cold winter areas, zones 4 to 6, plant as soon as bulbs are available in September and early October.

How to prepare the soil

Give daffodils a place with good soil that is high in organic matter — moist but well-drained. Although daffodils like moisture, lots of it, while they are actively growing, they don't want to be soggy in winter.

If you have a compost heap (and every serious gardener should), the organic matter can be compost or leaf mold. Otherwise, add bagged, dried manure from the garden center. Dig in a 2-inch layer of the stuff to prepare the soil before planting.

In general, bonemeal is a crummy fertilizer. If you prefer organic fertilizers, use rock phosphate and green sand. If inorganics are fine with your gardening philosophy, use a 5-10-10 granular fertilizer. If that's difficult to find in your area, use 5-10-5. Be sure to mix the fertilizer well with the soil at the bottom of the planting hole and then add some unamended soil to cover the fertilizer-enriched soil at the bottom of the hole before setting the bulb. Especially with inorganic fertilizers, it is important that the base of the bulb not touch the granules. Salt burns, so you need to take reasonable care to avoid damage to the bulb plate when planting.

How to plant

Plant daffodils in groups of ten or more. Make a sort of circle with six or seven bulbs along the perimeter and three or four in the middle.

For aesthetic reasons, don't mix different cultivars within each planting group — the effect will be stronger if you stay with one kind (such as a group of ten 'Ice Follies' or ten 'Spellbinder,' but not a group of 'Ice Follies' mixed with 'Spellbinder'). Where space permits you can plant in bigger blocks, 25 or even more. Daffodils in formal gardens look best in formal shapes, squares or circles. Informal plantings look good with tapered, fish-shaped drifts of daffodils.

- ✔ Plant daffodil bulbs with the pointy end up and the fatter, somewhat flattened end down.

- ✔ Plant daffodils twice as deep as the bulb is tall. If you have a bulb that's 2 inches from base to tip, dig a 6-inch deep hole (8 inches to base for a larger size bulb). No need to measure, you can just eyeball it. Bigger bulbs go deeper, smaller bulbs closer to the surface. Plant more deeply in sandy soil, more shallowly in heavy, clay-type soils.

- ✔ Cover the bulbs with soil and then water well after planting. Mulch with pine bark mulch, chopped leaves, or whatever you usually use as mulch.

Then wait — you'll soon see spring! In zones 6 and 7, garden daffodils bloom in April — sooner in mild winter regions (zones 8 and 9), later in colder areas (zones 4 and 5).

You may see photographs of great sweeps of lawn with daffodils in bloom. (In fact, we have one in the color section!) Remember, however pretty it looks in the picture, you cannot cut the grass until the daffodil leaves turn completely yellow. So the lawn's going to look shaggy, and take a while to recover after you cut the hay. It is much better to plant daffodils in rough grass than a lawn.

Don't use the cut grass mixed with daffodil leaves to feed your pet bunny, or any other animal. Daffodils are poisonous — that's probably why deer, rabbits, woodchucks, and other pests leave them strictly alone.

Companion Planting

Daffodils are reliable bulbs that come back year after year. Combining them with other kinds of plants — perennials, annuals, and shrubs — makes for a livelier and more interesting display.

Daffodils go dormant in very late spring to early summer. Do **not** fold, braid, rubber band, or otherwise mutilate their leaves. It may look tidier after the flowers have faded, but reduces the bulb's ability to make and store food for next year's display. After leaves turn yellow, you can remove them.

The best approach is to combine daffodils — and other bulbs, too — with plants that distract your attention from those yellowing daffodil leaves.

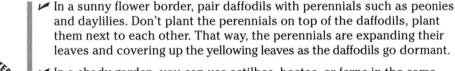

- ✔ In a sunny flower border, pair daffodils with perennials such as peonies and daylilies. Don't plant the perennials on top of the daffodils, plant them next to each other. That way, the perennials are expanding their leaves and covering up the yellowing leaves as the daffodils go dormant.

- ✔ In a shady garden, you can use astilbes, hostas, or ferns in the same way as the peonies and daylilies. *Note:* Although deer adore tulips and hostas, they leave daffodils and ferns alone.

- ✔ Certain spring annuals, such as pansies and primroses, make fine partners for the early color daffodils provide in your garden.

If you combine daffodils with shrubs, be sure to think about colors. Depending on personal taste, you may adore the vibrant color combination of a purple rhododendron and yellow daffodils, or you may think that the colors are screaming at each other. White daffodils would make a better partner. Yellow forsythia may seem like a good, safe choice, but yellow daffodils may disappear from view, camouflaged yellow into yellow.

Growing Daffodils Year-Round

Daffodils are good, multipurpose bulbs. As well as making a fine display in the garden, daffodils make great cut flowers (see Chapter 23). They can also be potted in autumn and coaxed into early bloom while winter is still outdoors (see Chapter 24).

Chapter 6
Don't Tiptoe — Run to the Tulips!

··

In This Chapter
▶ Choosing tulips for flower beds and rock gardens
▶ Deciding on permanent or annual cultivars
▶ Planning and planting for a rainbow spring
▶ Finding good companion plants to use with tulips
▶ Foiling pests

··

*T*ulips have a history as colorful as their flowers. Today their beautiful flowers make them welcome additions to our spring gardens. Yet they once were the junk bonds of early 17th century Holland (Tulipomania). Fortunes were gambled and lost on the potential beauty of an individual bulb still in the ground. People sold bulbs they owned only on paper. The wealthy and their servants all joined in. When the Holland bulb industry went bust on February 3, 1637, the Dutch government stepped in and suspended trading, though they couldn't suspend love for the beautiful flower. Today, however, the Holland bulb industry is a sound investment, supplying flower bulbs to the world.

Tulips: By Every Other Name

As with daffodils, tulips are classified by a variety of factors: number of flowers, shape of flowers, and time of bloom, among others. The following sections present the major *Tulipa* classifications.

Single early tulips

The name says it all — these are single-flowered *cultivars* (*culti*vated *vari*ety), early flowering, with strong 10- to 18-inch stems. Many are sweetly scented. Effective in beds, borders, and containers, these low-growing, early-blooming tulips are also good for cutting and forcing (see Chapter 23):

A bulb in the hand

Contemporary tulips are grown for their flowers, as garden plants, and in bouquets. But during the dark period of the German occupation of Holland in the winter of World War II, tulip bulbs served as food for the Dutch.

- ❀ **'Apricot Beauty':** These salmon and rose-pink flowers reach 18 inches. This sturdy, ever-popular, fragrant choice is ideal for bedding and forcing. *(You can see this one in a glorious garden setting in the color section.)*

- ❀ **'Flair':** Excellent, showy, bright red flowers with a hint of yellow on strong 14-inch stems give this selection plenty of landscape and container value.

- ❀ **'Mickey Mouse':** Dramatic, fringed "Rembrandt" type red-on-yellow flowers with feathered and striped petals that reach 14 inches are arresting accents in the landscape.

- ❀ **'Purple Prince':** Large lilac-purple flowers that reach 14 inches make a strong statement next to late daffodils and other late spring bloomers.

Double early tulips

Among the best bedding tulips — these large, double-flowered, early-blooming, peony-like blossoms provide a blanket of color on 10- to 12-inch stems. Somewhat formal in appearance, they look best in the front of the perennial border. In addition to beds and borders, these are also good for forcing and as cut flowers:

- ❀ **'Abba':** With tomato-red blossoms on 12-inch stems, fragrance and flaming color make this an excellent choice for cutting, bedding, and landscape use.

- ❀ **'Monte Carlo':** Bright yellow flowers top 12-inch stems. These fragrant blossoms are striking in beds, forced indoors, or in arrangements.

- ❀ **'Peach Blossom':** With rosy-pink blossoms that reach 12 inches, this old-fashioned favorite — known for its honey scent and soft color — is ideal for garden and indoor use.

Fringed tulips

Fringed tulips have one stem per bulb, a single flower per stem — but what an interesting flower. These tulips have petals intriguingly laced with crystal-like fringes (see Figure 6-1). You'll want to reach out and touch the crystal-like edges on these unique mid- to late-season beauties. Stem length varies from 16 to 26 inches.

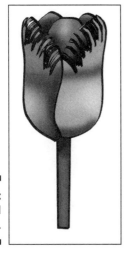

Figure 6-1:
Fringed
tulip.

Fringed tulips make a remarkable cut flower, or you can use them in beds, borders, or arrangements. Try these cultivars:

❀ **'Burgundy Lace':** Wine-red flowers reach 26 inches. Excellent for long-term plantings, this rich-looking flower provides a lasting display in beds, borders, or arrangements.

❀ **'Fringed Beauty':** Reddish-orange and yellow flowers extend to 22 inches. The intensity of the orange, accented with yellow make this flower truly unusual. Try it in beds and borders or arrangements.

❀ **'Fringed Elegance':** Primrose-yellow-edged-in-red blossoms top 22-inch stems. You'll get impressive repeat shows from year to year with this all-around favorite for indoors and out.

❀ **'Fringed Rhapsody':** Creamy-to-dark-yellow and red streaked flowers to 20 inches. A lavish blend of yellows and red, this flower offers variable beauty in the bed, border or vase.

❀ **'Swan Wings':** Pure white flowers grow on 20-inch stems. The pristine feathery petals combine well with other tulips in beds, borders, and arrangements.

Double late tulips

These double-flowered, late-blooming, long-stemmed tulips need some support in the form of staking, especially in wet weather when the extra petals soak up rain like blotting paper. They make an interesting cut flower.

Also known as peony flowering tulips, these offer striking, full blossoms well into the season, and plants reach 16 to 20 inches. With fragrance and long-lasting reliability, the following are useful in a variety of garden and indoor settings:

- ❀ **'Angelique':** Rose, pink, and white flowers crown 18-inch stems. Pale to dark rose double petals accented in white make this a most popular tulip for bedding.

- ❀ **'Carnaval de Nice':** Extra-large, showy white and red flowers on 20-inch stems mark this as an excellent landscape or bedding choice.

- ❀ **'Mount Tacoma':** White blossoms top strong, 18-inch stems. Vigorous, full flowers have subtle green accents and long lasting appeal in borders or clusters.

Darwin hybrid tulips

These hybrid tulips have a mixed past — Darwin tulips were crossed with *Tulipa fosteriana,* and then hybridized with other cultivars and other species of tulips. Huge, bright flowers on sturdy stems to 24 inches give this group much appeal. Plants bloom midseason and multiply in the garden, making them effective for use in beds and borders. Darwin hybrid tulips are excellent as cut flowers. Consider these cultivars:

- ❀ **'Apeldoorn':** With brilliant red flowers on 24-inch stems, this is the classic red tulip that is unsurpassed in the garden and in bouquets.

- ❀ **'Beauty of Apeldoorn':** This striped beauty with golden yellow and magenta flowers atop 22-inch stems offers a wonderful range of color. making it a striking addition to the garden.

- ❀ **'Daydream':** Like a changing sunset, these large flowers on 22-inch stems mature from yellow to apricot to orange. They're ideal in beds, borders, and bouquets.

- ❀ **'Elizabeth Arden':** Sturdy 24-inch stems stand up to the weather and hold arresting, bright pink blossoms that sparkle in a border or bouquet.

- ❀ **'Golden Apeldoorn':** Sturdy flowers on strong 24-inch stems, combined with vivid golden yellow color, make this selection perfect massed in a bed or planted as an accent.

- ❀ **'Gudoshnik':** With yellow, pink, and red flowers on 24-inch stems, no two of these multicolored beauties are the same. Feature them in a border or cutting garden.

- ❀ **'Olympic Flame':** Brilliant yellow petals brushed with red flaming accents and perched on 24-inch stems make for impressive, sturdy flowers in any border or indoor setting.

Triumph tulips

These popular hybrids of early and late single tulips have a single flower on medium-length (16- to 20-inch) stems and flower in midseason. This group produces large flowers that excel in containers and garden beds and do very well forced or cut.

- ❀ **'Attila':** Purple and violet flowers on 18-inch stems. Regal color and substantial stems make this cultivar excellent for bedding and cutting, especially when combined with white and purple accented 'Shirley.'

- ❀ **'Beau Monde':** Rosy red and ivory flowers on 22-inch stems. This unbeatable combination of rosy flamed markings on a creamy background is simply striking. It works well in many settings.

- ❀ **'Bellona':** Golden yellow flowers open on 18-inch stems. Sweetly scented, vibrant flowers are good bedding and forcing candidates.

- ❀ **'Golden Melody':** Yellow blossoms top 20-inch stems. Glowing like the sun, this standout offers classic good looks indoors and out.

- ❀ **'Ice Follies':** Yellow, red, and pink flowers reach 18 inches. Sparks fly from this 'Rembrandt' type striped blossom that fades from yellow and red to ivory and pink. Ideal in beds and borders.

- ❀ **'Judith Leyster':** Red and cream flowers on 22-inch stems. Strong, feathery light accents play well over a rosy-red base in this stunning flower perfect for borders and cutting.

- ❀ **'Negrita':** Deep purple flowers grow on 20-inch stems. This flower's dark color highlighted by classy silvery-blue tints make this one shine in the garden and indoors.

- ❀ **'Prinses Irene':** Apricot and purple blossoms top 14-inch stems. The pale orange base, brushed with dark flaming strokes give this tulip unique beauty. It's good in beds and as a cut or forced flower.

- ❀ **'Shirley':** White and purple flowers on 20-inch stems. Clean white petals edged in purple make this a standout in the garden or in a vase.

- ❀ **'Striped Sail':** Atop 14-inch stems, impressive flowers turn from creamy yellow to white, accented with purple flame markings. Use it in beds, borders, or indoors.

✿ **'Yokohama':** Golden yellow blossoms on 15-inch stems. Use these bright blossoms to add interest to a special bed, border, or arrangement.

Single late tulips

Single late tulips boast an awesome late season show from strong, reliable 22- to 30-inch flowers in amazing colors. Use these in mass plantings, beds, borders, and for cutting.

✿ **'Bleu Aimable':** Lilac and blue blossoms top 24-inch stems. This unusual flower color — a cool and refreshing shade — gains plenty of attention in beds, borders, and arrangements.

✿ **'Dillenburg':** Terra cotta orange blossoms top 24-inch stems. This unusual and attractive color integrates easily into the garden and adds warmth indoors.

✿ **'Esther':** Pale pink flowers top 18-inch stems. Wonderful pastel pink blossoms stand alone with class or combine elegantly in beds, borders, and indoors.

✿ **'Kingsblood':** Deep red blossoms reach 30 inches. Try these when you want bold, vibrant garden accents or impressive bouquets.

✿ **'Pink Jewel':** Pink and ivory flowers top 22-inch stems. This one is a gem with ivory flames over a soft pink base. Use it in beds, borders, and arrangements.

✿ **'Queen of Bartigons':** Blooms are salmon pink, 22 inches tall. Offering an elegant shade and shimmering highlights, this award winner is ideal for all-around use.

Rembrandt tulips

These were the tulips people bet their fortunes on. No longer commercially available, true Rembrandt tulips are the cultivars that caused the Tulipomania of the early 1600s that I mention in the introduction to this chapter. Their streaked, striped flowers are the result of a virus infection. You can, however, buy disease-free, genetically stable "rembrandt look-alikes" such as 'American Flag' and 'Sorbet.' They look great in the garden and are excellent cut flowers.

(If you ever admired those Dutch flower paintings with vases full of flowers from all seasons and wondered, "How'd they do that?" the answer is easy. Each painting was done over a period of months, with different flowers added to the painting as they came into bloom in the garden.)

🌸 **'Queen of Night':** Deep maroon flowers bloom on 24-inch stems. As one of the darkest tulips, this velvety cultivar is unsurpassed as a featured flower in the landscape and indoors.

🌸 **'Sorbet':** White and purplish-red flowers top 24-inch stems. Another 'Rembrandt,' this selection offers an excellent two-toned accent in beds, borders, and arrangements.

🌸 **'Union Jack':** Raspberry red and cream flowers top 24-inch stems. The striped uniqueness of this 'Rembrandt' gives it eye-catching appeal in beds, borders, and indoor settings.

Parrot tulips

With twisty, curled petals whose edges are snipped and clipped, the large, lush, late-blooming parrot tulips are sure show-stoppers in your garden (see Figure 6-2).

Figure 6-2:
Parrot tulip.

Use these showy, large flowers with the fringed petals crowning 14- to 20-inch stems for accent in beds and borders. They're great as cut flowers, too. We recommend these cultivars:

🌸 **'Apricot Parrot':** Apricot, cream, and green flowers top 20-inch stems. This fragrant cultivar offers soft colors ideal with green accents. Use them in borders, beds, and arrangements.

🌸 **'Black Parrot':** With deep purple, nearly black blossoms on 20-inch stems, this very fringed, velvety flower offers unusual color and impressive contrast in beds and borders.

❀ **'Blue Parrot':** Cool and rich looking, with blue-violet flowers on 22-inch stems, you can easily combine this flower with other tulips or feature it in beds, borders, and arrangements.

❀ **'Estella Rijnveld':** Spectacular flowers in vivid red and bright white on 20-inch stems will jazz up any bed or border or add unequaled drama to arrangements.

❀ **'Flaming Parrot':** Red and yellow blossoms reach 22 inches. Expect dazzling results from sunny yellow flowers brushed with bright red. It's truly outstanding in the garden and as a cut flower.

❀ **'White Parrot':** Fluffy white flowers edged in feathery green on 18-inch stems make this choice a winner in garden settings and with other cut flowers.

Viridiflora tulips

If they didn't flower in May, viridiflora tulips would be perfect for St. Patrick's Day! Also called green tulips, the plants have a single flower per 12- to 20-inch stem, with leaf-green edges or central streak on the petals, providing soft, feathery accents. These outstanding late-season pastel blossoms are long-lasting, making them ideal in borders. They also make interesting cut flower arrangements. Try these cultivars:

❀ **'Esperanto':** Dark pink and green flowers on 20-inch stems. This flower displays an arresting two-toned combination to star in the garden and in arrangements.

❀ **'Groenland' ('Greenland'):** Pink and green flowers on 20-inch stems. An ideal combination of soft pink and feathery green stripes give this bedding and cut flower tremendous appeal.

❀ **'Spring Green':** Creamy white and green flowers top 20-inch stems. Elegant, long-lasting flowers from this cultivar make a splash in the garden or in a vase.

Lily-flowered tulips

Lily-flowered tulips are simply elegant (see Figure 6-3).

Distinctive, slender flowers in vivid colors with pointed petals gently curved outward give these mid- to late-season blossoms status in beds and borders. Stem length varies from 18 to 24 inches, and each bulb provides one flower, with blooms appearing in mid or late season. Lily-flowered tulips make a classy cut flower.

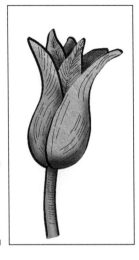

Figure 6-3:
Lily-
flowered
tulip.

We suggest these cultivars:

❀ **'Ballade':** These striking, stylish magenta and white blossoms on 22-inch stems make a bold statement in garden beds, borders, or arrangements.

❀ **'Mariette':** A white base flaring into satiny, rose-pink color on a 22-inch stem gives this cultivar elegance in the garden and in arrangements.

❀ **'Maytime':** This elegant late-flowering tulip featuring reddish-purple flowers edged in cream can reach 24 inches in height, adding a distinctive presence to beds, borders, and arrangements.

❀ **'Queen of Sheba':** With reddish-orange and yellow flowers on 24-inch stems, this tall, regal choice will stand out in the bedding or cutting garden.

❀ **'Red Shine':** Deep red flowers on 22-inch stems are perfectly formed and attractively colored. You can't beat this flower in the landscape or in a bouquet.

❀ **'West Point':** Use these sturdy and brilliant bright yellow flowers on 20-inch stems for accent in the garden or to enliven an arrangement.

❀ **'White Triumphator':** Pristine perfection characterizes these pure white blossoms with 24-inch stems. This is a classic choice for bedding and borders or the cutting garden.

Kaufmanniana hybrid (waterlily) tulips

Very early flowering *Tulipa kaufmanniana* and all its offspring — cultivars and hybrids — are dwarf tulips under a foot tall. The star-like flowers in striking colors open wide on sunny days, giving rise to the common name of waterlily tulip. These charming gems are an excellent choice for the rock garden. Compact and impressive, these flowers are also ideal for permanent plantings in beds and borders.

- ❀ **'Ancilla':** Soft pink, red, and white flowers on 6-inch stems. These large flowers offer a stunning blend of color and fine form. Use them to accent the border or rock garden.

- ❀ **'Johann Straus':** Rosy red and sulfur blossoms on 8-inch stems. Another impressive two-toned flower with spotted foliage, this one will add interest to the border or rock garden.

- ❀ **'Stresa':** Golden-yellow and carmine-red flowers top 8-inch stems. Absolutely vivid, these early, eye-catching flowers set off beds, borders, and rock gardens.

Try planting a handful of waterlily tulips in the same space with several siberian squills. When they flower all together, it looks like waterlilies afloat on a pool of blue water.

Greigii hybrid tulips

Tulipa greigii has given rise to an assortment of very early flowering charming cultivars, varieties, and hybrids that flower just a tad later than *T. kaufmanniana*. The dwarf plants, 8 to 14 inches tall, have leaves flat on the ground, often with wavy edges and chocolate-maroon mottled or striped markings reminiscent of supermarket bar-code price tags. The vivid flowers are good for forcing, great in the rock garden, and perfect for borders, containers, and cutting gardens. Reliably perennial in northern climate zones, this is a great group of tulips:

- ❀ **'Corsage':** These deep salmon pink and yellow flowers on 12-inch stems are unusual and appealing in their subtle colors. Use this one in beds, borders, and arrangements.

- ❀ **'Czar Peter':** Outstanding carmine-red and white flowers on 10-inch stems make a statement in the garden, in pots indoors and out, or in a vase.

- ❀ **'Donna Bella':** Carmine-red and pale yellow blossoms top 10-inch stems. Outer petals perfectly accent interior hues in this arresting flower for the garden and indoor uses.

- ❀ **'Oriental Splendor':** Carmine-red, yellow, and purple flowers on 10-inch stems make another unbeatable color combination that will accent a bed, border, container, or arrangement with style.

- ❀ **'Plaisir':** Carmine-red and cream blossoms on 10-inch stems make a stunning flower for use in the foreground of the garden or as a star in indoor arrangements.

❀ **'Red Riding Hood':** Bright red flowers top 8-inch stems. Expect early, dazzling results from this flower with a black base, perfect for use indoors and out.

Fosteriana hybrid tulips

Early fireworks are the payoff with these large, bright flowers offering impressive displays in mass plantings, borders, rock gardens, cutting gardens, and forcing jars. *Tulipa fosteriana* is parent to a number of early flowering cultivars, varieties, and hybrids noted for their large, long flowers on medium to long (8 to 18 inches) stems. Flowers open wide in sunshine. Their flowering period overlaps with late season daffodils. Check out these cultivars:

❀ **'Juan':** Orange and yellow flowers bloom on stems to 18 inches. Royal orange with a yellow base, this flower with purple, mottled foliage stands out in the border, landscape, or arrangement.

❀ **'Orange Emperor':** Orange flowers bloom on 16-inch stems. A deep orange center gives way to soft, satin exterior petals in this stunning flower ideal for garden and indoor use.

❀ **'Princeps':** Scarlet flowers top 8-inch stems. Tiny but mighty, this little show-stopper in vivid red is ideal for any rock garden, container, or cutting garden.

❀ **'Red Emperor' (Madame Lefebre):** Huge, regal, bright red blossoms opening on 18-inch stems simply command attention in this all-time garden favorite.

❀ **'White Emperor'(Purissima):** Glistening, pure white, fragrant flowers blooming on 18-inch stems will lend impressive elegance to your bed, border, or arrangement.

❀ **'Yellow Empress':** Large, golden-yellow flowers atop 16-inch stems add early sunny cheer indoors and out.

Bunch-flowering (multiflowered) tulips

If you like more bang for your buck, you should probably consider growing multiflowered tulips, where each bulb produces a single stem with four to six full-sized flowers. These varieties create a spectacular, long-lasting display in beds, borders, and bouquets. They bloom mid to late season on 8- to 20-inch stems.

Although not an "official" classification of the Dutch bulb growers, multi-flowered tulips are often grouped together in catalogs for your convenience.

Because bunch-flowering can occur in triumph, single late, and even greigii tulips, height and bloom time will vary from cultivar to cultivar. Try these varieties:

- ❀ **'Candy Club':** This single late tulip has ivory white flowers atop 20-inch stems. Subtle pink or purple accents on a white background provide classic good looks in the garden and in arrangements.

- ❀ *Tulipa praestans* **'Fusilier':** Several vivid hot orange-scarlet flowers accented with black anthers bloom on a 10-inch stem. These glowing flowers reliably reappear in the rock garden, border, or bowl.

- ❀ **'Georgette':** This single late tulip sports yellow and red flowers on 20-inch stems. Clear yellow petals and red highlights make quite a show in beds, borders, and bouquets.

- ❀ **'Red Georgette':** This single late tulip has late flowers in brilliant, arresting red that reach 18 inches and offer dazzling results in beds, borders, and arrangements.

- ❀ **'Toronto':** With salmon-colored flowers atop 12-inch stems, this gregii-type tulip sports mottled foliage and glowing flowers, making it ideal in beds and borders.

- ❀ *Tulipa praestans* **'Unicum':** Red-orange and white blossoms on 8-inch stems. Similar to 'Fusilier', 'Unicum' has bright flowers with white-edged leaves. It works well indoors and out.

Species tulips

Including such charmers as the candystick tulip, *Tulipa clusiana*, multiflowered *Tulipa tarda*, and others probably best grown in the rock garden or herb garden, these "wild" cultivars offer compact plants (6 to 8 inches) that star in rock gardens, along border fronts, in containers, in heirloom plantings, and naturalized in the landscape. *Tulipa bakeri* and *Tulipa batalinii* and their cultivars are excellent in the South. We recommend the following:

- ❀ *Tulipa bakeri* **'Lilac Wonder':** Lilac and yellow flowers bloom on 7-inch stems. Stunning, cupped, star-like flowers will spark the border or rock garden in midseason.

- ❀ *Tulipa batalinii* **'Apricot Jewel':** Apricot orange and yellow flowers on 6-inch stems. The golden centers and irresistible apricot color make these flowers ideal in beds and rock gardens.

- ❀ *Tulipa batalinii* **'Bright Gem':** Yellow and orange blossoms top 6-inch stems. The colors blend for a soft but appealing look, perfect in clusters or rock gardens.

❀ *Tulipa batalinii* **'Red Gem':** Vermilion and apricot flowers crown 6-inch stems. This popular choice offers perfectly-formed, long-lasting flowers for varied uses.

❀ *Tulipa batalinii* **'Yellow Jewel':** Soft, lemon-yellow flowers with a hint of rose on 6-inch stems provide unique appeal in gardens and indoors.

❀ *Tulipa clusiana* **'Cynthia':** Red-edged chartreuse and purple based flowers reach 12 inches. Dazzling candy-striped, feathery flowers in a star shape are a must in the garden.

❀ *Tulipa clusiana* **var. *chrysantha*:** These deep yellow and crimson flowers on 12-inch stems provide exquisite color and form, making this midseason bloomer a highlight in the rock garden.

❀ *Tulipa clusiana* **var. *chrysantha* 'Tubergen's Gem':** Midseason blossoms in a deep red and bright yellow combo atop 10-inch stems are ideal in rock gardens and containers.

❀ *Tulipa fostoriana:* Red and yellow-black centered flowers reach 20 inches. These flowers offer interesting colors and markings and provide interest in many garden settings.

❀ *Tulipa gregii:* Red and yellow flowers reach 18 inches. Early, cup-shaped flowers offer striking yellow-ringed black centers. Use these for naturalizing or planting in the border.

❀ *Tulipa hageri* **'Spendens':** These bell-shaped flowers in rich coppery and bronze tones sprout three to five blooms per 8-inch stem, making them a solid garden performer.

❀ *Tulipa kaufmanniana,* **'Waterlily':** Creamy white flowers top 8-inch stems. Excellent color blends make this species tulip a great rock garden, border, or container selection.

❀ *Tulipa tarda:* This easy to grow, ground-cover-like selection with white, green, and yellow flowers atop 4-inch stems will add distinction to the border edge or rock garden.

❀ *Tulipa whittalli:* Orange, green, and buff blossoms reach 12 inches. An unusual and showy flower, the graceful bell-shaped blossoms will shine in many garden settings or in containers.

Tulip-Planting Basics

Wild tulips are native to arid regions of Central Asia. The original species have a limited color range — primarily reds and yellows — and tend to be smaller in flower than modern cultivars and hybrids, whose rainbow hues include strong bright colors and pastel shades, providing options and possibilities for any desired color scheme. The bulbs you buy in fall already have an embryo flower tucked away inside, just waiting to begin growing in spring (see Figure 6-4). Plant the bulbs in groups of ten in the perennial border. Space them a couple of inches apart.

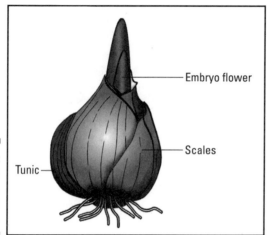

Figure 6-4:
Your tulip bulb, waiting to flower.

Choose tulips just like other bulbs — fat and firm. Avoid any that are soft, flabby, moldy, or whose papery brown tunic is missing. Buy tulip bulbs along with all your other bulbs in September, but wait to plant until October and November — even December if you live in mild winter areas. Tulips are so eager to grow that if you plant them promptly in the fall, they'll send their leaves up right away, only to have them frozen in winter. While you wait to plant them, store bulbs in paper bags, not plastic, and keep them in a cool place, away from heat ducts or furnaces, until you plant.

If you have the room, keep tulip bulbs in your refrigerator's crisper drawer, but away from apples and other fruit. Apples and bananas give off ethylene gas, which helps fruit ripen but destroys the flower bud inside the bulb. No room in the refrigerator? Don't put tulip bulbs in the freezer, it will kill them!

Keep the following points in mind before planting tulips:

✔ Keep tulip bulbs really dry and well ventilated if you dig and store tulips over summer when bulbs are dormant.

✔ Plant tulip bulbs in fall (September to December), or they send their leaves up in time to get frozen by winter.

✔ Good drainage is very important; bulbs rot in wet soil.

✔ Select a sunny site, tulips won't grow well in shade.

✔ The Dutch ate tulips from necessity; pests eat them for preference. Protect your plants.

Digging your tulip garden

Planting tulips is easy. First, prepare the soil:

1. **Choose a sunny site with good drainage.**

2. **Dig the area and loosen the soil a foot deep.**

3. **Add some compost or dried manure (you buy it at the garden center or nursery).**

4. **Add some 5-10-5 or 5-10-10 granular fertilizer.**

   See Chapter 21 for more about fertilizer.

5. **Mix all the ingredients — existing soil, soil amendments, and fertilizer, just like a cake batter.**

After the site is prepared properly, you can easily dig the individual planting holes:

1. **Dig each hole three times as deep as the bulb is tall.**

   There should be twice as much soil over the tip or nose of the bulb as from tip to base of the bulb, so if your tulip bulb measures $2^1/_2$ inches tall, dig your hole 8 inches deep, so you'll have 5 inches ($2^1/_2 + 2^1/_2$) of soil above the tip of your bulb.

2. **Set the tulip so the pointy end is up (see Figure 6-5).**

   Don't worry if you get some upside down, they'll flower anyhow, but it will take them longer to emerge in spring and they may not be as tall as they should.

3. **After the tulips are planted, water thoroughly and then cover with a mulch of pine bark or shredded leaves.**

That's all, unless squirrels or cats dig in the soft soil. In that case, lay an old window screen over the soft, freshly dug soil, or a piece of chicken wire or hardware cloth. After the ground is frozen, you can remove the protection.

If you want some tulips for cut flowers, plant the bulbs in a row in the vegetable garden or other out of the way place. Then, when you cut them, you won't spoil the appearance of the garden.

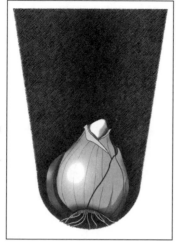

Figure 6-5:
Tulips grow
better
planted
right side
up.

Cut tulips when the buds are showing lots of color but before the flowers open — they'll last longer. Don't mix tulips and freshly cut daffodils in the same vase — fresh-cut daffodils give off a slime from their stems that makes tulips wilt faster.

Planting companions: Two (or more) for the show

Tulips are beautiful, and they look even better with the right garden partners.

- **Annuals.** Annuals provide quick color. Choose pansies and/or primroses, conveniently available at garden centers when the tulips are in bloom. Forget-me-nots are nice, too.

- **Bulbs.** That's right; why not use tulips with other bulbs? Because there are early, midseason, and late tulips, make sure that you choose companion bulbs with bloom times that match your tulips. Early tulips with late daffodils and/or siberian squill, midseason tulips with hyacinths, and late-season tulips with camassia.

- **Perennials.** Perennials that flower early in spring are another option, one that returns year after year. Choose bleeding heart with pink locket-like flowers, Virginia bluebells with soft blue bell-like flowers, or the yellow daisies of leopard's bane. Low-growing early tulips in the rock garden or at the front of the perennial border look great with yellow basket-of-gold alyssum, white candytuft, or creeping phlox in an assortment of pinks and blues.

Shrubs also make a nice background for tulips — yellow-flowered forsythia for example. Ask the folks at your local garden center or nursery what shrubs they recommend. Or, choose a shrub with unusual leaf color — coppery 'Crimson Pygmy' barberry, or greeny-gold spirea 'Lime Mound.'

Handling problem pests

Tulips are popular, not only with gardeners who enjoy their flowers but with critters who eat 'em up! City gardeners fight off squirrels, while suburbanites must deal with voles, chipmunks, rabbits, and often even deer!

Here are tips for dealing with the most common bulb pests:

- ✔ **Bulb eaters.** Squirrels, voles, and chipmunks burrow underground and eat tulip bulbs. Try planting tulip bulbs in a wire cage or coarse plastic mesh bag (you can find them in garden supply catalogs). But don't use onion bags from the supermarket because the holes are too small for the sprouts to grow through.

- ✔ **Flower eaters.** Rabbits and deer dine on tulip flowers. Rabbits are sometimes repelled by dried blood — which you can purchase at a garden center — sprinkled around on the ground. *Hint:* You'll need to reapply dried blood after rain or irrigation washes it away. Be stingy rather than generous when applying dried blood — it is a nitrogen fertilizer. Too much can overstimulate leaf growth and produce floppy stems. Various deer repellents are available that you can spray on tulips. Or, you can cage the plants with chicken wire so deer and rabbits cannot get at your "salad bar."

Caring for your flowers

Following are tips for caring for your tulips after they've flowered:

- ✔ **Off with their heads!** After tulips have flowered, their colorful petals wither and seed production starts. Perennial tulips such as the dwarf greigii, Darwin hybrids, and kaufmanniana hybrids should be deadheaded — clip off the spent flower and stalk. Energy goes into storage in the daughter bulbs for next year's flowers rather than seed production for the next generation.

- ✔ **Feed with fertilizer.** Tulip leaves aren't around for very long; plants are dormant by mid-summer. So a quick feed or two (or three) with a liquid fertilizer that bulbs can utilize right away is a good idea.

What happens if they seed?

Because seed production diverts energy from food storage in a bulb and this weakens the bulb, there's no point in letting them seed unless you're hybridizing tulips (which is too advanced for this book). Letting little bulbs such as scilla go to seed does not matter as much as it does with tulips and daffodils. Judy has more than 1,200 poeticus daffodils along a path into the woods and, that's right, she deadheads them all so they don't go to seed!

Those blue crystals that dissolve in water — for example, Peters and Miracle-Gro — are just the thing. Look for one where the nutrient numbers — N-P-K — are lower in **N**itrogen and higher in **P**hosphorus, the second number, and **K** Potash (K because if we used P for potash it would be confused with phosphorus), the third number. Make the solution weaker than suggested, half strength. (If the label says 1 tablespoon to 1 gallon of water, use 1 tablespoon to 2 gallons of water.) Splash it on tulip leaves and the ground right around the bulb and splash again in a couple of weeks. If you feel dedicated and solicitous, splash again a couple of weeks after the second feeding.

✔ **Turn off the tap.** Originally, tulips came from places where it never rained in summer. Unless you live in Colorado or someplace like that, chances are you occasionally have rain. If it doesn't rain, we water. Plant perennial tulips in the rock garden or herb garden, places with quick-draining soil and water-thrifty plants. In the perennial border, mix tulips with perennials such as lamb's ear and yarrow that can get by with less water. Then, when the tulips are dormant — asleep underground — you can water less because the plants that *are* still growing aren't thirsty.

Enjoy the flowers in the garden or as cut flowers. But after the tulips flower, make your life easy: Pull the bulbs out of the ground and throw them away. Not all tulips are as perennial as a gardener would wish. The big Darwin hybrids and triumph hybrids, fancy parrot, viridiflora, and lily-flowered tulips flower beautifully the first spring after you plant them. The second year, some send up a single huge leaf and no flowers. Even more won't flower their third year. Just think of them as annuals you happen to plant in autumn.

Of course, because robust growth is so dependent on proper drainage together with the variety of cultivar and how well it performs in your area, you may find that your tulips grow well year after year. If that's the case, keep 'em growing.

Chapter 7
Hyacinths — Fabulously Fragrant

In This Chapter

▶ Flower power with hyacinths — colorful and fragrant

▶ Tips and techniques for easy growing

*G*ranted, flowers should look pretty. But sometimes we get so caught up with their looks that we ignore other qualities — like fragrance. Hyacinths not only look good, they smell great — a floral perfume that's never cloying or heavy. This flower has a delicious scent that's great in the garden. It's also fine indoors, whether as a container of bulbs coaxed into early bloom or cut for a bouquet. (Directions for potting bulbs for early flowers are in Chapter 19, and cut flower information is in Chapter 23.)

Considering Hyacinths

The original wild hyacinths have pale-to-deep-violet-blue or pale-to-deep-pink flowers. With this foundation to build on, in the centuries since hyacinths were introduced to Western Europe from what is now Turkey, Syria, and Lebanon in 1562, hybridizers have developed an even wider range of colors. You can now find hyacinths with white, soft yellow, salmon orange, or red flowers, as well as in their original colors. There are even double- as well as single-flowered forms. (They're all suitable for growing in containers; but they're kind of top-heavy and fall over in rainy conditions or strong winds, so they may need support.)

Hyacinths are true bulbs. The flat bottom of the bulb goes at the bottom of the planting hole and the pointy end goes up. Just like an onion, if you cut hyacinths in half, you find rings, and hyacinths also have papery tunics or coverings.

Here's a handy hint if you forget to label the bags of hyacinths you bought at the garden center. Those with pink, violet, or blue flowers have a deep reddish-violet tunic; white- and yellow-flowered forms have white tunics.

The tunics of dry hyacinth bulbs contain acid that can make your skin itch. We recommend that you wear gloves when handling hyacinth bulbs, and that you moisten the bulbs right before you plant them.

Because hyacinths have a full, fat spike of closely clustered flowers, they are more appropriate for traditional garden schemes than naturalistic planting designs. We find them better in somewhat orderly plantings — in small groups rather than scattered about.

Think about a crisp, cool planting of white flowering hyacinths in repeating groups of five or ten — depending on the size of your planting area — underplanted with running myrtle as a ground cover. Then in summer you can follow the hyacinths with white leafed caladiums (a tender bulb, which we discuss in Chapter 14) and white flowering impatiens.

Hyacinths pair nicely with smaller bulbs, for a sort of jack-in-the-box design technique. Try dark blue flowering hyacinths with grape hyacinths, or pink ones with the pink daisies of Grecian windflowers (see Chapter 10).

Omar Khayyam, a 12th-century Persian poet and mathematician, wrote: "If thou hast but two loaves, sell one and buy hyacinths for your soul." This is still good advice in the new millennium.

Choosing the Right Hyacinth for You

The following sections recommend several choice cultivars to enjoy along the edges of beds and borders, or grouped in the landscape and, of course, in pots placed indoors and out.

Single hyacinths

Single flowered inflorescences (an arrangement of flowers along a single axis) make up the largest category of hyacinth, comprising a wide array of 8- to 12-inch flowers in a rainbow of colors. Each bulb sends up a single stalk covered in starry, fragrant florets (see Figure 7-1).

Figure 7-1:
The lovely, fragrant hyacinth.

Consider the following single hyacinth cultivars:

❀ **'Anna Marie':** Soft pink flowers top 12- to 15-inch stems. Clear pink blossoms cover the stalks of this bulb, which is sometimes sold specially prepared for early forcing for indoor Christmas displays.

❀ **'Blue Giant':** Pale blue flowers top 8- to 10-inch stems. This soft blue blends beautifully with darker shades of other hyacinths. These bulbs do very well in the garden and in pots.

❀ **'Blue Jacket':** Dark blue blossoms reach 8 inches. Impressive, cool, deep-blue flowers lightly striped with purple make a bold statement in the garden. Indoors, this variety can be forced for Easter bloom.

❀ **'Blue Magic':** Deep purplish-blue and white flowers top 10-inch stems. Dark, rich florets accented with white throats are arresting in beds, borders, containers, or arrangements. This cultivar definitely attracts attention.

❀ **'Carnegie':** White flowers top 10-inch stalks. This plant is the brightest, purest white of all the hyacinths. It offers an early, densely flowered spike and delightful fragrance. Use it in the garden, for cutting, or forced for Easter bloom.

❀ **'City of Haarlem':** Soft yellow flowers top 8-inch stems. The full-flowered spikes in soft yellow work well in combination with other pastels in the bed, border, or landscape.

❀ **'Delft Blue':** Pale, lilac-blue blossoms reach 8 inches. Especially good for forcing, this cultivar also serves well in the garden where its bright, clear color combines well with other bulbs or annuals.

❀ **'Gipsy Queen':** Dark salmon flowers grow on 8-inch spikes. The unique salmon-apricot color of this flower is simply hard to resist. It offers plenty of its own beauty and looks wonderful combined with other soft colors in the garden, in arrangements, or forced for a dining room table display.

❀ **'Jan Bos':** Almost-red florets cover 8-inch spikes. As red as they come, this hyacinth offers exciting vibrant color that is both unique and old-fashioned. Use it with success in the garden, in arrangements, and forced for display in pots.

❀ **'Lady Derby':** Soft pink flowers reach 10 inches. A wonderful pink, bordering on salmon, makes this flower an excellent choice to edge a bed or spark an arrangement.

❀ **'Paul Hermann':** Violet and dark purple flowers on 10-inch bronze-brown stalks. The combination of amethyst-violet flowers with dark purple streaks is outstanding in a variety of garden and indoor uses.

❀ **'Pink Pearl':** Deep, rosy-pink flowers on 10-inch spikes. Large, strong spikes make this hyacinth the best pink variety for forcing. Expect stunning results in beds, borders, and arrangements, too.

❀ **'Splendid Cornelia':** Pale pink and mauve florets cover 8-inch stems. Pleasingly fragrant blooms in a unique shade add class to the garden, container, or forcing jar.

❀ **'Violet Pearl':** Violet flowers cover 8-inch spikes. Elegant violet flowers with a hint of purple are bright and lasting in the garden, in your window box, or indoors.

Double hyacinths

Expect more of a good thing with this category featuring full, extra-fragrant flowers on compact but prolific spikes. You get double rewards because each floret has a second floret blooming in its center. Use these striking bulbs in beds, borders, containers, or for forcing:

❀ **'Chestnut Flower':** Light pink and dark pink flowers grow on 8-inch stems. Blossoms resembling horse chestnut flowers on this old-fashioned favorite offer delightful pink accents in beds, borders, tubs, or window boxes.

❀ **'General Kohler':** Lavender flowers cover 8-inch spikes. Another reliable and attractive heirloom plant, this hyacinth has been in cultivation since 1878. Use it for sure success in your garden or spring container collection.

❀ **'Hollyhock':** Crimson flowers top 8-inch stems. Arresting flowers with an awesome fragrance give this popular double plenty of value in a variety of settings.

❀ **'Madam Sophie':** White flowers top 8-inch stalks. This elegant hyacinth is a definite standout in the garden. It offers excellent fragrance and form indoors, where it is a good choice for early forcing.

Multiflora hyacinths

When you want a lighter, less formal hyacinth, try the cultivars in this category. Each bulb produces three to four loose spikes with up to a dozen fragrant flowers on each spike. Native to the south of France, these early bloomers come in white or blue and offer a soft, airy look. Try these in beds, borders, containers, and for forcing:

❀ **'Borah':** White flowers top 8-inch stems. As gardeners have known for generations, this heirloom beauty adds grace and charm to any border or indoor display.

❀ **'Blue Borah':** Soft blue flowers top 8-inch stems. This one is a winner in nature and a winner in your garden where this natural multi-flowering bulb offers wonderful fragrance in a delightful color.

❀ **'Snow White':** Pure white flowers grow on 8-inch stems. Often the earliest blossoms are the most special, as is the case with this delicate flower with sweetly scented blossoms. Try planting a drift of these hyacinths in the garden or forcing some for indoor fragrance.

Caring for Your Hyacinths

Plant your hyacinths in early fall so that they have enough time to grow a good mass of roots before winter. Choose a spot that has full sun in the north and light shade in the south with rich, moist, well-drained soil. The soil should be well prepared with plenty of organics and a complete fertilizer mixed in. Set the bulbs, flat side down, about 8 inches deep and space them 2 to 3 inches apart. You can also enjoy hyacinths in containers, as we describe in Chapter 19.

Don't forget to reserve at least a few bulbs for forcing so that you can enjoy these flowers indoors. Forcing is a snap if you use a special hyacinth glass that supports the bulb as it roots in water (see Figure 7-2).

Figure 7-2:
Hyacinths
grow
beautifully
in water.

Follow these steps for forcing hyacinths:

1. **If you don't buy prechilled (prepared) bulbs, cool bulbs for about 8 to 12 weeks in the fridge.**

2. **Set the bulbs, one to a jar, pointed side up so the water just touches the bulb.**

   Keep each bulb in a cool, dark place until you see a mass of roots and a 3- to 4-inch shoot with the flower bud in the center.

3. **When the shoot appears, move the bulb to a bright location (that maintains a fairly constant temperature of 60 to 70 degrees Fahrenheit) and maintain the same water level.**

In a few weeks, you should have a fabulous flower to enjoy. Unfortunately, the bulb uses all its energy on this process, so discard the bulb after the blooms fade.

As your outdoor bulbs emerge and grow, some may need staking, particularly double hyacinths, which may be top heavy. If you live in an area where the ground freezes or severe frosts occur, mulch the bulbs for protection. After the floral show, cut the flower stalks when the blossoms fade, but leave the foliage, removing it only when it has completely died. In the ground, your hyacinths should do fine season after season, but don't be surprised if the flower stalks look somewhat looser after the first year.

Chapter 8

Beautiful Blues: Grape Hyacinths, Scillas, Glory of the Snow, and Bluebells

Although flowers appear in lots of other colors, not many are in the hue of blue. Some of the perennials with blue flowers, gentians for example, are tough to grow. Once again, bulbs come to the rescue. You can find a handful of easily grown, readily available, inexpensive, long-lived little bulbs with blue flowers from electric to smoky. They've been grown in gardens for a long time, usually a century or two and even over four hundred years in the case of one type of bulb. Now that's reliability!

Grape Hyacinths

Grape hyacinths do look sort of like a miniature hyacinth, if you squint a little bit. The plants are shorter, only 6 to 8 inches high. The flowers look like small beads strung closely together up and down the stem (see Figure 8-1).

Grape hyacinths spread quickly; in fact, they can be invasive. We recommend that you plant them where they'll be welcome to spread freely, say under some shrubs rather than in a carefully designed flower garden.

Figure 8-1:
The grape
hyacinth.

Grape hyacinths are so eager to grow that they send their leaves up in fall — kind of scary when you think about it; after all, winter's on the way. They leaf reliably in the fall of every year after the first year of growing — Judy has even seen them leaf during the first year they're planted (when you might expect them to be a little confused). Don't bring out the electric blanket or otherwise worry about trying to cover them up. They're okay. The leaf tips get a little nipped and turn brown, but when spring rolls around the bulbs flower right on schedule.

You can find several varieties of grape hyacinth. The following are some of our favorites:

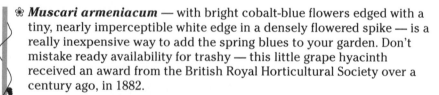

✽ *Muscari armeniacum* — with bright cobalt-blue flowers edged with a tiny, nearly imperceptible white edge in a densely flowered spike — is a really inexpensive way to add the spring blues to your garden. Don't mistake ready availability for trashy — this little grape hyacinth received an award from the British Royal Horticultural Society over a century ago, in 1882.

✽ *Muscari botryoides* is softer in color, sky-blue with a little white edge. This old-timer has been grown in gardens since 1594:

• **'Album'** is a pure white form, slower spreading. For maximum effect, plant bulb to bulb.

• **'Cantab'** and **'Christmas Pearl'** are other popular cultivars.

*❀ **Muscari latifolium*** has two-tone flowers — hyacinth-blue on top and a nice violet on the bottom part or portion of the flower stalk. Cultivated since 1886, plants grow only a single, rather large leaf, or occasionally a pair of leaves.

Planting grape hyacinths

Grape hyacinths grow from small fleshy bulbs. Remember that little bulbs can dry out easier than larger ones, so plan on planting early in autumn. Adaptable, grape hyacinths grow in sun or light shade. They don't like extremes, so avoid really dry or very wet sites. Just about anyplace else is fine.

Follow these tips for growing grape hyacinths:

1. **Loosen the soil, removing weeds, competing roots, and stones.**
2. **Plant bulbs in groups of ten or more, setting the bulbs twice as deep as they're high, and a couple of inches apart.**

Leaves will quickly make an appearance, but just ignore them. Flower spikes appear in mid-spring. Some color variation occurs depending on which ones you plant, but a soft smoky blue is most common.

Grape hyacinths need very little care after they flower. They seem to do fine with natural rainfall, and we don't bother to fertilize them — they multiply just fine without any kind of boost from us!

Because they're smaller, the leaves sort of wither away in a not-very-conspicuous manner. If the withered look does bother you, leaves can be cut off and thrown away when they become mostly yellow. Come fall, fresh leaves will again appear, a nice sort of reminder that something is waiting for spring.

Selecting grape hyacinth companions

 Companion plants always give a boost to the garden. And grape hyacinths are friendly associates for other early plants. Just remember to give them vigorous partners who won't be swamped by the increasing numbers of grape hyacinths that are sure to come! Consider these suggestions:

✔ Peonies are great companion plants for grape hyacinths. Their coral-red new shoots are a lovely contrast to the grape hyacinth flowers, and the expanding peony leaves disguise the grape hyacinth leaves both when they're aging in late spring and reappearing in autumn.

✔ Shrubs are super companions. One of the nicest combinations is grape hyacinths with coppery leaves of barberry, either *Berberis* 'Crimson Pygmy' or 'Rosy Glow.' The smoky blue grape hyacinth flowers get a nice boost from the leafy background.

✔ If you want to accent a seasonal display, how about using pansies? Choose blue ones for a more subtle effect, or yellow pansies for an effective contrast with more punch.

✔ Grape hyacinths are charming when they are growing through a ground cover of moss pink or a carpet of creeping dianthus.

If bulbs with bulbs takes your fancy, try grape hyacinths with hyacinths, perhaps a deep, dark blue-violet such as 'Blue Magic.' The play on scale, little 'uns and big 'uns, can be charming. Figure on using three times as many grape hyacinths as hyacinths, or the display will look skimpy.

Scillas Are Sensational

As long as you understand that scillas will happily spread, making more and more year after year, you can't go wrong with these plants. We're only pointing out their spreading nature in case someone is reading this book who doesn't like plants that volunteer. Most of us appreciate free bonus plants — especially if they're as pretty as these (see Figure 8-2). Blues from skim-milk pale to azure, and flowers like little bells make these spring beauties a welcome addition to the spring garden.

Several varieties of scillas are available:

❀ ***Scilla siberica*** is the most familiar, with bright-blue dangling bells of flowers that bloom in March. This type has been in cultivation since 1796:

  • **'Spring Beauty'** is an even more desirable cultivar. It is larger overall than its parent species, with somewhat richer blue flowers.

  • The **'Alba'** cultivar is a pure white form of *scilla sibirica,* but grows somewhat poorly.

❀ ***Scilla mischtschenkoana*** has a name that sounds something like a cat's sneeze. Maybe we'd better just call it "the other scilla." This other scilla flowers even earlier than the other types (in March in the mid-Atlantic region). It's so eager to display its nearly translucent bells of palest blue-white that flowers start to open as they poke through the ground. The exit-early blooming period means that not much else is available as a partner. Think about using ferns or hostas to cover the bare spots when this other scilla is summer dormant.

Figure 8-2:
Bell-like flowers make scillas super for spring.

Planting scillas

Scillas are true bulbs, small in size, so they are another candidate for early planting. They thrive equally well in shady woodland or a sunny lawn. Follow these steps for growing scillas:

1. **Choose a location where the soil is moist but well-drained, with reasonable amounts of organic matter and moderate fertility.**

2. **Plant in groups of 10, 25, or more.**

   Their small size suggests group planting, and modest prices make it possible. The pointier end goes up and the flatter base down. Set bulbs twice as deep as they're high.

3. **Water if conditions are dry at planting time, and then mulch with the smallest size pinebark or shredded leaves.**

After bulbs flower in early spring, allow leaves to grow until they are yellow; then either tuck them under the leaves of next-door neighboring plants, or cut them away when they're mostly yellow.

Selecting scilla companions

Finding companion plants for your scillas is simple — even your lawn will work. Just let the bulb make good leafy growth to nourish next year's display before you start mowing.

If you want to use your lawn as a backdrop for your scillas, start off with a reasonable number of bulbs, at least 50. Plant them close enough together so you can see them as a group, rather than evenly distributed in a sparse display.

Be careful with weed killers on your lawn — they'll knock out bulbs, too.

Some other good companion plants for scillas include the following:

✔ Small, early tulips such as the kaufmanniana or greigii types (see the descriptions in Chapter 6) are charming companions.

✔ Not much is going on in woodlands this early in the year — consider what is growing and add scillas to a patch of lungwort or early hellebores to brighten the scene.

✔ Shrubs are nice with a scilla-blue carpet. Either choose a type that blooms early or, perhaps easier, a shrub with left-over berries from last fall.

Glory of the Snow — an Electrifying Blue

Supposedly, the name glory of the snow was given because this plant flowered as snow melted in the mountains of Greece where it originates. However, whenever we've seen it in U.S. gardens, it flowers late enough in spring that snow would be unusual. Whatever the time, it's still glorious. Figure 8-3 captures the essence of this little gem; you can see it big and beautiful in the color section.

Check out these glory of the snow varieties:

❀ *Chionodoxa luciliae,* with its bright gentian-blue flowers accented with a white eye, is most readily available:

• **'Alba,'** as you would expect, has white flowers.

• **'Pink Giant'** is sturdy, taller growing at 6 to 8 inches, and has white-eyed, bright pink flowers. Relatively recent, 'Pink Giant' has only been around since 1942.

Figure 8-3:
Glory of the
snow.

- ❀ *Chionodoxa forbesii* has soft blue-violet flowers for an intense glowing effect, accentuated by a white eye.

- ❀ *Chionodoxa sardensis* produces flowers of a deep gentian blue without the white eye, for a very intense color. Although its flowers are smaller, this 4- to 6-inch plant has more of them.

Glory of the snow flowers earlier than scillas (occasionally a brief overlap occurs as one finishes and the other starts — the result is several upward-facing, widely flaring bell-shaped flowers in an intense, almost glowing blue). A side benefit of small size is smaller leaves, which are less obvious and displeasing when they wither away.

Planting glory in the snow

Glory of the snow is a true bulb, small in size, so planting early in the fall is desirable. Plant in shade or sun, but not where bulbs will bake in summer. Avoid soggy places. You want the usual — free-draining soil supplemented with organic matter and fertilizer.

This little bulb is another one that really looks splendid when planted with a lavish hand — especially if you're massing them under trees and shrubs.

The mechanics of planting are just the same as with other bulbs — pointier end up, flatter end down, and set twice as deep as the bulb is high. An inch-tall bulb gets 2 inches of soil over its pointy top.

Selecting glory of the snow companions

Many common varieties of bulbs work well with glory of the snow. Remember: One-third as many bulbs larger than glory of the snow is a good proportion; adding more of the smaller ones works well also. Judy once used ten *Tulipa kaufmanniana* 'Waterlily' with 50 glory of the snow creating a pool of blue underneath.

The following are some additional options:

- ✔ Pair glory of the snow with daffodils for a bright, blue and yellow splash of color, or a cool blue and white effect.
- ✔ Hyacinths and tulips offer more options — you can create a soft or strong color combination depending on the color of the larger bulb's flowers.
- ✔ Shrubs are another possibility — imagine a yellow forsythia with masses and masses of glory of the snow.

Remember: You don't have to plant thousands of bulbs all at once — unless budget, time, and energy allow — because glory of the snow is another little bulb that happily works away underground making more.

Wood Hyacinths: England's Bluebell and Its Spanish Cousin

The bluebells of England are known in song and story. Once upon a time, they were called scillas, now they're *Hyacinthoides* (hyacinth-like).

These fat, fleshy bulbs delight in a woodland location. They grow happily beneath trees and shrubs, and they multiply by offsets and seeds to carpet the ground in April and May. (If it sounds like they multiply in large numbers, you're right.) These bulbs are easy to grow, so you can create a little bit of England in your own garden (see Figure 8-4).

You may also want to consider trying the Spanish cousin to England's bluebells. In this section, we offer information on those closely related bulbs, as well.

Figure 8-4:
The wood
hyacinth.

English bluebells

English bluebells are *Hyacinthoides non-scripta*. The bulbs are bigger than a golf ball, but smaller than a tennis ball. They are fat and fleshy, without any papery tunic or covering. Plant promptly so they don't dry out. If you must store them — briefly — pack them in wood shavings to keep them from drying out.

Follow these steps for planting English bluebells:

1. **Select a moist but not soggy site with shade and moderately rich soil.**

2. **Because they multiply freely, space bulbs reasonably far apart — maybe a foot or so.**

   If you want a full display right away, group several bulbs close together and then leave a gap before planting the next group.

3. **Plant twice as deep as the bulbs are tall — 5 inches to base.**

   Find the small flat area on the bottom to help you discern which end goes down.

The spikes of pendant, bell-shaped, dark blue-violet, fragrant flowers grow about a foot tall and open in May. Leaves are rather conspicuous when they start to yellow.

Planting bluebells in combination with ferns or hosta helps disguise the awkward aging process as the leaves start to yellow. Other companion plants for English bluebells — besides leafy perennials to mask their untidy appearance as they go dormant — include tulips, late daffodils, and camassias (other bulbs that also have yellowing leaves that a gardener must cope with).

Spanish bluebells

Spanish bluebells are *Hyacinthoides hispanica*. The Spanish bulbs are about the same size as those of English bluebells, and get the same treatment. Flowers open in April or May — bell-shaped and drooping, violet-blue — and they are no where near as fragrant as English bluebells.

The wild type of Spanish bluebell has been in gardens since 1601. You may want to grow these colorful forms of lesser vintage, as well:

- ❀ **'Danube'** (also called 'Danau' or 'Donau') has very dark blue flowers.
- ❀ **'Excelsior'** is a fine dark blue-violet and is larger growing than the typical form.
- ❀ **'Rose Queen'** has deep rose-pink flowers that cluster toward the top of the flowering stem. She's been around since 1898.
- ❀ **'White Triumphator'** has clean, clear white flowers on a robust, tall plant.

Ferns, hosta, and astilbe are good companion plants that help disguise old bulb leaves before they fade away completely. Azaleas, flowering at the same time, also make a fine backdrop for Spanish bluebell flowers.

Sing a Song of Blues

Not a sad song at all, the early garden blues are beautiful. Several may be smaller in size than more well-known bulbs — daffodils, tulips, and hyacinths — but they create a great display that gets better year by year. Easy to find, easy to grow, and easy on the budget, these beautiful blues can improve every garden.

Chapter 9

Rainbow Beauty: The Iris

*I*ris was the goddess of the rainbow, and her flowers certainly come in a rainbow array of colors.

Iris flowers are different from most other blooms. The flowers consist of three upright petals, called *standards*. Think of them as "stand up" petals. Then three more petals kind of droop to the side. They're called *falls*. The *fleur de lis*, once a royal symbol of the French monarchy, is an idealized iris.

However, the bearded iris (see Figure 9-1) — the most colorful and possibly the best-known member of the genus — really doesn't fall within the scope of this book. Though bearded irises *do* have thickened, rhizomotous roots, they're usually classed as perennials. So you can find more information about bearded irises in *Perennials For Dummies* by Marcia Tatroe and the Editors of the National Gardening Association (published by IDG Books Worldwide, Inc.). That's where you can find out about the fibrous-rooted Siberian iris, too. In this chapter, we discuss the bulbous iris, the type with a lumpy underground structure much like a tulip.

Little Gems for Spring: The Rock Garden Iris

Rock garden irises are small, and flower very early in the year. Their dainty flowers often appear before the snow is gone, anywhere from January to April, depending on where you garden. You can grow them in zones 3 to 7. In zone 7, these little rock garden irises would flower in February. They do best in a sunny site with a somewhat heavy but freely draining soil.

Figure 9-1:
The
bearded
iris, the
most
familiar
member of
the genus,
is usually
considered
a perennial.

Standard

Fall

If your garden has average soil, that's good. If the soil stays kind of wet, you should amend with some coarse sand or fine gravel to improve the drainage before planting rock garden irises.

Avoid really dry, drought-stricken conditions. Even while dormant, these little irises don't want to dessicate (dry up). Avoid a windy site as well; it can dry up the silken petals.

Check out these rock garden irises:

✤ **Iris danfordiae** is a little sweetie, with golden yellow flowers about an inch and a half across, with some brown freckles on the falls. Flowers are fragrant, and this type is the earliest of the rock garden irises to bloom. The leaves are shorter than those of the other rock garden irises. A winter mulch is helpful in all except the mildest climates. *Iris danfordiae* has been in cultivation since 1876.

✤ **Iris histrioides** has beautiful blue flowers, varying in intensity between one *cultivar* (cultivated variety) and another, and in the darker tones surrounding the yellow streak down the center of the falls. Leaves are just peeking up when the flowers are open.

- **'George'** has plum-purple standards and somewhat darker falls with even darker purple veining, accented with a showy yellow blotch on a white ground, striped purple.

- **'Katherine Hodgkin'** has large, lovely flowers, and is difficult to describe. The standards are bluish-green (a soft yellow, sort of suffused or overlaid with pale blue), speckled and penciled in dark blue. Falls are more of a yellowish-green with a yellow blotch. As can be expected, you'll pay more for this beauty. Just one 'Katherine Hodgkin' costs the same as ten *Iris reticulata.*

❀ *Iris reticulata* flowers just a little later than *Iris histrioides,* and the leaves are more developed at flowering time, too. Although restricted to blues and violets (with a couple of stunning exceptions), this species contains more cultivars available for you to choose from.

- **'Harmony'** has bluebird-blue standards and royal-blue falls crisply marked with a white-edged yellow blotch.

- **'Joyce'** has deep sky-blue standards and falls, the latter accented by a yellow blotch mellowed with a gray-brown tint.

- **'J.S. Dijt'** has purple flowers with warm, reddish-purple falls. It is among the last of these little irises to flower.

- **'Natascha'** is strikingly different, with ivory-white standards and falls, the falls veined in green and marked with a golden yellow blotch. It costs twice as much as other reticulata cultivars.

- **'Pauline'** has petunia-violet standards and dark purple falls, marked with a blue-variegated white blotch.

- **'Purple Gem'** has pansy-violet standards and plum-purple falls, a purple blotch distinguishable from the color of the standards 'cause it's on a white ground.

The leaves of these irises are narrow, bluish green, and sort of square in cross sections, stiff and upright. Each leaf has a little white horny-looking tip. The leaves are nicely proportionate — just a few inches high — when the flowers appear, and they continue to grow after the flowers fade. The leaves are relatively inconspicuous, thanks to their narrow, grass-like look.

Planting rock garden irises

Plan on planting iris bulbs early in autumn.

The small bulbs have a coarsely netted *tunic* on the outside. A flattened basal plate where the roots emerge at the bottom lets you know which end is the top.

Follow these steps for planting rock garden irises:

1. **Plant in groups of ten, or more, about an inch or so apart.**

    Just one or two are easily overlooked.

2. **Set the bulbs relatively deep, with 3 or 4 inches of soil over the top.**

    Even more soil is okay, if your soil is free-draining (water doesn't puddle and moves freely through the soil).

One problem with the little rock garden iris, and most especially with *Iris danfordiae,* is that it flowers just fine the first year after planting, and then in subsequent years it just sends up leaves. Each original splits into little rice-grain-sized bulbs that don't have the food reserves to support flower production. Deeper planting helps, as does extra nourishment in the form of liquid fertilizer applied in very early spring while the leaves are actively growing. Another way around this problem is to just plant new ones each spring. They are inexpensive enough that this solution is not a budget-breaker.

Forcing rock garden irises

Rock garden irises are a piece of cake to force. Just pot some up in autumn at the same time as you plant other bulbs outdoors. Follow these steps:

1. **Acquire a bulb pan or azalea pot.**

    Bulb pans are half as high as they are wide, azalea pots are two-thirds as high as they are wide. They have the most pleasing proportions for these little irises, a standard pot (as high as it is wide) looks kind of massive.

2. **Whatever pot you choose, make sure that it has a drainage hole; cover the hole with a piece of window screening or pot shard (a chunk of broken clay flower pot) to keep soil from sifting out.**

3. **Use any regular potting compost, and fill the pot with rock garden iris bulbs, almost touching.**

    Cover with about an inch of soil.

4. **Water moderately right after planting.**

5. **Provide a chilling period lasting about 15 weeks for root formation; then bring into warmth and light for flowering.**

You can find more information about coaxing all sorts of bulbs into early bloom in Chapter 24.

For Borders and Bouquets: Dutch, English, and Spanish Iris

Whether you call these Dutch, English, or Spanish irises, *Iris xiphium, Iris xiphioides (Iris latifolia),* and their hybrids are fantastic for the summer garden, and also to cut for bouquets. In fact, you are probably familiar with them as supermarket or florist cut flowers. They're really easy to grow if you garden in zones 7 to 9, and even in zone 6 with some winter protection.

English irises are *Iris xiphioides (Iris latifolia).* They produce leaves in spring, and are the hardiest of the irises. Spanish irises are *Iris xiphium* (sometimes called *Iris hispanica*), and they bring forth leaves in autumn when they can easily be damaged by wintry weather. Dutch irises (see Figure 9-2) are hybrids between the two species, and they also usually produce leaves in autumn. They all have two or three flowers per stem.

Dutch irises flower first, usually in mid-June. Next are Spanish irises in late June, and still later are the English irises, in July.

Nicely "dressed" in a brown jacket, the good-sized bulbs of Dutch, Spanish, and English irises (much larger than bulbs of the little rock garden irises) are available in autumn.

Figure 9-2:
The Dutch iris is a hybrid of the English iris and the Spanish iris.

English iris

English irises have white or blue, violet, and purple flowers, all with a yellow streak on the center of the falls. Flowers are usually larger than those of Spanish or Dutch irises. They grow 18 to 30 inches tall. Often, catalogs offer only mixed colors.

The following are English iris cultivars:

- ❀ **'Isabella'** has rose-lilac flowers with broad standards and falls.

- ❀ **'Mount Blanc'** has white flowers, very faintly tinted with lilac. This heirloom variety was introduced about 1883.

- ❀ **'Queen of the Blues'** has deep indigo-blue standards with purple-blue falls.

Spanish iris

Spanish irises are somewhat daintier than English irises, with smaller flowers in a wider range of colors that appear earlier in summer. Flowers are light to deep blue or violet, and white. You can find other Spanish irises with yellow or bronze flowers, even bicolors with stands and falls of different colors. If you do find Spanish irises in a catalog, you usually see them as mixed colors only, rather than separate cultivars. Plants grow 12 to 18 inches tall.

Dutch iris

Dutch irises usually grow between 16 and 24 inches tall. They flower earliest, usually in the first half of May from bulbs planted in autumn. Sometimes you can find bulbs for sale in spring — these will flower in late summer. Dutch irises are nice sturdy plants with lots of cultivars available. Although easy to grow, they are not very cold-hardy and need winter protection; plant them late in fall whenever possible.

Try these varieties:

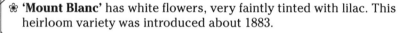

- ❀ **'Blue Magic'** has campanula-violet standards with deep heliotrope-violet falls accented with a brilliant yellow blotch.

- ❀ **'Casablanca'** has white standards and falls, with a narrow yellow blotch on the falls.

- ❀ **'Golden Harvest'** has golden yellow flowers shading to orange, with the standards lighter than the falls.

* ❀ **'Ideal'** has lobelia-blue standards and bluebird-blue falls accented with a yellow blotch.

* ❀ **'Marquette'** has soft creamy-white standards and primrose-yellow falls softly accentuated with an orange blotch.

* ❀ **'Oriental Beauty'** has wisteria-blue standards edged with paler flax-blue, and bluish-green falls marked with a sharply constrasting brilliant yellow blotch.

* ❀ **'Professor Blaauw'** has gentian-blue standards and falls, with a narrow yellow stripe accentuating the falls. It also flowers earlier than others in the Dutch iris group.

* ❀ **'Purple Sensation'** has violet-purple standards and falls, with yellow markings, edged in gentian blue.

* ❀ **'Royal Yellow'** has buttercup-yellow stands and sunflower-yellow falls.

* ❀ **'Sky Beauty'** has soft blue standards veined in darker blue and french-blue falls with somewhat darker veining, accented with a lemon-yellow blotch.

* ❀ **'Telstar'** has violet standards and blue falls with purple-violet accents where they narrow at the base, and a small brilliant yellow blotch.

* ❀ **'White Wedgewood'** has creamy white standards softly shaded in blue (think of skim milk) and greenish-white falls marked with a buttercup-yellow blotch.

Planting Dutch, English, and Spanish irises

Plant these irises in the flower border in groups of five to ten. Plant each group next to perennials such as peonies. This arrangement helps disguise their withering foliage.

If you want these late-spring-to-summer blooming irises for cut-flower use, plant them in a separate part of the garden. That way, they won't leave a hole and spoil the display when you cut them. You can find more information about flowering bulbs for cut-flower use in Chapter 23.

Follow these steps for growing Dutch, English, and Spanish irises:

1. **Choose a site with good, reasonably fertile soil and adequate moisture (soil that won't dry out in summer).**

   Dutch and Spanish irises need a sheltered environment due to their habit of producing leaves in autumn and winter. Good drainage will assist them in surviving the winter.

2. **Plant as early as you can buy the bulbs, and plant them deep, with 5 to 7 inches of soil over the top.**

   Dutch irises are an exception to the early-planting advice.

3. **Dutch and Spanish irises, unless grown in the warmer portions of their range, are best lifted (simply put, this term means dig 'em up after the leaves brown off) and stored out of the ground over the summer.**

   Lifting them provides the dry resting and ripening period they need for repeat flowering the next year. Don't sun-dry them; they're not tomatoes for cupboard storage! A warm, dry, and well-ventilated environment is fine.

4. **Replant them in late fall.**

Spanish irises originated in the Mediterranean region, and require similar climate and conditions to thrive as perennials. See Chapter 27 for other bulbs that like these conditions, similar to that of Southern California.

Chapter 10

The Lovely Little Dwarfs of Spring

● ●

In This Chapter

▶ Dogtooth violet: a lily-like spring beauty

▶ Grecian windflower: tiny blue, pink, or white daisies that bloom year after year

▶ Guinea hen flower: striking and unique checkered flowers

▶ Summer snowflake and Gravetye Giant: the cool, white bells of late spring

● ●

Small is beautiful, and some little bulbs really stand out for the special beauty they add to the garden. Those that are grouped in this chapter are easily found, but not that frequently grown. That's probably because people aren't as familiar with these underground treasures that produce such uncommon blossoms. Read on rather than skip over, if you want to enjoy these easy-to-grow dwarf bulbs that give you great results.

Dogtooth Violet: A Lily-Like Morsel for Spring

You'd need to be Superman with X-ray vision to see how this bulb got it's common name. Dogtooth violet, *Erythronium* species and cultivars, have a corm that really does look like a dog's canine tooth. You can see the dog-tooth shape of the corm when you plant it, but it's hard to see afterward when it's concealed in the dirt.

What makes this lumpy underground treasure special are its flowers. Dogtooth violets aren't anything like a violet; they're more like a miniature lily with curled-back petals in bright yellow, clean white, or soft rose-pink (see Figure 10-1).

We recommend that you try these cultivars of dogtooth violet:

Figure 10-1:
There's nothing hangdog about the dogtooth violet.

❀ *Erythronium dens-canis,* **'Frans Hals,'** is native to Europe dating back to 1596, and the imperial-purple or violet flowers make quite a show in modern gardens. It has fine form and each flower features a bronze-green spot near the base.

❀ *Erythronium dens-canis,* **'Pink Perfection,'** will reward you with clear, bright pink flowers that provide charming and welcome spring color amid your favorite shade plants.

❀ *Erythronium dens-canis,* **'Purple King,'** shows off with cyclamen-purple blossoms accented attractively with white hearts. With the open form and curled back petals typical of dogtooth violets, this richly colored cultivar holds much value.

❀ *Erythronium dens-canis,* **'Rose Queen,'** offers a regal display of vivid rose-pink flowers that combine well with cultivars in other shades, and provide plenty of interest and color when planted in a group in a shady rock garden or bed.

❀ *Erythronium dens-canis,* **'Snowflake,'** dances among the shadows with glistening white flowers that light up a shady spot to perfection. The nodding flowers blend beautifully with other spring bloomers.

❀ *Erythronium revolutum,* **'White Beauty,'** combines rare, pure white, reflexed flowers with handsome spotted foliage for a very lily-like and impressive display. Large, graceful blossoms can reach 2 inches across.

❀ *Erythronium tuolumnense* has rich yellow flowers and bright green leaves, reaching 12 inches in height.

❀ *Erythronium* **'Pagoda'** is a vigorous hybrid, with bright, lemon-yellow flowers rising from glossy green foliage. The nodding flowers are supported by sturdy 8-inch stems.

Several native North American dogtooth violet varieties are also available.

To successfully grow dogtooth violets, buy the corms early and plant them promptly. Ten is a generous number; five will make a nice start-up, first-time-to-see-if-you-like-them display.

Because the dogtooth violet corms dry out quickly, garden centers and nurseries often store them in wood shavings to retard moisture loss before they are sold:

- ✔ Choose plump solid corms with no sign of bruising such as soft flabby spots or mildew.
- ✔ Handle the corms gently because they are fragile and easily bruised.
- ✔ Partway down one side of the corm, closer to the fatter end, you should find a tiny, almost stubbly tuft of old roots. Don't fret if you can't find it. Just plant with the tapered end point upward.

Dogtooth violets like woodsy conditions: moist but well-drained soil high in organic matter, mulched with a nice layer of shredded leaves or wood chips. Blossoms appear when spring has arrived, adding their elegance to the shady garden. The leaves stay around for a couple of months, and then yellow and wither away until next year.

Deer like the leaves of dogtooth violets, munching the shoots as they come through the ground. Fences, large dogs, and sprays (repellents) can help ward off the deer.

Choose companion plants that like the same conditions and that add interest after the dogtooth violets are dormant. Ferns are a good choice, as are astilbe and hosta. True violets are sweet in combination while the dogtooth violets are in bloom.

Blown Away by Grecian Windflower

This little sweetie is a dainty daisy, so short that the flowers barely rise above the ground (see Figure 10-2). In its native home, Grecian windflower (*Anemone blanda*) blooms as the snow melts on the mountainside. In gardens, it waits until winter's over and spring is here.

Figure 10-2:
The
graceful
Grecian
windflower.

Yellow-centered daisies in blue shades, pink shades, or white, greet the gardener provident enough to have planted them the autumn before. Blue shades create a wonderful carpet of color ranging from pale to darker blue tones. These are ideal for mixing with daffodils, where they provide a striking contrast. Pink shades give you soft to deep pink flowers that blend well with annuals and other spring bulbs.

For all their small size, these are sturdy little tubers that happily come back year after year.

We suggest that you try these varieties of Grecian windflower:

- ❀ **'Charmer'** offers eye-catching color from radiant flowers that feature deep rose-pink petals and a yellow center ringed in white.

- ❀ **'Radar'** is unusual and attractive, with rose-pink to red flowers with white centers. Try combining this one with early tulips in white or similar hues or let it dazzle in the spring rock garden.

- ❀ **'Violet Star'** shines with amethyst-violet flowers borne in great profusion over many weeks.

- ❀ **'White Splendour,'** like new-fallen snow, glistens with bright blooms in pure white. When mixed with early tulips in bold colors, the effect is simply stunning. Plants form prolific, sturdy low mounds covered with very long-lasting flowers.

A windflower's tuber is a wizened little thing that looks like the trash that's left after you screen compost. Figuring out which end of the tuber is the top is impossible; just plant it sideways and let the tuber figure it out (which they do very nicely!).

You can improve the unpromising appearance of Grecian windflower tubers by giving them a quick soaking. The night before you're going to plant them, cover the tubers with damp peat moss. The tubers absorb moisture and plump up, making them more ready to root as soon as they are planted.

Remember: After they are soaked, you must plant the tubers right away. If they sit too long after soaking, they start to mildew:

- ✔ Plant this inexpensive tuber with a generous hand. Ten is kind of sparse; 25 is much nicer.

- ✔ Choose a bright, lightly shaded site. Full sun is okay, too, if it doesn't bake the ground in summer.

- ✔ Loosen the soil and add some organic matter in the form of dried manure (available bagged at the garden center; it emits hardly any odor) or compost. Fertilize as we suggest in Chapter 21.

- ✔ Set the tubers just 5 inches below the soil surface.

- ✔ After planting, mulch with wood chips or shredded leaves.

In our experience, the Grecian windflower seems pretty much left alone by pests.

Companion plants need to be in scale with the little windflower. Pansies and primroses make a wonderful combination if you are looking for annuals. Small daffodils are great if you are mixing your bulbs, as are the dwarf early tulips. In autumn, dig the hole deep enough for the larger bulbs, and set them in the ground. Then back-fill the hole to the proper depth for the Grecian windflower, set them in place, and then finish filling the hole.

Summer Snowflake: Too Soon for Summer, Too Late for Snow

The name "summer snowflake" is a real misnomer for this bulb. Because it flowers with the late daffodils and early tulips, blooming in snow is the exception, but I'd hardly call its season summer. True, the spring snowflake variety does flower earlier (see Chapter 4 for information), but that hardly seems to justify the name "summer" for this species.

Sneak a peek at the guinea hen flower: Something completely different

Guinea hen flower, *Fritillaria meleagris*, is un-like anything else you've ever grown. It grows 12 to 15 inches tall, with a slender stem and narrow, somewhat grayish-green leaves. The single flower (occasionally two flowers) seems too clunky and heavy to be held up by the delicate-seeming stem.

Broad and nodding, each flower is checkered like a chessboard. (You can see a drawing in Chapter 11, where we discuss this and other fritillaries.) The combination can be a striking set of small purple and white squares, a more subtle darker/paler purple, or even a cool white/green. Why such a striking, handsome plant is so rarely grown escapes us. We can only surmise that what people don't know, they're not likely to grow.

In any case, summer snowflake, *Leucojum aestivum,* is a well-behaved bulb that flowers nicely in late spring, producing a few cool white bells of flowers, tipped with green and dangling from a 12- to 18-inch-tall stem. In fact, this version of snowflake grows so well that it often shows up mislabeled "spring snowflake." Summer snowflake likes moist sites and is excellent near a pond or slow-moving stream.

Here are some hints for successfully growing summer snowflake:

- A true bulb, plant summer snowflake in autumn like most spring-flowering bulbs.
- Ten bulbs will make a pleasant showing.
- Plant bulbs twice as deep as they are tall, with about 6 inches of soil over the bulb.
- Improve the soil with organic matter, and add fertilizer.

This bulb is good for naturalizing; consider planting it in greater numbers to create large drifts.

Why Try New?

If you're happy with the tulips and daffodils you already grow, stay with them. In fact, I'm not saying that you should stop growing old favorites. But there's always room for new favorites. Widen your horizons and find some new bulbs to enjoy along with your old stand-bys to refresh and enliven your garden's spring look.

Gravetye Giant

"Handsome is as handsome does" says the old folk saying, and here's a pretty bulb, more subtle than blatant in its appeal, that deserves wider use.

Leucojum aestivum 'Gravetye Giant' is sometimes called giant snowflake or Loddon lily. With this particular cultivar, you get large, pure white flowers of the typical nodding type. This vigorous free-flowering plant produces up to nine flowers per stem and when mature can reach 22 inches. It makes a wonderful display naturalized in the garden and also performs well as a cut flower.

Chapter 11

Fantastic Fritillaries
from Small to Tall

Fritillaries are different from any other flower you may have grown — not in how they grow, but in appearance. Their flowers — from few to many, depending on the type — are bell-shaped and dangle in a most interesting manner. That description sounds simple and straightforward, but the plants have rung in changes in size and color that result in remarkable diversity. The four different fritillaries we cover in this chapter would never be mistaken for one another, so strikingly different are they from each other.

What all fritillaries do have in common — large and small alike — are that they are true bulbs, few-scaled, and lack a papery tunic or covering. The result is that they dislike being out of the ground for any length of time. Purchase and plant all fritillaries as early in the autumn as they're available. They'll repay your efforts with an outstanding display in spring.

Guinea Hen Flowers Flock to the Garden

Guinea hen flower, *Fritillaria meleagris,* has one or two rather chunky bell-shaped flowers, marked like a checkerboard in somber purple and white (see Figure 11-1). Plant a bunch, and you may find the occasional white one, with faint green markings. Like most albino forms, these are a bit less vigorous and somewhat shorter. They are even offered separately, as *Fritillaria meleagris alba.*

Figure 11-1:
The guinea hen flower gets its name from the speckled feathers of the Guinea hen bird.

The flowers dangle from a slender stem about 8 to 12 inches tall in mid-spring. The few leaves are also slender, and plants look so delicate you wonder how they support the square-shouldered flowers. Clearly, the plants know what they're doing — guinea hen flowers have been grown in gardens since 1572!

The only variation you are likely to find available is 'Alba' with white and green checkered flowers. A few will even pop up in a bagful of plain guinea hen flowers. Deeper-colored named forms (such as, 'Poisodon' and 'Artemis') are available in Europe.

Like so many other small bulbs, guinea hen flower is inexpensive (we would say "cheap" but that sounds disparaging), so you can afford to plant in quantity. Ten is a minimum number if the small plants are to make a display you can see at a glance. And several groups of ten are even nicer.

The ivory-white bulbs of guinea hen flower are just an inch or so wide, and have only two scales. Because these bulbs are both small and have no tunic, they dry out really quickly. If you have to keep them between time of purchase and when you plant, store them in a paper bag mixed with a handful of wood shavings to reduce *desiccation* (drying). Make the waiting period until planting as brief as you can.

Guinea hen flowers luxuriate in constantly moist soil. They grow in average conditions, too, but die out if the soil gets too dry, even when bulbs are dormant. They prefer lightly shaded conditions, in tall grass or woodland.

Most bulbs rot if they're kept wet. Guinea hen flower is one to keep in mind for that soggy spot in your lawn or garden. But you can't cut the grass until the inconspicuous leaves start to yellow and wither away. Follow these steps for planting guinea hen flowers:

1. **Plant bulbs right side up (using the dried-up tuft of roots as your guide), 5 inches to base, and 1 inch apart.**

   You can recognize the top of the bulb from the bottom because a little tuft of wiry brown roots is usually at the base, left over from last year.

   The planting method varies slightly depending on the site for your bulbs:

   - If you are planting the bulbs in a lawn, dig up a square of turf and set it aside. Loosen the soil, adding organic matter and fertilizer. Set the bulbs, and then replace the grass and gently press on it, using your hand. You don't want to squash the bulbs you've just planted.

   - If you are planting the bulbs in a lightly shaded spot under a small tree or shrub, mulch with small pine bark chips or shredded leaves.

2. **In either situation, water after you're finished planting.**

Given conditions to their liking — light shade and nice moist soil — guinea hen flower will multiply by seed and offsets.

Nothing seems to think of guinea hen flower as salad, so this bulb is safe from the depredations of deer, rabbits, squirrels, and other pests.

Companion plants for guinea hen flower are somewhat limited because it flowers in early spring. Violets are nice, but what Judy really likes in her own garden are Lenten roses, *Helleborus x orientalis,* especially in the deep pink and oxblood red shades. The deep-purple form of this hellebore also makes a pretty combination. Another good companion in woodland situations is the primrose.

Guinea hen flower is probably the easiest of the fritillaries to grow. You've perhaps never seen this bulb growing or even heard of it; however, the flowers are better than just unusual, they're quite charming. Anything that has been in gardens for over four centuries certainly deserves a turn in yours.

The New Frit on the Block (With an Unpronounceable Name)

The only thing wrong with this plant is its name: *Fritillaria michailovskyi*. It doesn't have a common name, either. It was discovered for the very first time in 1904, lost, and then rediscovered in 1965 (which is kind of romantic). Very easily cultivated and readily propagated by bulb growers in Holland, the frit with the unpronounceable name has rapidly gone from a collector's expensive rarity to a moderately priced, easily grown addition to anybody's bulb repertoire.

Michailovskyi has one or two boxy bells of flowers, with the petals somewhat curled outwards at their tips (see Figure 11-2). For their small size, the flowers are very impressive. Near the stem, the flowers are a rich, deep-purple maroon, and the last third is a vividly contrasting golden yellow. Sturdy stems stand 4 to 6 inches tall, so select a site for suitably close-up viewing.

Figure 11-2:
Michailovskyi, a sturdy little frit.

Recently, some plants are available with more flowers (up to seven on a stem), no doubt a result of selection by Dutch growers.

A little frit, michailovskyi has small, two-scaled bulbs that dry out quickly.

Plant early in autumn in a gritty soil that drains well. A rock garden is most suitable. This frit likes cold winters and cool, dryish summers.

If conditions are too warm in winter — southeastern states along the coast, southern California, and mild southwestern states — the flowers get stuck underground and, if they appear at all, are misshapen.

Try planting this frit under a ground cover of thyme or creeping phlox. These plants will suck up water while they grow in summer (when the frit bulbs are dormant).

Michailovskyi is easy to grow if you remember what it likes: good drainage, dry summers, and cold winters. To plant michailovskyi, follow the same instructions that you would use for guinea hen flower (see the previous section). Although this frit doesn't multiply very quickly in gardens, specialized micropropagation techniques have produced ample quantities. The result: an attractive flower for the mid-spring garden, and an interesting choice for curious gardeners.

Crown Imperials Cap the List

There's no ignoring crown imperials, *Fritillaria imperialis*. To begin with, they're big — big bulbs with a largish price. In spring they grow into tall plants you can't miss. And then there's their scent — sort of foxy, skunky, and pungent. Phew!

Actually, the smell isn't bad at all outdoors in the garden, but we suggest that you enjoy these flowers there — the strong odor is overwhelming indoors. Perhaps the sharp odor protects crown imperials from pests — such as rabbits, woodchucks, deer, mice, voles, and chipmunks — which leave both bulbs and growing plants alone.

This bulb has quite a history. Paintings by Dutch masters often include crown imperials. Another name for crown imperial is "Tears of Mary." A folktale says that when Christ was on the way to Calvary this plant did not mourn. And ever since that time, its once-white, upright flowers blush orange and nod for shame. The fat drops of nectar inside the flowers are unshed tears.

The stunning flowers are typically a brick orange-red color, very showy and conspicuous. You can see this flower in Figure 11-3; you can also see it in the color section. Tulips in a softer orange make a nice companion plant.

These bulbs are expensive. Expect to pay about as much for one crown imperial as you would for five hyacinths or ten tulips. One crown imperial makes an accent, three make a statement, and more are wonderfully lavish.

Figure 11-3:
The crown
imperial.

The crown imperial has been around for a long time, grown in gardens since 1580. That history tells you that it's easy to grow. And if the regular crown imperial itself isn't enough of a showstopper for you, several cultivars are available at similar or higher prices. Some have different color flowers, or two tiers of flowers, or the flowers are double, or the leaves are variegated. Some of the cultivars have been around for a long time, too. Check out these varieties:

✤ **'Argenteomarginata'** offers double delights from bright red flowers that rise above arresting white-edged leaves. Gardeners have valued this striking cultivar since its 1771 beginnings.

✤ **'Aureomarginata'** has dazzled in gardens since 1665, sending up impressive stalks ringed with bright red flowers set above outstanding gold-edged leaves. This one makes a wonderful accent.

✤ **'Aurora'** sports eye-catching, apricot-orange flowers on 2-foot stems. The nodding flowers fairly glow above the dark foliage.

✤ **'Duplex'** is the choice when you simply want more of a good thing. Two tiers of outstanding orange flowers give this cultivar plenty of appeal. It's been grown since 1594 when it was cultivated in Leiden, Holland, by Carolus Clusius, who is famous for the introduction of tulips to the West.

❀ **'Lutea'** is another impressive old-timer — since 1665 — sporting vivid yellow flowers with faint purple veins on stems that top out at about 2 feet.

❀ **'Prolifera'** or **'Kroon op Kroon'** offers distinctive double flowers in bright orange on stems that reach 2 to 3 feet.

❀ **'Rubra Maxima'** sparkles with very large flowers in an unusual burnt orange shade tinted with red and accented with light purple veins. These dark flowers have delighted gardeners since 1665.

Crown imperials have huge bulbs, five inches across and three and a half inches thick. Big as they are, the bulbs are made of only two or three scales, with a gap in the middle from last year's flower stalk, now withered away. No tunic protects the fleshy scales from drying out, either.

Growth begins early and each bulb — usually offered for sale individually wrapped in tissue paper — often has roots starting into growth by late August. The size of a pencil lead, the new white roots are easily broken, setting back the bulb's growth. If the tissue-wrapped bulb is upside down in the box or bin where it awaits purchase, roots start growing in the wrong direction.

When you plant, dig a good deep hole, about a foot deep. Crown imperials like the same sort of soil as potatoes — rich loam well prepared with ample organic matter and fertilizer. The site should have good drainage but not dry out. Aim for moist but free draining.

You may see recommendations to plant these big bulbs sideways, so water won't collect in the hole in the middle of the bulb. Ignore any such suggestion. If the site is that wet, the bulbs won't do well anyway. And besides, roots pull downward and shoots grow upward. Over time, the bulbs (knowing which way is up) are going to straighten themselves out.

Growth starts in mid-spring — a fat bronze shoot that quickly elongates into a sturdy 3-foot-tall stem. Leaves grow on the bottom half of the stem, and then there's a bare space, a whorl of 4 to 6 large bell-like flowers, and a tuft of leaves (like those on a pineapple) topping the whole thing off.

Crown imperial goes dormant in very early summer. Because it is so stately, few perennials are large enough to disguise its natural decline. Plant something like yarrow in front of it to distract attention away from the yellowing foliage.

Persian Fritillaria for Subtle Beauty

The Persian fritillaria looks different from guinea hen flower or crown imperial. In fact, Persian fritillaria, *Fritillaria persica,* doesn't look like any other fritillaria. The bulb is as big as a crown imperial's, but more egg-shaped than flattened. The stout stem has gray-green leaves about two-thirds of the way up. The upper part of the stem has up to 30 small, dangling, somewhat conical bell-shaped flowers in a charming, rather Victorian, dark-plum purple with a silvery grey-purple bloom. So the similarities, and the differences, explain why this bulb has been moved out of the *Fritillaria* classification four times, but keeps getting put back in.

Big bulbs equal big price. The high cost isn't due to the size, it is because of the scarcity and time necessary to bring the plant to blooming size. (This bulb emits no skunk-like scent, though.) Again, like the crown imperial, one plant is enough to catch attention, three are excellent, and more are lavish.

Eager to begin growing, Persian fritillary starts root growth in late summer, in the ground or out of it. The bulbs are covered by two fat fleshy scales and no protective covering, so they can wither pretty quickly. Buy early and plant promptly, providing the same sort of conditions as for the crown imperial (see the preceding section).

Growth begins in spring, with a sturdy stem quickly growing 3 feet tall, or even a bit more. Unless it is in a site sheltered from wind, you may want to provide support with a stake and ties (see Chapter 21 for more about staking).

Remember: A big bulb is underground. Put the stake in place before filling the hole so the bulb is still visible. Be sure to push the stake in the ground far enough from the stem to avoid spearing the bulb, but close enough to provide secure support.

Keep the leaves growing as long as you can, sending food back underground to nourish the bulb for next year's display. Only cut off the stem when leaves are yellowed and withering.

Persian fritillary has a wonderfully refined color scheme of foliage and flower. If you use it to add a focal point to a bed of bulbs, choose pale pink and deep purple-black tulips. Because the bulb has tall flower stalks, you can display Persian fritillary with shrubs, planting the bulbs just in front of late azaleas.

Though they flower reasonably close to the same time, we wouldn't mix crown imperials and Persian fritillaries. They're too different in appearance to look good together.

Fritillaries for a Touch of Class

Fritillarias are definitely not ordinary bulbs. But don't think that just because you don't find them in the supermarket with discount tulips that they're troublesome bulbs — quite the reverse. They're simple enough to grow that they belong in ordinary gardens where they add a touch of class, and sometimes even a historical connection.

Part III

Bulbs That Flower in Summer and Fall

The 5th Wave   By Rich Tennant

Dutch Lily **VERY COLORFUL**

3-Mile Island Lily **GLOWS IN THE DARK**

NURSERY

In this part . . .

Don't you just love plants with initiative? In this part, we tell you about some feisty bulbs that just won't wait until spring to bloom their little hearts out. You can enjoy these bulb varieties in summer and throughout autumn.

As the gardening year winds down, these bulbs are just getting started.

Chapter 12
Garden Royalty, the Lilies

• •

In This Chapter

▶ Choosing lilies for the garden

▶ Planting lilies in containers

▶ Using lilies as cut flowers

▶ Planning and planting for a great display

▶ Foiling pests

• •

*W*ith its regal, elegant good looks, it's no wonder that the lily has been called "Queen of the Garden." But you don't need a butler (or even a head gardener) to enjoy these beautiful flowers in your own backyard. Lilies are wonderful winter-hardy bulbs that bloom in early to midsummer. Their panache and sheer grace provide visual appeal, while their sturdy nature makes them suitable for everybody's garden.

Selecting Lilies for Beauty and Grace

Lilies once had a reputation as tricky plants to grow. That was true around the beginning of the twentieth century when bulbs collected wild, often infected with a debilitating virus, were all that was available. That was then, this is now. Currently, commercially propagated, healthy bulbs are offered for sale. Additionally, hybridizers have developed sensational colors that go beyond the wild species — from delicious pastels to bold, vivid colors.

Not everything that's called "lily" really is one. Lilies grow from true bulbs, with many fleshy scales that have no papery covering or tunic. Scads of other plants masquerade as lilies, daylily being the one most commonly confused.

Named lilies, which are cultivars and grexes, have some rather tricky classifications:

✔ A *grex* (Latin for a flock of sheep) covers all lilies that came out of an individual seed capsule. They have the same parents, but look no more alike than you do to your siblings. The name of a grex — Dummy's Delight, for example — is written in ordinary roman type rather than italics and has no quote marks around it.

✔ A particularly worthwhile individual plant may be selected and given *cultivar* (cultivated variety) status. That means the cultivar — 'Dummy's Wonder' for example (if there were one) — is an asexually propagated cultivated variety and, as a clone, everything with that name is identical. The name, also in ordinary roman type, always appears in single quotation marks.

Remember the difference between a grex and a cultivar so that you won't be surprised when your grex lilies share only their name and not their looks (they'll still be beautiful).

Choosing lilies for the garden

Lilies are native to the United States as well as to Europe and temperate Asia. Some native species make a charming addition to gardens.

✔ Canada lily, *Lilium canadense,* blooms in mid-summer with pendant, orange to red flowers black-speckled inside, in a candelabra-style arrangement on 3-foot-tall plants.

✔ *Lilium superbum* is taller, 5 to 6 feet or more, with numerous red-orange turk's-cap flowers — the petals curl back tightly toward the stem — yellow in the throat and speckled black inside. It likes moist sites.

One you'll see growing wild that isn't native is tiger lily, *Lilium lancifolium.* It used to be named *Lilium tigrinum.* It looks sort of like *L. superbum,* only sturdier. Native to Eurasia, it happily grows wild in the northeastern United States.

Just as with tulips and daffodils, lilies have several classifications, which are based on parentage. Knowing the species of the parentage gives you an idea of what the flower shape, bloom time, height, and so on might be. The original wild parents of the modern hybrid lilies gave rise to seven divisions, the most interesting of which for gardeners are the

✔ Asiatic hybrids of Division I

✔ Trumpet hybrids of Division VI

✔ Oriental hybrids of Division VII

Some divisions have subsets, but we're not going to worry about that. The lilies in this book will give you a good start. Later, you may want to try your hand with other varieties. We stick to the basics.

Asiatic hybrids

Asiatic hybrids flower in early summer, mostly in June or July, but some also spill into August with late color. Ranging in height from 2- to almost 4-feet tall, they feature abundant, upward-facing, bowl-shaped flowers mostly in yellow through orange to red, with a few white and pink ones available (see Figure 12-1). Flowers may be unspotted or else charmingly speckled with darker freckles.

Figure 12-1:
An Asiatic hybrid lily.

Although not fragrant, these wonderfully reliable garden plants reproduce freely. They also make eye-catching container plants and perform beautifully as cut flowers. Try these cultivars:

- ❀ **'America'** has crimson flowers that bloom on 30- to 40-inch stems in July and August. This lily offers rare color and outstanding garden performance. The regal, deep red petals are softly sprinkled with dark spots for a classy and unique look. Use this one as a special garden accent, or combine it with other lilies for a stunning display.

- ❀ **'Batist'** with white blossoms reaches 20 to 24 inches in July. It's simple — perfect white flowers are the payoff with this cultivar. Each flower offers impeccable form with flawless petals accented charmingly with a light dusting of freckles in the center.

❀ **'Cinnabar'** has maroon flowers that open on 24-inch stems in July and August. Rich and refined, the vivid maroon flowers dusted with dark spots, give this lily distinction. As a low-grower, it's one of the Asiatics well suited for growing in pots or for forcing indoors.

❀ **Citronella Strain** has lemon-yellow flowers atop 46-inch stems in July and August. Petals curl back on this flower to nearly touch the base in an unusual and attractive circular formation. (***Remember:*** These are lilies produced from a single seed capsule and so offer variations in flower color.) The abundant flowers in soft yellow tones, are peppered with dark dots and nod gracefully from tall stems. These bulbs are ideal in the back of the border or grouped with shrubs and perennials.

❀ **'Connecticut King'** offers golden yellow blossoms and reaches 36 to 48 inches in June and July. This flower offers flair from its vivid yellow petals that turn to gold in the flower center. It offers true garden elegance, excellent reliability, and is considered "the" yellow lily by many.

❀ **'Cote d'Azur'** has bright pink flowers open on 30- to 35-inch stems during July and August. Expect plenty of outstanding color and fine form with this lily. An abundance of flowers makes this one splendid in borders. Note, however, that you may come across a lower-growing 'Cote d'Azur' that reaches only 18 inches. This is a dwarf pot lily used for container culture and forcing. It produces awesome color — also in bright pink — blooming indoors approximately 10 weeks after planting.

❀ **'Dreamland'** has bright yellow flowers flushed with apricot and gold atop 30- to 40-inch stems in July and August. Big, bold flowers with enchanting color and superb style are your reward here. Many impressive flowers bloom on each sturdy stem.

❀ **'Enchantment'** has red-orange flowers bloom on 36- to 48-inch stems in June and July. This flower offers radiant color from nasturtium-orange flowers dotted with dark freckles. A most popular selection, this cultivar produces especially long-lasting flowers and may just be the most vigorous and most rapid multiplier of all lilies.

❀ **'Grand Paradiso'** boasts ruby-red blossoms atop 35- to 45-inch stems in July and August. Grand is the best way to describe the intense and arresting flowers produced on tall and robust plants. As an accent, this one is hard to beat.

❀ **'Montreaux'** has light to dark pink blossoms reach 24 to 36 inches in June and July. A lightly spotted, dark pink center gives way to soft pink near the petal tips in this selection. It combines beautifully with white, rose, or other soft two-toned lilies and is one of the best large-flowering, early varieties.

❀ **'Roma'** offers cream to white flowers atop 35- to 40-inch stems in July and August. Strong and reliable performance and stately flowers make this cultivar an outstanding choice. Its height and large flowers command attention in the garden, and offer exceptional life in arrangements.

❀ **'Sterling Star'** has white flowers atop 36- to 48- inch stems in June and July. Stunning white blossoms with tiny dark spots over a glowing yellow center really do offer sterling results. It's adaptable and attractive in garden settings, and valuable indoors as well.

❀ **'Vivaldi'** sports pink blossoms that reach 24 to 36 inches in June and July. If it's big and bold you want, you'll be hard pressed to find a better pink lily. The clear color and showy star-shaped flowers make a strong statement anywhere.

Trumpet (Aurelian) hybrids

Trumpet hybrids are like opera divas — tall and stately, with tremendous stage presence (see Figure 12-2).

Figure 12-2:
A trumpet lily.

Trumpet hybrids bloom in midsummer, July to August. Their large, intensely fragrant flowers are, well, trumpet-shaped. Their fragrance is most emphatic at dawn and dusk. Plants grow anywhere from 4 to 7 feet tall. Flower color ranges from white through pinks to deep, almost purple-black hues, and from a range of yellows to apricot, peach, and orange. Some whites and yellows are flushed with brown on the outside; some yellows have an alluring touch of lime-green in the throat.

Check out these varieties:

- ❀ **African Queen** flowers are yellow-apricot inside, apricot-brown outside, and reach 36 to 48 inches in July and August. Two-toned and terrific, these large flowers offer an impressive color statement and alluring scents for a spectacular show. Because this is a grex, you'll find some variation from one individual to another.

- ❀ **Aurelian Hybrids** offer as a group, all the good things other trumpets feature, including an easy-going nature and the ability to naturalize well. They range from 4 to 8 feet tall and are deliciously fragrant.

- ❀ **'Black Dragon'** with white flowers inside, maroon outside, reaches 4 to 8 feet in July and August. Extra-large and dramatic flowers categorize this cultivar. The bright white flower interior is accented with a vivid yellow throat, set off by the maroon of the reverse side of the petals for an overall special look.

- ❀ **'Black Magic'** flowers in July and August with blossoms that are white inside, purplish outside on 4- to 6-foot stems. Similar to 'Black Dragon,' this one offers a creamy white and yellow interior and purplish-brown exterior. You'll enjoy wonderful fragrance from this elegant and stately flower.

- ❀ **Copper King Strain** offers golden yellow flowers flushed with orange on top of 4- to 6-foot stems. This is a grex selected from the Golden Clarion Strain with fragrant, outstanding, trumpet-shaped flowers attractive for their warm tone.

Choose trumpet lilies when you want a bold look in the rear of the bed or perennial garden. Mass plantings make an astonishing display. Support the tall stalks and protect flowers by staking the stems.

What to do with the Easter lily

The Easter lily is widely familiar — it's frequently brought along more quickly or held back in greenhouses to suit the calendar vagaries of the holiday. Native to southern Japan, *Lilium longiflorum* grows okay in regions with moderate winters but needs heavy mulching to protect the dormant bulbs in regions where it's really cold. (Commercial production in the United States is along the coast in California and Oregon.) We wouldn't buy this specially for the garden except in mild-winter regions, but if you receive it or buy it as a potted Easter flower, it's worth planting in your garden afterward.

Oriental hybrids

Oriental hybrids continue the lily season, flowering from mid-to-late summer — late July through August into September. Each sturdy 2- to 4-foot stem supports from 6 to 12 outward facing or upright *recurved* (petals are curled back) flowers, as shown in Figure 12-3. Intensely fragrant, these lilies' flower color ranges from white through rosy pinks to deeper red, ornamented with raised *papillae* (wart-like bumps) at the base of the petals. Good for cutting and containers, their perfume can be overwhelming at close quarters.

Figure 12-3: An Oriental hybrid lily.

Here are some other types of Oriental lilies:

❀ **'Casa Blanca'** offers white flowers atop 36- to 48-inch stems in August and September. This cultivar is world-famous and often ranked as the most spectacular and fragrant of all the Oriental lilies. Its pure white flowers can reach 10 inches across offering fragrance throughout the garden.

❀ **'Con Amore'** is 12 to 24 inches tall with soft pink flowers that appear in July and August. The translation is "with love" but it could just as easily read "with style" for this glowing pink lily. The large flowers are borne on strong but short stems making this an exceptional choice for containers.

❀ **'Creation'** has light to dark pink flowers in July and August, reaching 30 to 35 inches. The flowers are a perfect blend — rosy-pink dotted centers fading to soft pink along the petal edges. Plants produce an especially high number of showy and elegant flowers over a long period.

❀ **'Emily' (or 'Emmely')** has rosy to pink to white flowers that crown 30- to 40-inch stems in July. Graceful, 7-inch flowers with deep pink centers and creamy edges give this flower tremendous value. Each stem produces an abundance of buds so plants massed in the garden make an impressive display. Or, a single stem loaded with buds will provide a complete bouquet in a vase.

❀ **'Gold Band'** has golden yellow and white flowers topping 30- to 40-inch stems in July and August. Huge pure white petals are accented by a central golden band in this unique and attractive flower. The band and sprinkle of freckles against a light background accentuate the flower's star shape and give it a glowing, radiant look.

❀ **'Hit Parade'** has pale pink and white blossoms open on 20- to 24-inch stems in July and August. Chosen as a 1992 Oriental Hybrid Lily winner, this flower shows off flawless, soft pink curling petals fading to pure white in the center. Try this one for fragrance and beauty in containers.

❀ **'Le Reve'** offers pink and yellow flowers that bloom in July on 24- to 30-inch stems. This lily has been admired and prized for years, making it a popular and worthy choice. The clear pink petals dashed with yellow deep in the center are stunning in the garden or in a vase. It really does live up to its name as "a dream" cultivar.

❀ **'Marco Polo'** offers white and purplish-pink flowers, reaching 24 to 36 inches in July and August. When you want very large and very unusual flowers, try this selection. The clear white flowers shade to a purplish-pink along the wavy edges of each petal. Expect as many as 20 fragrant blossoms per bulb.

❀ **'Star Gazer'** has crimson and white flowers atop 36-inch stems in July and August. Bold and joyful with a bright center and pale edges, this lily will give you double delights with reliable color in the border or in containers. It offers outstanding fragrance typical of all the lilies in this group, so it's an awesome cut flower as well.

Because most of these are stem-rooting plants, you need to plant them a bit deeper than other types of lilies.

As mentioned previously, Oriental hybrids finish the summer show, offering large, impressive, perfumed flowers in late summer and providing welcome color in the garden for a perfect follow-up to the summer perennial show. On a deck or patio, they're ideal in containers with plenty of late season color and fragrance. Include at least a few in this group in your cutting garden or use them as outstanding companions to late-blooming annuals or perennials.

Choosing lilies for containers

Lower-growing (shorter) lilies are excellent when planted in containers to decorate a patio or terrace. Here are some things to consider when choosing lilies to plant in a container:

✔ How tall does the particular lily grow?

A 7-foot-tall trumpet lily in a pot is highly accident-prone — it falls over. Shorter is better.

> ✔ Will you keep the lily in a pot for the rest of its life?
>
> Conditions in a pot are harder on bulbs in winter than for the same kind of bulb in the ground. After the lily flowers in the pot, plant it in your garden in fall and get new ones for pots.

For more about growing bulbs in containers, see Chapter 19.

Choosing lilies as cut flowers

As cut flowers, lilies are very popular — and expensive. You can buy the bulbs cheaper and grow your own lilies for cutting. Just remember that taking away too many healthy green leaves reduces the bulb's ability to store food for the next year. So keep at least 50 percent of the leaves or more, if possible. In addition, cutting lilies with long stems weakens the bulb. So does cutting the same bulb year after year.

Chapter 23 has more information about using bulbs for cut flowers.

Planning and Planting for a Great Display

Lilies are easy to plant, just like most other bulbs. But lily bulbs need prompt planting and gentle handling — no pinching, dropping, or throwing around — because the bulb always has some fleshy roots at its bottom, and the scales are not covered with a papery, protective tunic.

Lilies go dormant late in the growing season — November and sometimes even December. Bulbs shipped in fall can arrive kind of late; any time after October in zone 6 is considered late. If that's the case, prepare the area ahead of time, and then cover it with an unopened bag of mulch. That way, if the weather gets really cold the site will be protected. Even if the bag of mulch freezes, you can still pry it up and flip it out of the way, and then plant in the nice unfrozen soil beneath.

Lily bulbs are also available in spring. They need to be planted right away, because they're primed to grow. If you leave a bulb in the bag for too long, the shoots are liable to begin growing. If the bulb is upside down or sideways in the bag, you can imagine the contortions the expanding shoot goes through! Also, the new shoot is very fragile, easily broken when you're planting. So be sure to plant the bulbs within a day or two of purchase.

An even easier way to get lilies is to buy them as growing potted plants in spring. Just take them home from the garden center, pop them in the soil, and — voilà! — instant display. The drawback is that your selection will be more limited.

Choosing a place for lilies in the garden is pretty simple. Because they are moderate to tall plants — anywhere from 2 to 7 feet high, depending on the type you've chosen — they go to the middle or back of the border.

Lilies don't have great foliage — narrow little leaves sticking out from that tall stem — so mix them with perennials, such as summer phlox and bee balm, that disguise the lily's rather stick-like nature.

Because lilies like to have their heads in the sun and their roots shaded, combining lilies with perennials suits this to a "T" as well, although low shrubs, such as dwarf spireas and barberries, work well too.

Although lilies don't like soggy soil, lilies also don't like drought. If necessary, amend your soil so it is moist, yet drains freely, and has good levels of organic matter. We discuss amending in more detail in Chapter 21.

Some lilies, such as most of the Asiatic and Oriental hybrids, are *stem-rooting* — they make seasonal roots along the portion of the stem that's underground. You need to plant these lilies deeper than non-stem-rooting lilies, which are generally planted to a depth of three times the bulb height. During the growing season, the seasonal roots take up moisture and nutrients while the lily is actively growing leaves and flower. These roots wither away when the stem does at the end of the growing season.

Make sure that any fertilizer you add to the soil is well mixed with the dirt. Inorganic fertilizers in particular can harm the scales or roots if they come in direct contact — this ultimately can affect the growth of the bulb. See Chapter 21 for more detailed information on fertilizer.

Foiling Pests

Unfortunately, lilies are tasty treats for all sorts of varmints. Deer eat the flowers while the flowers are still in bud, for a tasty head-high snack. Rabbits like to nibble on lily shoots as the shoots are just starting to grow. And voles and the like dine on the bulbs. Well, people used to eat lily bulbs, too.

To help control pests, follow these suggestions:

- ✔ Use repellent sprays for deer and rabbits. Make sure that all the plant is covered because as the lily grows any unsprayed portion is unprotected. Continue to spray as the plant grows.

- ✔ Plant lily bulbs within a wire cage or mesh bag to foil the underground pests. You'll have to make the wire cages yourself out of hardware cloth — wire mesh with a small, square pattern of holes. Wear gloves, the cut ends of wire are sharp. Bulb-planting bags are available from some mail-order sources.

Although tending to these jobs is a nuisance, you'll find it worthwhile in the long run. Lilies are such exciting flowers that the maintenance chores fade from mind while you enjoy their regal splendor.

Chapter 13

Ornamental Onions

. . . .

In This Chapter

▶ Selecting ornamental onions for the flower garden

▶ Deciding where and when to plant

▶ Choosing companion plants

▶ Using ornamental onions in bouquets

▶ Beyond flowers, beautiful seed heads

. . . .

*O*nions? In the flower garden? You bet!

Ornamental onions have beautiful, unusual flowers that are different from anything you've ever grown. Imagine a dandelion gone to seed. Now picture it purple. Basically, that's what an ornamental onion looks like — a splendid pale-to-deep purple soap bubble tethered on a sturdy stem (see Figure 13-1).

Figure 13-1:
The surprisingly beautiful ornamental onion —
this one's
Allium christophii.

Ornamental onions vary from the size of a small to large grapefruit and even larger. They don't even smell oniony, so their long-lasting flowers are great for cutting. And the onion's beauty goes beyond bloom: The seed heads that follow the flowering have an elegant beauty of their own.

Flowering as they do after tulips and before lilies, you can use ornamental onions to fill this gap in your bulb display. Just remember to disguise their lack of leaves at blossom time.

Selecting Ornamental Onions

Following are various ornamental onions you can grow:

* *Allium aflatunense,* 'Purple Sensation': Dramatic color and form reward gardeners who plant this newer hybrid, which has 4- to 5-inch purple flowers on 2- to 3-foot stems. Plants perform very well in the garden, offering abundant blooms in May, and they shine when combined with perennials. Feature this one in the cutting garden because the flowers are outstanding cut or dried.

* *Allium caeruleum* (also known as *Allium azureum*): Discovered in Siberia in 1830, this cultivar offers striking color with charming plants that bloom in May, having 1- to 2-inch cornflower-blue flowers atop 12- to 20-inch stems. They produce distinctive globes, which work well as garden accents. This versatile bulb naturalizes easily, integrates beautifully into a perennial bed, and serves well in the cutting garden.

* *Allium christophii* (also known as *A. albopilosum*): Also called "Star of Persia," this cultivar sends up spectacular spheres that rank among the largest ornamental onion flowers, with 8- to 12-inch light lavender flowers that reach 18 to 30 inches. *(You can see a picture of it in the color section.)* The June blossoms have star-shaped, somewhat metallic florets in a loose arrangement. As a cut flower, this one may be the most dramatic of all the cultivars. You can also use it in borders, naturalized, and as a dried flower.

* *Allium flavum:* This cultivar has bell-shaped yellow flowers that top 12-inch stems. With a look all its own, this ornamental onion offers a loose, pendulous cluster of up to 30 small but radiant lemon-yellow florets. It blooms late — in June or July — and will grow in light shade. Use this unusual cultivar to create a special look in the rock garden or border, or naturalized in the landscape.

* *Allium giganteum:* For an impressive upright accent with June blossoms, choose this cultivar, the stateliest and tallest ornamental onion with deep purple 4- to 6-inch flowers that bloom on 3- to 5-foot stems. The huge bulb, about as big as a crown imperial bulb (see Chapter 11),

produces hundreds of richly colored florets that form a tight ball. Expect dramatic results when you plant this bulb with perennials, in borders, as a cut or dried flower, or in a grouping in the landscape.

❋ *Allium karataviense:* With pale pink to almost white 4- to 6-inch flowers on 8-inch stems, you can enjoy double rewards from this exceptional allium, which offers handsome leaves as well as distinctive ball-shaped flowers in May or June. Two or three broad, pleated, silvery gray-green leaves hug the ground, making a great backdrop to the silver-mauve flower head. This compact grower is especially attractive near border edges, in the rock garden, with perennials, as a cut or dried flower, or even forced late.

❋ *Allium schubertii*: Huge 12- to 14-inch pale rose flowers top 18- to 24-inch stems. Like fireworks bursting in the sky, the impressive May or June blossoms of this cultivar feature a loose spherical cluster of huge 12- to 14-inch pale rose flowers open on stems of varied lengths, from 18 to 24 inches. The result is a striking, airy, almost dill-like flower that's ideal for cutting, and long lasting (up to two years) when dried. This may not be the tallest ornamental onion, but in terms of diameter, it has the biggest flower head. It is tender in cold winters, so plant it near a house wall or some sheltered site for a little extra protection.

❋ *Allium sphaerocephalon*, **Drumstick allium:** With reddish-purple 2-inch oval flower heads atop 15- to 30-inch stems, this cultivar has a long history, with references to it noted as far back as the late 1500s. The egg-shaped May and June flowers feature about a hundred tightly packed florets per flower. These long-lasting flowers are especially attractive when planted in groupings and allowed to naturalize, because they offer a carpet of color. They're also effective in beds and borders, and for cutting and drying.

❋ **'Gladiator'**: This hybrid has lilac-purple 4- to 6-inch flowers atop 3- to 4-foot stems. For early summer color in the landscape, try this ornamental onion. The blossoms are very showy and long lasting, offering ideal contrast and unique form when used with perennials. Also save a spot for this cultivar in the cutting garden.

❋ **'Globemaster'**: Deep-violet 10-inch flowers top 2- to 3-foot stems on this striking hybrid. Spectacular is the only word for these huge globes that bloom for weeks — from June on. Each large cluster is made up of over 1,000 florets. The waist-high blossoms are unsurpassed for drama and offer a bonus of acceptable foliage during the bloom period. They make ideal focal points in a bed, border, or landscape, and mass plantings will naturalize with flair.

❋ **'Lucy Ball'**: Lilac-purple 4- to 6-inch flowers top stems that reach 3 to 4 feet. Reliable and richly colored, this hybrid offers impressive early summer flowers in a cool and inviting shade. The softball-sized blossoms provide plenty of interest in a variety of garden settings and add drama to arrangements.

❀ **'Mount Everest':** White 6-inch flowers top 3-foot stems. The pure white blossoms sit atop straight and sturdy stems in this cultivar. Plants are especially vigorous and flowers are long lasting. Save a special place in your bed or border for these gems, which combine beautifully with other ornamental onions or perennials and stand out in bouquets.

❀ **'Rien Poortvliet':** Amethyst 6- to 8-inch flowers top 3- to 4-foot stems. Huge, early summer flowers are not to be missed in this special cultivar named for a famous Dutch artist. The melon-sized globes offer regal color and intense drama. This ornamental onion is versatile indoors or out, so consider it when you want early color.

Planting Ornamental Onions

Ornamental onions are true bulbs with papery white tunics. You can plant them in a flower bed or cottage garden mixed with perennials of suitable size, and they're good in the cutting garden, too. There's really very little to growing ornamental onions, no special tricks or techniques you have to know — other than that you want them in the first place!

Ornamental onions are sun lovers and prefer a well-drained site. Many of them originated in the steppes of Central Asia and prefer its cold winters and dry summers. These bulbs really hate soggy soil in summer.

You plant ornamental onions in fall, just like tulips and daffodils. Plant the bulbs with the flat basal plate downward and the pointy end up. You should plant the bulbs in a hole two to three times their height — deeper in sandy soils, more shallow in loamy soils. Small growing bulbs (which are small in stature, not flower size) are best if you plant them in groups of ten; the larger ones are okay as ones and threes. Plant small bulbs 5 inches to base, and large bulbs 8 inches to base.

The onion bulbs can be costly. In general, you may want to try unusual bulbs in small numbers the first time that you grow them. Then, when you're captivated by their charm, you can buy more bulbs the next year.

Deer and rabbits leave ornamental onions alone, as do voles and chipmunks.

Choosing Companion Plants

Ornamental onions, especially the tall-growing, large-flowered ones, do have one drawback: Their leaves wither away about the time they flower, leaving a purple globe balanced on a stem with no leaves to dress things up. Companion plants for ornamental onions provide the necessary embellishment. Fortunately, a number of fibrous-rooted perennials grow and flower at the same time that ornamental onions do.

When you choose companion plants, think about the effect that you want to create. Ask yourself the following questions:

✔ Do you want the colors to be contrasty — for example, yellow hues would provide the most distinct color contrast?

Yarrow is one possibility. It is an easily grown perennial with fern-like leaves and flat-topped clusters of numerous tiny daisy flowers that also grows in sunny sites with well-drained soil.

✔ Do you want a more subtle harmony — for example, lavender, lilac, and blue to delicately accent the ornamental onions' colors?

Hardy geraniums, the larger growing ones such as 'Johnson's Blue,' would be a good choice. Perennials with silver foliage, such as lamb's ears, are agreeable also.

Ornamental grasses are a great choice, too — their thin, linear leaves make a good contrast to the more definite shape of the ornamental onion's flower.

Smaller ornamental onions, with their round flower heads, contrast nicely with daisies and flowers like liatris, which bloom in spikes, and make good companions.

Displaying the Beautiful Flowers and Seed Heads

We like plants and flowers that have multiple uses. It's nice to enjoy them in the garden, but more handy if they're good for something else as well. And ornamental onions fit the bill most attractively.

Beyond flowers, ornamental onions have beautiful seed heads. Wait until the seed heads are fully developed and turn brown before you cut them. They're amazingly sturdy. Judy has some that she cut two years ago, and they're just fine — they last naturally. We prefer their natural color, but you can spray paint them any color you like — Christmas colors, glittery gold, whatever. And don't worry about cutting the seed heads, the bulbs should flower just fine next year.

Ornamental onions are a case of having your cake and eating it too. You can enjoy their flowers in the garden; you can cut them as fresh flowers when the flowers are just approaching full open and the color is well developed. And then, after the seed heads appear, you can also cut them for bouquets. Using just one of the big beautiful flowers, in a sturdy glass vase, gives a modern, contemporary look.

A wine bottle is a good size and shape to use as a vase for a large ornamental onion's flower or seed head.

Chapter 14

Tender Summer Beauties

*J*ust because the most familiar bulbs — daffodils, hyacinths, snowdrops, and so on — easily sleep through winter and come up each spring, we think that it's normal for *all* bulbs to manage snow and cold. But a bulb may have originated in response to alternating cycles of dry and rainy seasons rather than cold and warm weather. And these warm-weather bulbs can't survive prolonged freezing weather. These tender beauties are great for summer interest. Sure, if you leave them in the garden after hard frosts arrive, they won't survive until spring. But they are easy to dig and store. Maybe you should think of these tender bulbs as annuals, with the option of keeping them from year to year.

Gardeners who live in mild winter areas have it made because these bulbs enjoy the kinder, gentler winters where snow and cold are the exception rather than the norm — sort of compensates those who have to refrigerate hardy bulbs, such as tulips, in order to convince them that winter has arrived.

Glorious Gladiolus for Indoors and Out

Gladiolus is a great warm-weather corm with which to start your garden or flower bed. The 3- to 4-foot-tall spikes of summer flowers (see Figure 14-1) are easy to produce in sequence, just by planting corms every couple of weeks. Flowers come in a rainbow array of colors. They're great as cut flowers, too. In fact, Judy thinks that they make better cut flowers than flower-border companions.

Gladiolus corms look like oversize crocus corms: They're covered in a fibrous brown wrapper with a small, flat place at the bottom and sometimes have pointy shoots already showing at the top.

Some mail-order sources offer you a choice of sizes: the larger, top-size corms have somewhat longer flower spikes, which sometimes produce two flower spikes and bloom a bit earlier than the smaller ones.

Choosing glads by color

You can choose your glads by the color you want in the garden or for bouquets, as well as for their height and beauty. Glads are often sold by mixed colors, too.

You may want to try the following gladiolus cultivars:

 ❀ **'Arabian Night'** offers dark good looks in an unusual combination of deep red with brownish tones highlighted with a white flair on the lowest petal of each flower. Plants reach 3 to 4 feet and should be spaced 5 inches apart.

❀ **'Home Coming'** boasts an impressive two-toned creamy white with a delicate purple throat on 3- to 4-foot plants. Combined with dark purple glads, this makes a smashing display.

❀ **'My Love'** offers elegant beauty from 3- to 4-foot spikes featuring white flowers edged with deep pink splashes. The tinted flowers have a unique, lacy look.

❀ **'Nova Lux'** has an easy-going nature and an abundance of color from clear, golden yellow flowers on spikes reaching 4 feet. Velvety, ruffled petals give this cultivar high marks.

❀ **'Peter Pears'** sports large showy flowers up to $5^1/_2$ feet tall in a delightful apricot-salmon accented with red throat marks, making it a standout in arrangements or exhibitions.

❀ **'Priscilla'** is simply stunning with tricolored flowers featuring a white background accented with bright pink along the wavy petal edges and finished with a soft yellow throat.

❀ **'Saphir'** lends a cool elegance to the garden with its deep blue flowers accented with pure white throats. Plants may reach 4 feet tall.

❀ **'Spic and Span'** sends up perfectly formed 4-foot spikes with overlapping deep pink flowers, each with a creamy white center. This one is an old-fashioned favorite and top choice among commercial growers.

❀ **'Victor Borge'** offers dramatic color from brilliant vermilion-orange flowers on 5-foot stems. The blossoms open to reveal creamy white throat markings on this cultivar, which excels in arrangements.

❀ **'Windsong'** shines with vivid flowers in a soft pastel pink with slightly darker, ruffled edges and sparked with a prominent pure white central spot.

❀ **'Wine and Roses'** is an inspiring two-toned variety featuring pale pink blossoms decorated with a deep wine-red throat. The unusual look makes an impressive accent.

Perhaps you don't like staking, or you prefer shorter plants and smaller bouquets. In that case, you may want to try butterfly gladiolus. They grow only 2 to 3 feet tall and are ideal tucked in among perennial plantings. You'll find them sold individually and as a mix with an array of colors including two-toned flowers. They are hardy in zones 7 to 10. The following is a list of some butterfly gladiolus varieties:

❀ **'Blackpool'** offers an impressive trio of colors — white, red, and yellow — on flowers that open to offer sheer delight in the garden or in a vase.

❀ **'Green Bird'** is graceful and refined with clean white flowers flushed with green. Imagine a dozen or so of these popping up with fresh, crisp color among your favorite summer perennials.

❦ **'Perky'** delivers robust, perfectly formed flowers in arresting red with white throats.

❦ **'Perseus'** is hard to resist with glowing deep pink flowers delicately dabbed with white in the center.

If you want even more of a selection, be aware that some mail-order nurseries specialize in gladiolus, with hundreds of cultivars available. You can find a list of mail-order nurseries in Appendix A.

I'm especially fond of the "hardy gladiolus," *Gladiolus nanus*. It is more cold-tolerant than the other gladiolus and can stay in the ground year-round in zone 6 and warmer, zone 5 with the added protection of a winter mulch. It is more graceful and airy in bloom than the glads previously described, harmonizing nicely with perennials and shrubs.

The following *Gladiolus nanus* cultivars make lovely additions to the garden:

❦ **'Albus'** shows off glistening crystal white flowers with yellow stripes and blue anthers borne on 12- to 18-inch foot stems.

❦ **'Aranea'** sends up regal spikes gracefully decorated in rich purple flowers. Its height range is 15 to 20 inches.

❦ **'Atom'** commands attention with its vivid poppy-red flowers accented boldly with a violet spot and white center. Plants reach 18 inches.

❦ **'Charm'** does simply that as the bright purplish flowers open to reveal white centers. Flowers are arranged loosely on 18-inch stems.

❦ **'Nymph'** is a strong grower with impressive white flowers sporting cream to pale pink blotches edged in crimson. The effect is at once stunning and delicate in this popular variety.

❦ **'The Bride'** grows 18 to 24 inches rewarding growers with glistening white flowers with a hint of pale yellow to light green in the center. Blossoms have an interesting, open form with star-shaped florets.

Growing glads

Follow these tips for successfully growing glads:

✔ Glads prefer sandy, well-drained soil in a sunny location.

✔ Because glads have a tall sheaf of sword-like leaves, plant them deeper than usual for a plant this size to help anchor them against strong winds that may push them over.

To plant glads:

1. **Dig a trench about 8 inches deep, long enough that you can space the corms about 6 inches apart.**

   That spacing may look kind of odd in the flower border, so plan to plant them there in a rounded, somewhat tapered oval, making it big enough to accommodate 10 corms. Plant glads in a row if you're growing them for cutting.

2. **Feed corms with 5-10-10 or 5-10-5 granular fertilizer.**

   Add the recommended amount at the bottom of the planting area, and mix well with the soil. Add a layer of unfertilized soil, so the corms won't be in direct contact with the fertilizer granules.

3. **Start planting, either groups or rows, in mid-spring (April in northern areas and February in southern regions).**

   - Make new plantings every two weeks.

     Because glads take 70 to 100 days from planting to flowering, that approach gives you flowers right through summer.

   - If the glads are growing in a location that is exposed to wind, stake them.

     Use a pair of 30-inch stakes at each end of the row, and down the sides as necessary. Support the plants with string strung between the stakes, midway and just below the top of the stakes.

   - Stop planting in summer, late June or mid-July in northern regions and May in southern areas.

4. **Keep glads well-watered while they are growing and mulch to help keep the soil moist.**

   Just cover the soil with a couple of inches of light, airy, weed-seed-free organic matter: shredded leaves; coarse chunky compost; or small-size, mulch-grade pine bark. (You need to produce the first two mulch materials; the pine bark is commercially available.)

Glads are only winter hardy in zones 8 to 11. They are often hardy in zones 6 or 7 with the protection of a thick mulch in winter or next to a house where enough warmth comes through the foundation to protect them. If you live in these zones and grow glads as a permanent addition to your garden, or if you plan to dig and store the corms for next year, fertilize again to produce bigger corms for next year's display. Fertilize when the flower spikes begin to show, and again when you pick the flowers. Add the fertilizer in a band next to where the glads are growing, and gently scratch the granules into the soil, using a *cultivator* (a three-pronged claw-like hand tool).

Cut glads for bouquets when the first few flowers at the bottom of the spike are fully open.

Storing corms

You can dig the corms for storage 4 to 6 weeks after you pick the flowers, or 4 to 6 weeks after they fade.

1. **Shake as much soil as possible off the corms and then trim back the leaves to within an inch of the corm.**

2. **Let the corms dry for a week or so and then gently brush off any remaining soil.**

3. **Store glads dry, in a mesh bag or old panty hose, in a dark cool (35 to 41 degrees Fahrenheit) place.**

   Remember that mice love gladiolus corms as a tasty snack. Make sure that you store the corms in a vermin-proof place.

If you live somewhere with cold winters where glads are planted fresh each year, don't replant them in the same place they were growing the year before. A new site gives better results. Cycle them around the garden, returning to a previous location in three to five years.

Considering the peacock lily: Gladiolus or not?

Officially called *Gladiolus callianthus,* other times referred to by the formal name of *Acidanthera murialae,* peacock lily grows in much the same way as a gladiolus and needs the same sort of handling. Follow these tips:

- ✔ Peacock lily has smaller, more pointed corms. Plant in groups of ten with the pointy end up. Space the corms 3 inches apart. Choose a sunny, well-drained site just as you would for gladiolus.

- ✔ Plants have a sheaf of sword-like leaves, 20 to 30 inches high.

- ✔ In summer, each corm produces a spike with six to eight beautiful white flowers that display a showy maroon blotch in the throat.

   They look stunning in front of a dark-leafed canna such as 'Red King Humbert' or 'Wyoming.' Peacock lily makes a great cut flower.

In mild winter areas, zones 7 to 10, corms can stay in the ground year-round. Even so, in zone 7, these Ethiopian natives benefit from a winter mulch. In colder regions, lift and store the corms over the winter just like glads (or let them freeze out and just buy new corms the next spring).

Dazzling Dahlias

Dahlias are fabulous plants, as flamboyant in flower as you may expect from their colorful Mexican and Guatemalan origins. They were grown by the Incas, and you'll feel like royalty, too, when they produce their stunning flowers (see Figure 14-2).

Figure 14-2:
Dahlias
deserve a
place in
your
garden.

Deciding on a dahlia

Dahlias come in all sizes, and all colors, too. You can find window-box dahlias under a foot tall on up to dinner-plate dahlias, which are 4 feet tall or more. The shorter dahlias are great in the garden at the front of the border, in window-boxes, and in containers. Tall dahlias are stunning at the back of the border where their summer and early autumn flowers add fabulous color. All dahlias make great cut flowers (though the dinner-plate dahlias, with flowers a foot across, can be tricky to arrange!).

Dinner-plate dahlias

These dahlias reach 4 feet tall or more and plants produce abundant flowers that are, yes, truly as big as a dinner plate. Some may even rival your serving platter! Expect a dozen or more 9- to 11-inch flowers per plant. You may also see these referred to as "Extra Large Decorative" dahlias in some catalogs. Space these giants 3 feet apart. Try these varieties:

- ❀ **'Barbarossa'** offers arresting, enormous flowers in rich red. Not only are these striking because of color, but the blossoms exhibit outstanding form.

- ❀ **'Jean Marie'** produces distinctive blossoms with vivid violet-rose petals accented with pure white tips. This two-toned combination is an ideal accent for a burst of color.

- ❀ **'Kelvin's Floodlight'** just may be one of the largest dahlias you'll find. When you see the glowing, deep yellow flowers, you'll understand why this cultivar has won awards in both the United States and Holland.

- ❀ **'Lilac Time'** is a regal cultivar, displaying impressive deep lavender flowers with a bluish tint. Sturdy stems support the large flower heads, which can be cut and floated in a bowl for an unbeatable table decoration.

- ❀ **'Mistery Day'** (sometimes spelled "Mystery Day") has showy fuchsia-red flowers with white edges. The combination of deep red and sparkling white is a simply stunning contrast.

- ❀ **'Mrs. Eileen'** offers a bold, bright display from huge flowers in as vivid and bright an orange as you can imagine.

- ❀ **'Night Queen'** is a giant among giants with its dark good looks coming from rounded claret-colored flowers on tall stems.

- ❀ **'Otto's Thrill'** provides plenty of excitement as one of the largest dahlias ever. Its apricot pink flowers are a study in perfection.

- ❀ **'Rosella'** has such a bright and glowing pink hue it looks like it is lit from within. For elegance in the garden and in arrangements, this one fills the bill.

❀ **'Seattle'** blooms with clouds of huge, pure white flowers on sturdy 3- to 4-foot stems. They're absolutely ideal in combination with other two-toned dahlias or mixed with a variety of solid-color flowers.

❀ **'Thomas Edison'** sports rich, dark purple flowers with both outstanding form and an irresistible velvet-like texture — a combination that has served to make it a garden favorite for generations.

❀ **'White Perfection'** lives up to the dinner-plate billing with magnificent white flowers nearly a foot across. Buds show a light yellow blush but open to snowy white. It's excellent combined with almost any other dahlia.

Border decorative dahlias

Choose these 15-inch flowers when you want a burst of color for near the front or in the middle of your bed or border. Flowers reach 3 to 4 inches across and are produced in great numbers — up to 40 per plant. The border decorative form and compact size make these ideal choices for containers, too. In the garden, space these cultivars 12 inches apart. Check out these varieties:

❀ **'Aspen'** dazzles with bright white flowers sporting slightly curved petals. Prolific plants may give you dozens of flowers.

❀ **'Berliner Kleene'** is a well-known and popular cultivar because plants are nearly covered in deep pink blossoms. Its versatile nature makes it valuable for nearly any setting.

❀ **'Claudette'** displays very double, vivid flowers in a purplish-pink hue. This one produces an abundance of reliable blossoms.

❀ **'Zingaro'** offers a big payoff from exquisite flowers that start pale yellow in the center and unfold to a clear pale pink along the outer petals. The added bonus here is a long bloom time from summer into fall.

Border cactus dahlia

Cultivars in this category reach 2 feet tall and display impressive double flowers with narrow, pointed petals that curve slightly inward. This gives a somewhat looser more spiked look than other dahlias. The unusual form and vivid colors provide striking contrasts when combined with other dahlias in the garden or in arrangements. Blossoms are 4 to 5 inches across and a single plant may produce 40 buds. Space tubers 12 inches apart. We recommend these cultivars:

❀ **'Park Princess'** has tightly rolled blush pink petals. Each flower offers a range of color from pale to dark pink, making it a winner whether it's planted alone or combined with perennials, annuals, or other dahlias.

❀ **'Saba'** is rich with arresting spiky red petals. This one adds drama and flair wherever you use it.

❀ **'Yellow Happiness'** offers abundant cheer from lemon-yellow flowers that lend a bright but soothing look to the late summer garden.

Decorative dahlias

This distinction refers to flower form. Flowers under this heading are fully double with short, broad, pointed to rounded flat petals that curve slightly along the margins. Some have a very formal, tailored look, and others are slightly looser — almost fringed on the edges. Size can range from 15 inches to 4 feet. Expect a range of production too, because some will produce as many as 25 flowers. Tubers should be planted 12 to 18 inches apart.

Here are two beautiful decorative dahlias:

❀ **'Key West'** puts on an impressive show with 5-inch flowers in a warm orange changing to yellow at the base of each petal. Each 3-foot-tall plant will reward you with up to 25 buds.

❀ **'Miami'** is an exquisite cultivar showing strong white flowers with faint pink coloring at the petal tips, especially in the center of the flower. It grows 3 feet and produces 5-inch flowers.

Spider dahlias

These unique cultivars have narrow curled petals that are almost tube-like as they radiate from the center of the flower. Similar to cactus dahlias, these are more spiked and slightly looser resembling, maybe, a spider if you are in the right frame of mind. They're ideal for an unusual accent. Plants produce about 25 flowers, each one 4 to 6 inches across. Set tubers 12 to 18 inches apart.

Consider these two cultivars of spider dahlia:

❀ **'Alfred Grille'** is a cultivar of many colors. The yellow center gives way to peach pink and pale pink petals along the flower's margins. It grows 2 to 4 feet and produces an abundance of healthy blossoms.

❀ **'Yellow Star'** is a burst of bright yellow from layer upon layer of slender, vivid petals. It reaches 30 inches and offers a long bloom time.

Mignon patio dahlias

Sweet and simple, these dahlias offer classic good looks from single flowers on compact, bushy 2-inch plants. Blossoms are 3 to 4 inches across with golden centers and the flowers are flatter with fewer petals than other dahlia varieties. Prolific plants may give you as many as 40 plants each. Try these for cheerful color along border fronts or in pots, planters, and window boxes. Plant these cultivars 8 to 12 inches apart.

The following are impressive mignon patio dahlias:

- ❀ **'Irene van der Zwet'** is a bright golden yellow that will spark any border or container garden. It combines well with other varieties and is ideal among perennials and annuals.

- ❀ **'Murillo'** sends up striking bright pink flowers with a dark pink ring around the golden center. The effect is eye-catching anywhere and may remind you of a cosmos flower in miniature.

- ❀ **'Red Riding Hood'** adds plenty of zip from bright red flowers that nearly cover the neat, tidy clumps of foliage.

- ❀ **'Sneezy'** is an unbeatable pure white with a yellow heart. It's ideal for late summer color just about anywhere in your garden, and it combines beautifully with other dahlias or late-blooming annuals in containers.

If you really fall in love with dahlias, you can find some mail-order nurseries that specialize in dahlias, offering hundreds of cultivars. A list of mail-order nurseries is in Appendix A.

Growing dahlias

Dahlias are really easy to grow, if you pay attention to their particular needs by heeding the following advice:

- ✔ Dahlias like a sunny site.

- ✔ Although dahlias need ample water while they are growing, they hate wet feet. Make sure that the site has good drainage.

- ✔ Fertilizer is good, but don't use too much or the plants will grow more leaves than flowers.

- ✔ Dahlias hate frost; it turns their flowers, leaves, and stems to limp, blackened mush. Don't rush them outdoors too early, before the weather is frost-free. If you cover them for the first frost or two in autumn, you can often get another few weeks of beauty before cold weather comes to stay. Plant dormant dahlia tuberous roots two weeks before the last frost date in your area. By the time they are up above ground, the weather should be frost-free. If you're planting dahlias that already have leafy shoots showing, wait until the same time you'd plant tomatoes outdoors.

If you live in zones 8 to 10, you can leave dahlias in the ground year-round. In zone 7, you need to provide a protective winter mulch. Dahlias are great garden flowers even in zone 4. But anywhere colder than zone 7, you need to lift the tuberous roots out of the ground after the first killing frost or plan on buying new tuberous roots in spring.

To plant dahlias:

1. **Dig the soil a foot deep where you intend to plant the dahlias.**

2. **Add peat moss and compost to improve the soil and coarse sand or fine gravel — $^3/_8$-inch size — to improve drainage if necessary.**

    Return the removed soil to the hole so that it is level with the surrounding ground.

3. **Dig a planting hole (easy, now that you've prepared the soil) deep enough to hold the spread-out clump of tubers and to cover them with 2 to 4 inches of soil.**

4. **Space dahlias 1 to 3 feet apart, depending on how big the particular variety will grow.**

    Handle the clump of tuberous roots gently, to avoid breaking any off. After you place them, cover the tubers with 2 to 4 inches of soil.

Tall dahlias get top-heavy because they produce so many flowers, so they need staking. Placing the stakes at planting time is much better, because you can see where the tubers are, rather than running the risk of spearing through them later on.

Enjoy the dahlias in your garden and as cut flowers; the more you cut, the more they bloom. If you don't cut the flowers for bouquets, be sure to deadhead. No, don't become a rock-band groupie. *Deadheading* means to remove old flowers when they start to look yucky.

- ✔ After the first mild frost has blackened the above-ground growth, cut the bloom away close to ground level.

- ✔ Carefully dig up the clumps of tuberous roots.

    The roots will have grown bigger over the summer, so be sure to dig wide enough to avoid damaging them!

- ✔ Shake off the loose dirt. Let the tubers dry for a few days (about a week) and then gently dry-brush (no water, please) to remove more soil. Pack the tuberous roots in dry peat moss, buckwheat hulls, or sawdust — you get the idea.

Don't let the clumps touch each other, but keep them separate with packing material.

Keep the box of tubers in a cool (35 to 45 degrees Fahrenheit), dry, frost-free place. Then next spring you can start them again.

Cannas with Panache

Either you love them or you don't, but not very many gardeners are indifferent to cannas. We think that it is the boring way that we all-too-often see them used — a canna sort of plopped into the middle of a lawn surrounded by concentric rings of yellow marigolds and red salvia. Think of cannas instead as bold, lush, tropical plants, and they become much more interesting (see Figure 14-3).

Figure 14-3: With vibrant colors and bold, tropical foliage, cannas add zest to your garden.

Selecting cannas for your garden or flower bed

Cannas come in different sizes, different leaf colors, and many have lush flowers offering you a choice of colors.

Some dynamite color combinations (at least we think so) include dark purple-leafed cannas with

 ✔ Bright red flowers such as zinnias, dahlias, or salvia

 ✔ Clear pink flowers such as zinnias and dahlias, or petunias

✔ Purple flowers such as *Verbena bonariensis* with its bobbles of soft purple on tall stems

✔ Green flowers (yes, there are such things!) such as *Zinnia* 'Envy' or *Nicotiana langsdorffii*

✔ Maroon-blotched white flowers of peacock lily, which we describe earlier in this chapter

'Tropicana' (a multicolor canna), which we describe later in this chapter, is absolutely stunning with *Brugmansia* 'Charles Grimaldi,' a huge sort of woody tropical plant with dangling 10-inch, apricot-peach trumpets. 'Tropicana' is also a blast with black-leafed plants such as a sweet potato vine (called 'Blackie') or chartreuse (for example, another sweet potato vine named 'Marghrita').

'Praetoria' is a canna with green-striped yellow leaves that looks great with flowering maple, *Abutilon pictum* 'Thompsonii,' with yellow-speckled leaves and apricot, bell-like flowers. We tossed in a dwarf apricot-flowered dahlia to complete the picture.

The following sections list some excellent canna varieties.

Green-leafed cannas

We recommend the following green-leafed cannas:

❀ **'City of Portland'** grows 3 to 4 feet and flowers in a regal salmon pink. The large blossoms against the gray-green foliage make quite a show.

❀ **'Cleopatra'** offers true garden drama from bold yellow and red flowers set above unusual leaves marbled with chocolate. Petals run the gamut from solid yellow to half yellow and half red to yellow with red specks — all on the same plant! This mid-sized canna reaches about 3 feet.

❀ **Futurity** dwarf cannas are smallest of all, and are excellent in containers.

• **'Pink Futurity'** sports wide clear pink blossoms that bloom all summer long. The bright blossoms set against dark burgundy leaves give this 2^1/$_2$-foot cultivar lots of class.

• **'Red Futurity'** shows off vivid scarlet flowers that reach 3 feet tall, rising above bronze foliage.

• **'Rose Futurity'** offers a unique blend of colors from flowers ranging from coral to rose. It's an even more appealing combination when you add in the dark burgundy leaves. The total package tops out at about 3 feet.

• **'Yellow Futurity'** is lush and attractive and at the same time exciting and dramatic. Why? Because the vibrant and abundant bright yellow flowers are striking above the rich green foliage and because the old blossoms fall away, never detracting from the show.

❀ **'Harvest Yellow'** is a giant canna, growing about 4 feet tall with large, deep yellow flowers and dark green leaves which, you can imagine, provide lovely contrast.

❀ **'Journey's End'** may remind you of a tropical sunset with its striking flowers in creamy yellow splashed with glowing pink accents. With such color atop rich deep green foliage, this 3 footer is a sure winner.

❀ **'Miss Oklahoma,'** also known as 'Pink President,' will give you an admirable early show from big, bold flower heads in pink to watermelon shades. Plants are compact at 2 to 3 feet.

❀ **'Omega'** is a giant, easily 10 to 14 feet tall when fertilized. This robust plant stands up to winds and produces dainty apricot-orange flowers set against green foliage. It's best when viewed from above.

❀ **Pfitzer** series are more dwarfed than many other cannas, good for container use.

- **'Chinese Coral'** combines lush green foliage with coral pink blossoms to make quite a display even though it only reaches $2^1/_2$ feet tall.

- **'Crimson Beauty'** dazzles with bright red flowers set against deep green foliage. It's ideal for containers because it tops out at under 2 feet tall.

- **'Primrose Yellow'** delivers soft, canary yellow blooms and rich green foliage on quite compact 2-foot plants.

- **'Salmon Pink'** isn't a mystery with salmon flowers over green foliage, but it is attractive and versatile as a 2-foot cultivar.

❀ **'Richard Wallace'** ensures a double take, once you see its golden yellow flowers accented with a touch of red in subtle streaks and spots. Together with the bright green foliage, it definitely makes a statement in the garden. This mid-sized canna grows 3 to 4 feet.

❀ **'Rosamund Cole'** is the choice when you want big flowers with unique flair. The blossoms are bright red with yellow backs and margins and this $3^1/_2$ foot cultivar features broad, dark green leaves.

❀ **'Salmon Pink'** is a delightful 3-foot cultivar (not to be confused with the Pfitzer dwarf) that sports coral flowers that brighten to yellow. It makes an impressive display combined with either pink or yellow cannas.

❀ **'Stadt Fellbach'** offers choice color from vibrant, deep orange flowers that are guaranteed to enliven the garden. This giant canna tops out at about $3^1/_2$ feet.

❀ **'The President'** may be the most popular canna of all, and its extra-large, extra-bright red flowers set against handsome deep green foliage tell you why. Plants reach 3 to 4 feet.

✿ **'Yellow King Humbert'** proves more is better when the sturdy, 5-foot plants send up torches of oversized glowing yellow flowers accented with red splashes near the throat. This large cultivar will fill garden spaces with flair.

Red-leafed cannas

The following are red-leafed cannas:

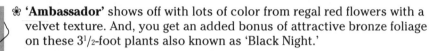 ✿ **'Ambassador'** shows off with lots of color from regal red flowers with a velvet texture. And, you get an added bonus of attractive bronze foliage on these $3^1/_2$-foot plants also known as 'Black Night.'

✿ **'Black Knight,'** not to be confused with 'Black Night' mentioned in the preceding bullet, also blooms in bright red and offers impressive deep mahogany to purple foliage on 3- to 5-foot plants.

✿ **'Red King Humbert'** is among the tallest cannas with a height range of 4 to 8 feet. It features scarlet flowers and dark leaves tinged with red which, overall, makes for a winning combination.

✿ **'Wyoming'** simply proves how contrast can conquer when the tangerine flowers open above dark bronze leaves touched with purple. It's another tall one — reaching 4 to 7 feet.

Yellow-leafed cannas

The following are yellow-leafed cannas:

✿ **'Bengal Tiger'** will stop you in your tracks with arresting variegated leaves striped with bold bands of cream, green, and gold. The 4- to 5-foot plants also send up huge orange blossoms. Set behind gold-leaved shrubs, this cultivar is simply stunning. You may find it listed as 'Pretoria' in some catalogs.

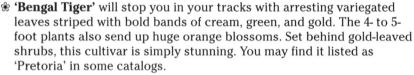 ✿ **'Striped Beauty'** commands attention with leaves streaked with yellow, but the big payoff is that the leaves are perfectly matched to bright canary-yellow flowers. And, the 2- to 3-foot compact nature of this canna makes it better in smaller spaces than many larger cultivars. Some catalogs also link 'Striata' to 'Striped Beauty' and 'Striata' is very similar with gray-green leaves streaked with creamy white, but it offers soft orange flowers.

White-blotched canna

'Stuttgart' is an impressive 7-foot-tall cultivar with medium green, narrow (for a canna) leaves attractively blotched with white and gray. It needs shade, especially at mid-day or the leaves burn.

Multicolored canna

'Tropicana' is a show in itself as the striped leaves unfurl to reveal burgundy stripes and a greenish-yellow center vein. But that's only the start, for the stripes quickly go from burgundy to red, pink, yellow, and gold — all against a dark green background. Top this with impressive bright orange flowers and you have a dazzling display from 2- to 4-foot plants.

Water cannas

These love to grow wet, in pools and ponds with water lilies. You may want to try them in large non-draining pots, which you can overwinter in a protected spot indoors. Try these cultivars:

- ❀ 'Erebus' is a graceful 4-foot-tall plant with delightful salmon-pink flowers.
- ❀ 'Ra' sports bright, cheerful yellow flowers which are ideal against the wide, bold leaves that reach 4 feet.
- ❀ 'Taney' adds sparks from radiant apricot-orange blossoms borne on 4-foot plants.

Raising cannas

Here are some hints for successfully growing cannas:

- ✔ Cannas like rich, moist, wet soil. In fact, you can even plant them in a pond!
- ✔ Cannas don't like frost, so wait until the weather is close to frost-free to plant tubers, and the weather must be mild and settled if you're planting started plants.
- ✔ Add generous amounts of compost, leaf mold, and/or dried cow manure — cannas like this kind of stuff! Feed them fertilizer, too.
- ✔ Space plants about a foot and a half apart, laying the rhizomes horizontally about 4 inches deep.

If you want to jump-start the season, start cannas indoors about a month before planting-out weather (mild and frost-free) arrives. Just make sure that you have somewhere sunny and protected to keep the pots until you can plant them.

- ✔ Keep cannas well watered in dry weather, and fertilize them once a month up to about September.
- ✔ When cold weather comes and a frost blackens the above-ground growth, dig, clean, and store canna rhizomes just as you would dahlias.

Leafy Splendor with Caladiums

Tired of this focus on summer bulbs for sun? Then caladiums are just the thing for you. These tubers came from tropical jungles and positively adore the dog days of August, when the weather's hot and humid and caladiums can flaunt their large, flamboyant, arrow-shaped leaves in the shade (see Figure 14-4). After all, who needs flowers if the leaves look this good!

If you're trying to find something for a window box or container in the shade, think of caladiums. Also, consider using caladium leaves in your summer bouquets. The following are just as attractive cut as they are in the garden, and they last pretty well, too:

❀ **'Aaron'** is a versatile, sun-tolerant variety with medium green leaves decorated with creamy white centers and veins. It reaches 16 inches high.

❀ **'Blaze'** dazzles with outstanding bright red foliage elegantly edged in deep green on 18-inch plants.

❀ **'Candidum'** offers stunning accents from its snowy-white leaves with medium green veins and borders — all on 18-inch plants.

❀ **'Candidum Jr.,'** as you might guess, mirrors the green and white beauty of the preceding cultivar, but it's shorter — 16 inches or less — with smaller leaves that show off more white. *(You can see this one in the color section.)*

Figure 14-4:
Caladiums flaunt their flamboyant foliage.

❀ **'Carolyn Whorton'** combines awesome color with sheer size on extra-large crimson leaves with splashes of pale pink and rose veins with dark green margins. Vigorous plants top out at 18 inches.

❀ **'Fanny Munson'** is a study in pink, displaying large leaves in bright pink with dark green edges. This 16-inch cultivar grows somewhat lower than other caladiums.

❀ **'Frieda Hemple'** is a lady with style as you'll see when you grow this cultivar with vivid crimson leaves bordered elegantly with soft gray-green. This one looks hand painted and reaches 18 inches.

❀ **'John Peed'** shows off in bright red with a broad, rich green border — a combination that draws the eye. Plants reach 18 inches.

❀ **'Lord Derby'** offers classic good looks from deep rose leaves highlighted with green veins and a deep green border. Expect plant to grow about 18 inches.

❀ **'Miss Muffet'** is an unusual and graceful lance-leafed caladium with smaller, narrower, and more pointed leaves — and it's not short on color, either. This 12- to 18-inch cultivar starts out chartreuse and pales to a creamy white, with added zip from dappled red spots.

❀ **'Mrs. Arno Nehrling'** is a low-growing white about 12 inches or so, and its claim to fame is arresting bright pink veins that command attention. Leaves also have occasional greenish markings.

❀ **'Pink Beauty'** will light up your shade with tricolored leaves that start with a gray-green background overlayed with light pink speckling and accented with rose veins. This cultivar, which takes well to sun, grows to 14 inches.

❀ **'Pink Symphony'** is another lance-leafed caladium so its leaves are smaller and narrower, but not short on drama. Pale pink foliage is accented to perfection here with dark green edging and veins. Plants reach about 18 inches.

❀ **'Postman Joyner'** dazzles with large deep red leaves elegantly edged in deep green. Was this 12- to 18-inch grower named for some famous letter carrier? Who knows?

❀ **'Red Flash'** may knock your socks off with its scintillating scarlet leaves set off with loads of bright pink spots. Expect results with this 12- to 18-inch cultivar.

❀ **'Rosalie,'** another lance-leafed caladium, shines with luminous deep red leaves edged in dark green. Try this, or any of the lance-leaved caladiums in hanging baskets or shady planters.

❀ **'Scarlet Beauty'** takes a bit from all the best, because this dramatic selection sports large upright leaves in blazing pink with scarlet overtones and olive-green dappled edges. At 18 inches, this cultivar easily stands alone as an accent, or it's stunning combined with other single or two-toned varieties.

❀ **'White Christmas'** also offers bright beauty for shady spots, because it displays clear white foliage with deep green veins. The color and texture make this a choice cultivar.

❀ **'White Wing'** is our last, but not least, lance-leafed selection, and it offers glowing creamy white foliage with a hint of green along the margins. For a spectacular mixed display, make this one a must.

Follow these tips for growing caladiums:

✔ Don't plant caladiums outside until the weather is consistently warm and soil temperature reaches 60 degrees Fahrenheit. They get chilled very easily.

✔ Started plants are available at nurseries, garden centers, and home centers. If you want more of a selection, check out the nurseries specializing in caladiums, which we list in Appendix A. You need to start the tubers indoors in a warm place, about 70 degrees Fahrenheit, at least two months before they'll go into the garden.

✔ If you start the tubers just as you receive them, they'll produce fewer, but larger leaves. If you use a grapefruit spoon (or your thumbnail) to scoop away the growing points, you can grow shorter, bushier, leafier caladiums.

✔ Caladiums love shade and appreciate rich, moist soil.

Caladiums are only hardy in really subtropical regions (zones 10 and 11) that replicate their tropical South American home. Elsewhere, you need to lift and store them dry and frost-free over winter. Containers can be brought indoors as is, and kept in a dark closet until late winter or early spring when tubers need to awaken and begin growing again. Store caladiums at 70 to 75 degrees Fahrenheit.

Good combinations include caladiums with perennials such as ferns and astilbes with lacy leaves. We find that hostas, which have a bold, blocky leaf, don't offer enough contrast of shape to caladium, but that's our own taste — some folks think that the two are fine together. Impatiens are a good annual companion, because they thrive under the same conditions.

Playing with Tender Bulbs

Tender bulbs give gardeners the opportunity to play in the garden. Tall or small, sunny or shady, bulbs provide seasonal summer color. Some for flowers, others for foliage, enjoy them in the garden or cut for bouquets. If you live in a place with mild winters, bulbs make a permanent addition to your gardening palette. And if winter arrives with a chilling blast, you can provide a place for them to hibernate in your house.

Crocus 'Blue Pearl'

Iris
'Shepheard's
Delight'

Striped Squill *Puschkinia libanotica*

Crocus tommasinianus

Daffodils naturalized in a lawn.

Hyacinth 'Delft Blue'

Tazetta narcissus
'Geranium'

Crown Imperial
Fritillaria imperialis

Summer Snowflake
Leucojum aestivum

Grape Hyacinth *Muscari*

Tulip
'Prominence'

Tulip 'Pax' with deep blue viola

Mixed Tulips (fringed and parrot types)

Kaufmanniana Tulip 'Heart's Delight'

Double Late Tulip 'Angelique'

Dahlia 'Madeline's'

Canna

Star of Persia
Allium christophii

Caladium
'Candidum'

Lilium, Asiatic hybrid lily

'Star Gazer'— Oriental hybrid lily

Gladiolus
'White Prosperity'

Begonia 'Sweet Dreams'

Dahlia 'Park Princess'

Montbretia Crocosmia 'Lucifer' with kniphofia

Peruvian daffodil *Ismene festalis*

Oxalis *Oxalis triangularis*

Nerine manselli

Naked Lady
Amaryllis belladona

Lords and Ladies
Arum italicum

Nerine bowdenii

Rain Lily *Zephyranthes grandiflora*

Colchicum
'Waterlily'

Colchicum
Colchicum autumnale

Glory-of-the-Snow
Chionodoxa 'Blue Giant'

Amaryllis Hippeastrum 'Apple Blossom'
(flowers outdoors in summer)

Winter Aconite
Eranthis hyemalis

Snowdrops *Galanthus nivalis*
(common snowdrop), snowdrops,
with *Crocus tommasinianus*

Freesia

A festival of flowers, this border garden of perennials and bulbs features tulips 'Mrs. J. Scheepers' and 'Westpoint' with wallflower and cloth of gold and 'Purple Queen' forget-me-nots.

Tulip 'Apricot Beauty, 'Alabaster Carrara' with *Cytisus x kewensis.*

A field full of crocuses at Kew Gardens, England.

A living portrait in Rembrandt tulips with narcissus 'Dove White' and viola 'Sorbet Yellow Frost'.

A floral
fantasy of
lilies and
perennials.

Chapter 15

Tender Southern Bulbs: African and American

- -

In This Chapter

▶ Crocosmia: a surprisingly hardy beauty

▶ Amaryllis: big, bold blooms or pretty, petite flowers

▶ Veltheimia: long-lasting, dusty pink flowers

▶ Peruvian daffodil: not really a daffodil at all

▶ Guernsey lily: nerines from South Africa

- -

*I*f the idea of growing exotic bulbs from foreign countries seems intimidating, you can relax. Gladiolus, that familiar backyard, farm-stand flower, originally grew wild in South Africa. Today, it is an easily grown addition to summer gardens everywhere. We discuss it in Chapter 14.

The one vestige of gladiolus ancestry is an inability to survive cold winters. This legacy is because the South African bulbs developed in response to a cycle of rains and drought, rather than warmth and cold. We also discuss another South African bulb, naked ladies or *Amaryllis belladonna,* in Chapter 16 on autumn bulbs. Gardeners living in regions with matching, mild climates — where seasons are determined by rainfall rather than temperature — can grow these bulbs as permanent garden residents. Where temperatures decline below freezing, and stay there for a while, these bulbs will need a vacation indoors.

Crocosmia: Hardier Than You May Think

When you first grow plants from winterless places, the tendency is to think that they're delicate, needing all sorts of cosseting and protection. Sometimes, you'll be pleasantly surprised at how sturdy these plants can be. That's exactly the case with crocosmia.

Sometimes crocosmia are called *crocosmiiflora* or *montbretia*. Because the cultivars (cultivated varieties) are hybrids, hardiness varies depending on which parent they most closely resemble.

A gladiolus-like plant in leaf, crocosmia has a tall sheaf of sword-like leaves. The flowers are quite different, a spray of smaller blossoms in hot reds and oranges that really light up the late summer garden. When these South African plants were first introduced, gardeners in wintry regions went through that tedious business of digging and cleaning the corms, sacking them up and storing them through winter, and then trying to remember to get them planted at the right time in spring. Lo and behold, someone said, "Forget this, too much work!" (Or maybe frost just snuck up on them.) And the following spring, here came crocosmia. Consider them hardy in zones 6 to 10 (use a winter mulch of pine boughs at the colder end of the range).

Try these varieties of crocosmias:

- ❀ **'Constance'** offers electric summer color from very showy nasturtium-orange blooms. Expect dozens of funnel-shaped flowers in double rows on graceful, arching stems. Plants range from 2 to 3 feet and bloom from August through September. This one makes an impressive cut flower.

- ❀ **'Emily McKenzie'** does it with style with extra-big deep-orange flowers accented with dark-red or mahogany throats. The impressive flowers are arranged in dense spikes above deep green leaves on this compact 2-foot cultivar.

- ❀ **'James Coey'** strikes quite a pose and offers a lighter alternative with its brilliant yellow flowers with vermilion accents. Plants grow 2 to 3 feet tall and produce over a long bloom time.

- ❀ **'Lucifer'** is the hardiest of the lot, even surviving zone-5 winters with protection. Its robust nature and regal deep red flowers simply command attention. Your reward will be dozens of blossoms on 3-foot plants, and when you plant them in groups of 10 or more, you'll have a spectacular mid-summer display. Provide a generous layer of mulch to ensure winter survival in coldest regions.

- ❀ **'Queen Alexandra'** has been a winner for generations following its 1925 introduction, and when you see the cadmium-orange flowers with red highlights, you'll understand why. For an arresting, warm garden accent, try this 2- to 3-foot cultivar in any sunny or lightly shaded spot.

- ❀ *Crocosmia mansonorum* dazzles with bright reddish-orange flowers with lighter orange-yellow flames. Set against the pleated, deep green foliage, this one displays plenty of exotic beauty.

Follow the growing information for whichever cultivar you choose and whatever name your vendor gives it. Your caution is the better part of their survival during winter conditions.

Here are some tips for growing crocosmias:

1. **Plant crocosmias in spring, even in places where you are sure that they are hardy; wait until after the last frost, and then plant in a sunny, well-drained site.**

   If the corms are showing signs of growth when you receive them, and the weather's still too chilly to plant them outdoors, pot them. It's important to let them begin growing if that's what they show you that they want to do. Then you can just transplant them to the garden when the weather's mild and settled.

2. **Plant the corms 5 inches deep, and space them about 6 to 8 inches apart.**

3. **Fertilize as you would gladiolus: Add granular fertilizer to the bottom of the planting hole and mix it in well.**

   Add some unfertilized soil and then the corms, pointy end up. *Side dress* once or twice during the growing season (that term simply means applying a little fertilizer next to the growing plants and scratching it lightly into the soil).

4. **Keep the corms well-watered during the growing season if natural rainfall is limited.**

Enjoy the late summer flowers in the garden, or cut them for bouquets. Good companion plants are ornamental grasses tall enough (2 to 4 feet tall) to partner the crocosmias. Sneezeweed, *Helenium autumnale,* is a good choice. No, it doesn't cause hay fever — early colonists dried and powdered the leaves to use for snuff. Sneezeweeds have numerous small daisy-like flowers in colors that blend beautifully with crocosmias.

Amaryllis: South Africans for Awesome Flowers

Just to keep poor gardeners confused, what we in the United States call amaryllis, the taxonomists insist are *Hippeastrum*. (Technically, the naked ladies plants from South Africa are *Amaryllis*. It's a good thing the plants know who they are!)

The U.S. amaryllis originated in South America. Popular in autumn, their huge bulbs, a real handful, are sold at home improvement stores, supermarkets, garden centers, and through catalogs.

Sometimes you can find an amaryllis already potted. All you need to do is take it out of the box, stand it on a window sill, and add water. A huge, rather phallic bud quickly emerges and grows to a top-heavy height. Four, sometimes six, huge, wide-open trumpet-like flowers appear. The biggest bulbs frequently send up a second, sometimes even a third, flowering stem. Then the long, strap-like leaves appear. You water; you feed the plant fertilizer, and then the leaves go dormant. Later, the bulb wakes up and starts making leaves, but no flower stem. This result causes frustration on your part and dogged determination on the part of the amaryllis — it needs to make seven leaves before it regains the strength to flower again. If it doesn't produce that many leaves at once, it does so sequentially.

Here are some tips for successfully producing beautiful amaryllis flowers in pots:

1. **Pot so the bulb nose and shoulder of the bulb are above soil level.**

   The bigger the bulb, the better the display. If you buy loose bulbs, choose a pot just bigger by an inch diameter than the bulb.

2. **Soak the potting mix thoroughly once, but not again until growth begins.**

3. **Keep in a moderately warm, brightly lit place.**

   If the location is too sunny, the flowers won't last as long. Staking may be necessary to keep the top-heavy flower stem from falling over.

4. **After the flowers fade, move the indoor plant to a sunny place to encourage the most vigorous leaf growth possible; fertilize with a liquid plant food.**

   The leaves are so large, they may need staking — use a pair of stakes on either side of the bulb and a supporting corset of soft twine.

5. **When weather is mild and settled, move your amaryllis, pot and all, outdoors for a summer vacation.**

   Choose a bright location sheltered from intense mid-day sun.

6. **When the days begin to shorten, bring the plant back indoors.**

   Cut back on watering. Remove the leaves as they wither. Store the pot on its side — that position reminds you not to water. Keep dry for eight to ten weeks.

7. **Scrape off the top inch or so of soil and replace with fresh soil (this process is called *top-dressing* and is useful for plants that don't like to be disturbed).**

8. **Commence watering.**

Amaryllis are garden plants only in temperate, warm, subtropical climates, zones 7 to 11. Amaryllis make great cut flowers (see Chapter 23).

Amaryllis (= *Hippeastrum*) come in two forms: the familiar huge blooms from large bulbs, and daintier flowers from more moderately sized bulbs. The latter are quite easy to rebloom.

Full-size amaryllis

Here are some excellent cultivars of amaryllis bulbs that produce large, impressive blooms:

* ❀ **'Apple Blossom'** sends up stout stems, each with 2 to 6 flowers in creamy white with pink blush on the petal tips. These star-shaped blossoms offer simple elegance on 12- to 20-inch stems.

* ❀ **'Beautiful Lady'** is an excellent choice with perfectly shaped flowers in salmon orange. Bulbs may produce 2 to 3 stalks that reach about 24 inches.

* ❀ **'Bestseller'** produces very large, exquisite blossoms in a clear, light pink. The satin-like flowers will add charm and style to any indoor setting, and become celebrities in your warm spring garden. Blossoms open on 18- to 24-inch stems.

* ❀ **'Double Record'** proves more is better on outstanding fully double flowers with twice as many petals in creamy white with delicate rose along the outer edges. This pattern gives a wonderful highlight to the star-shaped nature of the flower. You can often get two stems with three to four blooms each on this 2-foot cultivar.

* ❀ **'Dutch Belle'** sets a high standard from impressive open flowers in an irresistible combination of luscious white with pink accents. Reliable stems reach 18 to 24 inches.

* ❀ **'Fantasica'** is a dazzling cultivar, sporting bright-red petals highlighted with white stripes. The two-toned combination is eye-catching and elegant, especially against the deep green leaves. Stems may reach 18 to 24 inches.

* ❀ **'Lady Jane'** offers unsurpassed delights from double flowers in unique apricot rose with just a touch of white striping in the center of each petal. The result is a lovely, layered effect on 18- to 24-inch stems.

* ❀ **'Lucky Strike'** is regal and refined with distinct flowers in dark blood red. Imagine this one as a dazzling centerpiece, rising to nearly 2 feet on your dining room table.

* ❀ **'Ludwig's Goliath'** also goes red — this time with scarlet overtones on absolutely stunning, bold blossoms. The large flowers offer unsurpassed color and form on 18- to 24-inch stems.

❀ **'Maria Garetti'** is perfect anywhere, because the large blossoms open to reveal flawless white flowers with glistening good looks. Guaranteed to attract attention, the multiple flowers open on stems that may reach 24 inches.

❀ **'Minerva'** earns plenty of style points as the red-and-white-striped flowers begin their show. Bright red edges give way to pure white center markings with light feathering on every petal, every time. The result is a full flower with definite flair. Stems top out at 24 inches.

❀ **'Pasadena'** is another worthy red-and-white cultivar, only this time the double ring of regal red petals with white stripes offers festive beauty. Expect stems to grow 18 to 24 inches.

❀ **'Red Lion'** offers top-notch rewards from radiant red flowers in a speedy 3 to 5 weeks following planting. The yellow anthers add a subtle touch of contrast on the impressive blossoms, which open on 15- to 20-inch stems.

❀ **'Sandra'** sends up appealing blossoms in warm peachy rose with darker veins, accented by a white brush stroke down the center of each petal. Multiple stems should reach 18 to 24 inches.

❀ **'White Christmas'** will grace your holiday table, or send up stately blossoms in your warm spring garden as the plump buds open to display pure white flowers with outstanding form on 18- to 24-inch stems.

Look for **'Orange Sovereign'** as another good-looking cultivar worth growing.

Miniature amaryllis

If you really want a show, try planting three to five bulbs of one variety of miniature amaryllis in a suitably sized pot. Try these varieties:

❀ **'Butterfly'** is a cultivar of *Hippeastrum papilio,* with exotic flowers in creamy white, flushed with green, and highlighted in the center with generous burgundy feathering. The bulbs are smaller — at 20 centimeters rather than the 32 centimeters of the larger hybrid amaryllis — as are the flowers, which have looser, narrower and more pointed petals, but retain the star-shaped form. Multiple stems should produce six flowers each on compact 12- to 18-inch stems.

❀ **'Donau'** is a cultivar of *Hippeastrum gracilis,* with magnificent rose-colored blossoms half the size of standard cultivars. Ideal for forcing, this smaller cultivar offers easy table-top displays from charming, abundant flowers that open on 12- to 18-inch stems.

❀ **'Double Picotee'** delights with glistening white flowers edged with a pencil-thin band of red outlining every petal. A final brushstroke of pink at the petal tips gives this bulb simultaneous drama and elegance. Stems reach 18 inches with multiple flowers.

❀ **'Germa'** offers unusual soft yellow flowers with a hint of green in the heart. The starry blossoms have lily-like similarity on stems that reach 18 inches. Choose this one when you want that rare look.

❀ **'Picotee'** is stunning with white flowers edged delicately with a fine line of dark red and finished with pale green centers. One of the most popular cultivars, it produces a cloud of elegant beauty when planted three or four to a pot. The tallest stems may reach 18 inches.

❀ **'Scarlet Baby'** is a remarkable performer displaying many brilliant red flowers with faint white dashes and compact stems that stay 12 to 18 inches. The long-lasting color gives long-lasting rewards.

❀ **'Yellow Pioneer'** is a *gracilis* amaryllis with particular beauty from satiny yellow flowers that bring loads of sunshine and cheer during those dreary days of spring. Expect multiple stems (to 18 inches) and multiple flowers on prolific plants.

'**Pamela**' is a readily available cultivar that's also worth a look.

Veltheimia for Great Winter Flowers in the House

If you've ever grown an amaryllis, *Hippeastrum* cultivar, had it flower once, and ever after produce only leaves, the South African veltheimia bulb (commonly called the Veldt lily or the Forest lily) is for you. It blooms much more easily.

Veltheimias are planted in autumn. Almost everybody grows them as a potted bulb. Follow these tips:

1. **Choose a pot just a little wider than the diameter of the bulb.**

2. **Cover the hole in the bottom of the pot with a piece of window screening or a piece of a broken clay pot to keep soil from sifting out.**

3. **Use a good commercial potting soil, setting the bulb so its skinny neck and the top of its shoulders are above soil level.**

4. **Water thoroughly once, and then don't water again until growth starts.**

5. **Keep the pot in a bright sunny place, with cool temperatures (high 50s or low 60s Fahrenheit are ideal).**

   The bulb makes a rosette of bright green leaves a foot or so long. The flower spike begins to form in January, and the bulb blooms in February, producing a tall spike of numerous, closely packed, drooping tubular flowers in a soft dusty pink. They last for a long time.

6. **After the flowers fade, cut the stem as low as you can.**

7. **Keep watering as necessary, and fertilize with a liquid plant food lower in nitrogen (the first number) and higher in phosphorus and potash (the second and third numbers on the label).**

8. **When the bulb shows signs of wanting to rest — the leaves will start turning yellow — stop watering.**

   Keep the bulb dry. Remove the leaves when they wither.

9. **Keep the bulb, still in its pot, in a warm, dry, dark place all summer long.**

   Come autumn, the bulb will start to wake up. You'll see a green nubbin start to show in the center of the bulb.

10. **Top-dress (scrape off the top inch or so of soil and replace with fresh soil), water, and feed with fertilizer as described for amaryllis.**

Some bulbs don't flower the first year. They may be a little small, and they may not like the disturbance. Just keep watering and feeding, and after their summer rest, they will flower during their second winter.

When they become established, veltheimias often make offsets. Don't separate them, just move them up to a larger pot in autumn when signs of growth are apparent.

Peruvian Daffodil: A Super South-American Bulb with Unique Flowers

The *Peruvian* portion of the name makes sense, because Peruvian daffodils are native to Central and South America, and warmer parts of the southeastern United States as well. But it's anyone's guess where the *daffodil* part of the name came from — the flower isn't daffodil yellow, and you'd have to squint quite a lot to see any resemblance.

This is another plant masquerading under a variety of common names. You may find it as spider lily or ismene as well as Peruvian daffodil. *(You can see a photo of one in the color section.)*

We recommend these varieties of Peruvian daffodils:

❀ **'Advance'** shows off the unusual form of all Peruvian daffodils — featuring a central trumpet surrounded by narrow, curly ivory petals for an elegant but spidery look on airy flowers that reach 6 inches across. The fragrant blossoms are nearly all white with faint green markings. Plants reach 2 feet in height.

❀ *Hymenocallis festialis* blooms with a look of swirling ballet dancers in dazzling white dresses. The pure white flowers have narrow, curving outer petals that surround a fringed white cup with a pale green center. Four or more flowers open on every 15- to 20-inch stem for a truly unique and fragrant display.

❀ *Hymenocallis festialis* **'Zwanenburg'** is a vigorous and sterling variation of the preceding entry — with exceptional white form on sturdy 18- to 24-inch stems rising from amaryllis-like foliage.

❀ **'Sulphur Queen'** has a much more daffodil feel, with a large golden-yellow trumpet with feathery edges and a green star-like central marking surrounded by narrow, lance-like outer petals. These 2-foot plants produce numerous flowers that are standouts for fragrance and form in any arrangement.

Peruvian daffodils are hardy in zones 8 to 10. In cooler regions, they can be grown in the ground, lifted, and stored over winter. Or grow them for summer display in containers that are brought indoors in winter. Here are some hints for growing Peruvian daffodils:

1. **Plant bulbs in spring when the weather is mild and settled; choose a sunny site sheltered from wind, with sandy, well-drained soil.**

2. **Fertilize before planting, mixing well with soil at the bottom of the hole.**

   Peruvian daffodils prefer an evenly moist, but not wet, soil.

3. **Set bulbs 6 inches apart and 6 inches deep.**

4. **Fertilize once a month, either side dressing with a granular fertilizer or watering with a liquid fertilizer.**

   Bulbs flower in summer, with striking, funnel-shaped flowers surrounded by a crown of six delicately curled petals on 18- to 24-inch tall stems.

5. **At summer's end, bring potted bulbs indoors and dry off for their winter rest.**

   If they are not hardy, dig bulbs from the garden, being careful to preserve the fleshy, thong-like roots. Store in dry peat-moss, perlite, buckwheat hulls, or similar material, in a frost-free area that is about 60 to 70 degrees Fahrenheit.

   Some authorities suggest packing the bulbs upside-down in the storage material.

Guernsey Lily (or Nerine): A Traveling Plant for Many Places

There's a great story about how nerines came to be called Guernsey lilies: A ship wrecked off the Guernsey coast, and the bulbs washed ashore to root and grow on the sandy beaches. Whatever the true story, nerines originated in South Africa. They grow in sunny, sandy, mild-climate regions — zones 8 to 11. They make great cut-flower bouquets and are good in containers, too.

Check out these varieties of nerine:

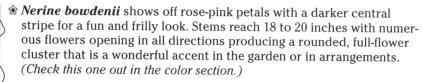

- ❀ *Nerine bowdenii* shows off rose-pink petals with a darker central stripe for a fun and frilly look. Stems reach 18 to 20 inches with numerous flowers opening in all directions producing a rounded, full-flower cluster that is a wonderful accent in the garden or in arrangements. *(Check this one out in the color section.)*

- ❀ *Nerine bowdenii* **'Pink Triumph'** sports a softer, silvery pink tone on petals accented with a darker pink central stripe to create a remarkable and distinct floral show.

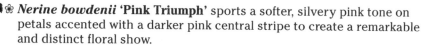

- ❀ *Nerine crispa* has a distinct look with looser flowers featuring very thin, wavy petals in a delicious shade of pale pink. The narrow petals bend artfully backward, bowing to fringed pistils and stamens in the flower center.

Follow this advice to successfully grow nerines:

1. **Plant nerine bulbs in spring, and choose a sunny site with well-drained soil, well supplied with organic matter.**

   Nerines are primarily summer dormant, and grow better if kept on the dry side. They need warm summer temperatures while dormant if they are to flower well.

   Nerine bulbs do not like to be disturbed. Where they are not winter hardy, plan on growing them in containers rather than planting and digging annually.

2. **Space bulbs about a foot apart, and 3 inches deep. About $\frac{1}{3}$ of the bulb should be above ground.**

3. **Water and fertilize only while leaves are in active growth.**

   Cut back on watering when they show signs of yellowing and approaching dormancy.

Nerines flower in August to September or October, producing 18- to 24-inch-tall stems of clustered flowers with narrow, recurved petals that are pink with an almost glittery, crystalline appearance. The leaves are strap-like, untouched by deer, rabbits, woodchucks, or other vermin.

Garden companions should be plants that also flower late in summer or early in autumn. Try fall asters with purple or lavender flowers, especially lower-growing forms such as 'Purple Dome.' *Sedum* 'Autumn Joy' produces tiny flowers in tight clusters resembling pink broccoli — it would make an interesting pairing.

Chapter 16

Hardy Bulbs for Autumn Flowers

*A*utumn is traditionally a busy time for planting bulbs, but the payoff for all your hard work isn't immediate: You stick 'em in the ground, wait patiently through winter, and then watch flowers pop up in spring. A few bulb species, however, provide savvy gardeners with more instant gratification, pushing at the edges of the season and flowering as the gardening year winds down. Plant these bulbs in late summer or early fall, and you see flowers within weeks rather than months.

Not the sort of thing that waits for you on a rack next to the supermarket check-out counter, these less familiar bulbs require a little effort on your part to find them. Try a garden center or mail-order catalog. Once they're planted, though, your sleuthing pays off: These autumn flowering bulbs come back as reliably as spring flowering bulbs. (Several species are also cold hardy and reappear year after year, even in regions where winter reigns. And if you live in a Mediterranean climate, don't despair — you have your pick of autumn-blooming beauties as well.)

Because they're just about ready to flower when they arrive at the store, fall-flowering bulbs need to be planted PDQ (pretty darn quick for those of you not into alphabet soup). These bulbs jump the planting queue and must get automatic priority over your spring-flowering bulbs. Handle them gently: Fall flowering crocuses, in particular, often have shoots emerging from the corm, which can be easily damaged. Water right after you plant. This rule is true for all bulbs, but especially for those that flower in the fall. These bulbs need to replace moisture used during growth, but they can't quench their thirst without roots — and roots need moisture in the soil to start them off.

Don't worry if you see only flowers at first: Several fall-blooming bulbs are smart enough to hold off on growing leaves — after all, winter's coming, and leaves could be damaged. The leaves will come along next spring.

This chapter offers a few of our favorite fall-flowering varieties.

Autumn Crocuses

Fall-flowering crocuses are a unique accent to the garden, blooming when perennials and shrubs are shutting down for the season. They open wide in sunshine and close toward evening or when the weather is cloudy — it's as if their looks change with their moods. Figure 16-1 shows an autumn crocus.

Figure 16-1:
Autumn
crocus.

Autumn crocuses are as easy to grow as their more familiar spring-flowering cousins; you just need to make more of an effort to find the fall-flowering bulbs (mail-order catalogs are usually the best place to look; see Appendix A for a list of these resources). Most fall crocuses have no common names. You can make up your own names for them, but that doesn't help when you order from a catalog — using Latin names make sure that you get what you want. Because of their impetuous nature, autumn-flowering bulbs have shorter shelf lives than other bulbs. That's why nurseries often prefer to stock bulbs such as daffodils, tulips, and spring-flowering crocuses that can wait around.

Crocuses grow from corms (see Chapter 4 for more about crocuses). They have definite right sides up that are easy to distinguish, especially because many have new shoots emerging by the time you buy them. If you're in doubt, just remember that the bottom of the corm is flatter than the top.

Plant the bulbs in a gritty, free-draining soil in groups of ten or more, and in areas where you can view them at close range (crocuses are small wonders; make sure that they get the attention they deserve).

Having tracked down these choice little treasures, protect them. Chipmunks and voles devour the bulbs. The gritty soil helps protect the bulbs, as does planting them in wire mesh cages, pint-size plastic mesh strawberry baskets, or mesh bags — that way, the corms are secure and free to multiply, and the flowers return autumn after autumn. Figure 16-2 shows the way this can work.

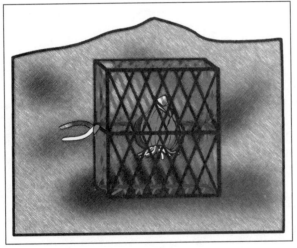

Figure 16-2:
Use mesh cages and strawberry baskets to protect the corms.

For added protection, plant the corms with a carpeting ground cover. It ties the flowers (especially those that bloom without leaves) to the site and also keeps the corms drier in summer, when they are dormant. Thymes (woolly thyme, gold-edged thyme, and so on) are a good ground cover choice; so are moss pink — also known as creeping phlox, *Phlox subulata*. For something a little more unusual, plant low-growing *Sedum sieboldii*, which also flowers in autumn.

Crocus speciosus

Crocus speciosus is often the most available of the fall crocuses. At only 5 to 6 inches tall, this plant produces charming, goblet-like flowers that appear from late September into October. Blooming without any leaves, the violet-blue flowers make an attractive addition to rock or herb gardens. Adaptable to a wide geographical range, this crocus can be grown from zones 4 to 9. As you'd expect with a plant that's been in cultivation for nearly two centuries (since 1800), several forms have been selected for flower color and form:

❀ **'Aitchinsonii'** offers delicate, distinctive large flowers with soft blue petals accented with darker veins. This one is striking along the border's edge and is somewhat later in flowering than other cultivars.

❀ **'Albus'** brightens any fall landscape with its pure white tulip-like flowers accented with orange anthers and a yellow throat. Rare color and form highlight this cultivar, which offers sparkling contrast when planted with the cool tones of most other autumn crocuses.

❀ **'Artabir'** is a lightly fragrant cultivar with a wonderful display in each blossom. The cream-colored throat blends into the pale blue petals contrasted with dark blue veins. And all this is set against a white background and accented with orange pistils. Imagine grouping several dozen of these for a spectacular naturalized effect.

❀ **'Cassiope'** provides impressive aster-blue flowers with a yellow base, which in itself is nice, but this cultivar offers the largest flowers — at 4 inches across — of all autumn crocuses. Expect blooms late in the season, just as the constellation Cassiope becomes visible in the night sky.

❀ **'Conqueror'** is excellent for contrast in the warm-colored fall garden. This sky-blue bloomer sports clear, rich tones for bright accents perfect in compact spaces.

❀ **'Oxonian'**'s violet-blue blossoms offer a delightful but subtle range of pastels as flowers show off pale centers and darker tips to give this cultivar distinction and value anywhere you plant it. It naturalizes very well, and makes an excellent container plant.

Crocus kotschyanus and other season extenders

Crocus kotschyanus used to be called *Crocus zonatus* (which had the advantage of being easier to pronounce!). At 3 to 5 inches high, it's somewhat smaller than the *Crocus speciosus* (see previous section), but its appeal is greater than its stature. Just wait until you see its flowers — and the wait won't be long, because this crocus flowers in September or October. Soft lilac flowers are feathered outside with darker markings and have cheery yellow throats inside. Not quite as cold tolerant, this wee charmer grows in zones 6 to 9. (We even suggest trying zone 5 if you have a nice sheltered spot.)

Crocus goulimyi extends the season even further, flowering in October or November. This crocus's ground-hugging flowers are only 3 to 4 inches tall. Variable in color, the blooms shade from pale to deeper lilac purple, usually paler inside. Hardy from zones 6 to 9, this plant does best at a sheltered site where winters are colder.

Crocus sativus is one crocus that has a common name, but its blossoms are far from ordinary. This is the saffron crocus of culinary fame — the three bright orange stigmas plucked from the center of the dark feathered, lilac-purple flower are used in cooking. But don't think that you'll raise your own saffron supply: It takes *lots* of flowers to flavor enough paella for a crowd.

Unfortunately, we've also found this plant to be a poor performer in most gardens — it flowers well the first year but disappoints in following years. Hardy in zones 6 to 9, the saffron needs the warmer end of its range to really grow well, we suspect — after all, it is of Mediterranean origin and is picky enough to prefer places with a similar climate.

The saffron crocus has a really strong urge to grow. We once saw this poor baby flowering in a bin where unsold bulbs had bravely put forth their flowers.

Crocus laevigatus 'Fontenayi' is a crocus that is really frost-proof. The first flowers, soft lilac with darker feathering stripes, open in October. Every time the weather hovers above freezing, the corms bravely send forth new flowers, right through February. If you cup the flowers in your hands — bend over, they're close to the ground — and warm them with your breath, they're fragrant. Hardier than the zones 7 to 9 catalog suggests, the bulbs have grown successfully for us in a sheltered zone 6 site with good drainage.

Crocus longiflorus may be last on this list and small in stature, but it's sturdy enough to send up leaves with its flowers. The lilac-colored flowers have rich yellow throats and a delicious fragrance, like violets. This crocus blooms from October into November.

Colchicum

If crocuses don't suit you — perhaps the flowers are too small, or you don't want to deal with pests — then go for colchicums. The large flowers look like those of a crocus on anabolic steroids (see Figure 16-3). Confusingly, you'll sometimes see colchicums offered as "fall crocuses," but they're not even distantly related. The colchicum has an unusual corm, pointed sort of like a tulip bulb on top, with a foot-like protuberance at the bottom; the whole package is wrapped in a crisp, smooth, brown tunic.

Figure 16-3:
Colchicums may resemble crocuses, but they're not related.

Colchicums are costly enough to be priced individually, rather than by tens, but you don't need many of them. Just three will give you a good display, and they multiply quite nicely.

What's their drawback? Because colchicums send their leaves up in spring just as the flowers are bigger than those of crocuses, so too are the leaves — big, coarse, strappy things that start growth in March and turn yellow and collapse all over their neighbors in late June. Plant colchicums where foliage crash is not a problem, such as near sizable perennials or shrubs — colchicums are poisonous, so nothing eats the corms, leaves, or flowers.

Colchicums will flower in the bag that you bring them home in, on the kitchen table, or on a windowsill if you leave them there. Allowing this flowering to occur is definitely a poor idea — it weakens the corm, resulting in flowers that are smaller and paler in color. Purchase and plant colchicums with as brief an interval as you can manage, but preferably no longer than a week.

Colchicums prefer bright shade, but they'll also accept a sunny site that's not drought-stricken. Plant colchicums in a site where the soil is loamy, high in organic matter, and moist but well-drained. Three to five corms make a good start. After they've been in the garden for a couple of years, you can start dividing them — late spring to early summer, when their leaves are just starting to go "off-green," is a good time. Dig, separate, and replant promptly. (See Chapter 21 for more on planting bulbs.)

You won't find as much diversity in colchicums as in the fall-flowering crocuses. Most colchicums produce soft pinky-mauve goblet-like flowers up to 12 inches tall that swoon when pollinated and then loll on the ground. You can see some in the color section.

Some colchicum blossoms are checkered, although not as intensely as the guinea hen flower. A couple of double-flowered forms also exist.

Colchicum autumnale

Colchicum autumnale (autumn colchicum) is the dainty one. Each corm sends up from one to six purplish-pink flowers from late summer into autumn. This variety has appeared in gardens since 1561. This reliable, easily grown beauty is hardy from zones 5 to 8.

Cultivars include the following:

❀ **'Album'** produces white flowers blooming in profusion on this tiny but mighty cultivar that is very easy to grow. It sends up slightly smaller flowers than other colchicums, but its clear and bright color will attract attention wherever you plant it.

❀ **'Alboplenum'** features double white flowers that are both rare and beautiful to give this cultivar plenty of class. Each multi-petaled bloom reaches an impressive 4 to 6 inches across. Although individual bulbs can be expensive, the effect in the border or rock garden is a stunning payoff.

❀ **'Pleniflorum'** rewards you with double pinkish-purple flowers that are both unusual and refreshing in the fall. The numerous amethyst segments of the blossoms form attractive double flowers that show off well in the rock garden or border edge.

Colchicum speciosum

Colchicum speciosum is larger than *Colchicum autumnale*. The coloring of mature flowers varies from pale violet to a rich amethyst, accented with a white throat. Flowering in September or October, they look great in front of beautyberry *(Callicarpa japonica)*, a shrub with clusters of vivid violet colored berries wreathed along the branches.

Cultivars include:

- ❀ **'Album'** is regal and revered with pure white, well-formed flowers that resemble tulip blossoms. The flowers are sturdy and each bulb eventually develops into a prolific clump. This one was originally introduced in the late 1800s.

- ❀ **'Atrorubens'** is distinctive because of its richly colored reddish-purple blossoms accented in white, which in the typical goblet shape of all in this group. It makes quite a show late in the season.

Other colchicums worth cultivating

In addition to the named forms of the two species previously described, you can also find some hybrid cultivars whose parents aren't mentioned in catalog descriptions but are well worth adding to your garden:

- ❀ **The 'Giant'** lives up to its name with showy flowers each with a large white throat and amethyst-violet petals atop compact creamy stems. This is definitely one that will perform admirably on a windowsill or in a pot, but put it in the garden and you'll see an impressive display with a long succession of early fall flowers. It's adaptable and easy to grow, too.

- ❀ **'Lilac Wonder'** offers a bonus of very large, very numerous, goblet-shaped flowers in a glowing shade of amethyst-violet accented with narrow white lines in the center. The corms produce great masses of color on plants that reach 10 inches. Some consider this to be the most free-flowering of all colchicums.

- ❀ **'Violet Queen'** is unique because each flower displays an arresting checkered pattern in rosy-violet and white. Light in the center, the flowers darken at the petal tips on this early flowering cultivar that beats others to the punch in September.

- ❀ **'Waterlily'** looks just like, you guessed it, a waterlily. The dramatic 4- to 5-inch double flowers in vivid lavender-pink are very showy and offer a unique effect in the October garden. You might gaze down on this one and wonder what happened to the pond.

Some additional species are also more or less available; check the specialty catalogs. Once you become fascinated with the following easily grown, undeservedly little-known corms, you'll want to watch for

- ❀ *Colchicum bornmuelleri,* with large rosy purple, white-throated flowers in September or October.
- ❀ *Colchicum byzantinum,* with up to 20 soft lilac-to-mauve flowers from September on, all from a single corm.
- ❀ *Colchicum cilicium,* with narrow-petaled, starry looking petunia-purple flowers.
- ❀ *Colchicum giganteum,* with funnel-shaped soft, pale purple flowers that appear a little later than the previously mentioned species, in October or November.

The first year that you plant them, colchicums often bloom a little out of sync with their scheduled appearances. They quickly settle down and arrive on time in following years.

Lords and Ladies

These jack-in-the-pulpit relatives grow from a tuber. In autumn, attractive foot-tall arrow-shaped leaves appear, dark green and handsomely marked with white along their veins. *(You can see a picture in the color section.)*

Although dormant tubers are available in autumn, you also find lords and ladies, *Arum italicum* 'Marmoratum,' as potted growing plants in spring.

Lords and ladies are hardy in zones 5 to 9, although a year or two may pass before they develop their attractive markings. Plant the tubers in woodland shade. Lords and ladies prefer a soil high in organic matter that never dries out — not soggy soil, though; good drainage is important.

Leaves remain through the winter unless conditions get really cold. If leaves are killed off, new ones appear in spring. That's also the time when established plants flower, producing a yellow-green blossom reminiscent of the jack-in-the-pulpit. This flower isn't especially exciting, but the showy cluster of bright orange-red berries that follows is.

For winter interest, combine lords and ladies with other evergreen plants, such as running myrtle *(Vinca minor),* or shrubs and trees with attractive bark. Red twig dogwood, *Cornus stolonifera,* is one option; the pure white-barked birch, *Betula jackmontiii,* is another.

A Begonia for the Fall Garden

Believe it or don't, begonias can be grown outdoors in your garden not just in summer, but all year round. Hardy begonia, *Begonia grandis* or *Begonia evansiana* (you can find it offered by both names), is so prolific in milder zone 7 areas that it has almost an "oh, that old thing" cachet. Even so, we still think that it puts on quite a show from August through October, when the 2-foot-tall stems (featuring large tapering triangular leaves that are beefsteak red underneath) produce masses of charming pink flowers (see Figure 16-4).

Figure 16-4:
Hardy
begonia.

Because the hardy begonia is a woodland plant that's late to appear, you're probably better off planting actively growing plants from pots in spring. Dormant tubers planted in fall in colder climate zones tend to rot.

Plant in a moist yet well-drained soil that's high in organic matter, and then mulch with shredded leaves or chopped bark. This begonia is hardy from zones 6 to 9, but adding some extra mulch or covering the ground with pine boughs after plants go dormant is a good idea in zone 6.

Unless frosts come early, a hardy begonia multiplies by means of tiny tubers that form where leaves join the stem. You can improve the odds of achieving a successful increase by collecting these tubers when they're "ripe" — that is, when they fall off the stem into your hand at the gentlest nudge — and planting them in loosened soil, covering lightly.

For an extra splash of visual interest, combine your hardy begonias with other beauties: Ferns look really great with hardy begonias, and so does astilbe.

Autumn Cyclamen

The autumn cyclamen's flowers appear suddenly in August, dancing above the ground like little pink butterflies. (White is also possible, but the color is a rarity.) In September, leaves begin to appear. Shaped like ivy leaves and handsomely marked in silver, these leaves persist through the winter and then fade away in late spring.

If you can find them, potted plants in active growth are your best planting option. Dormant tubers are sometimes available in spring, but these remain dormant until late summer. (Self-sown seedlings from happily established plants should be removed to a nursery area to grow for a year or so before planting.)

To successfully grow autumn cyclamen, you need to accommodate their somewhat unusual growth cycle (green through winter, but not evergreen because it's dormant in summer). A tender ground cover that fades away with frost is ideal to add summer interest. (We suggest the silver- and purple-leaved inch plant, most often used in hanging baskets indoors. The inch plant also likes shade and is very tender to frost, and its color harmonizes well with that of the cyclamen. It then dies away with frost, just when the cyclamen is reaching its peak display.)

Rot can be a problem if the planting site is too wet. Remember that good drainage is more than a good idea; it's vital. Mice adore the corms of very young plants, but leave those of older tubers alone.

Also suitable for shady, woodland conditions with well-drained soils high in organic matter, ivy-leaved cyclamen *(Cyclamen hederifolium)* is hardy from zones 6 to 8. This plant requires drier conditions when dormant than when in bloom, but planting it on a slope or nestling it among tree roots often takes care of these moisture requirements. Because they're only a couple of inches tall, plant ivy-leaved cyclamen where they're easy to enjoy, perhaps near a path.

Bulbs Ideal for Temperate Climates

All the autumn blooming bulbs discussed so far are winter hardy, but there are a couple of tender beauties that don't want to know about winter cold and snow. Ideal for more temperate climates, magic or rain lilies and naked ladies are reliable autumn flowers for zones 7 to 9.

Rain lilies

Summer is on the wane, you get a heavy rain, and bingo: Within three or four days — definitely less than a week — you have flowers in the garden. Because of their timing, these true bulbs are called rain lilies. You may also find them called magic lilies because of the magical rapidity with which they bring forth their flowers. They may take one, two, or even three years to settle down and start to flower after planting. But it's worth your patient wait, because after they settle in, the bulbs send up 18- to 30-inch stalks with elegant soft pink trumpet flowers in July or early August. (**Hint:** They make great cut flowers.)

Lycoris squamigera is sometimes confused with the naked lady, another bulb of the same common name. This is the hardier of the two and can be grown in a sheltered site in zone 6. (We've even heard of one success story in zone 5 but suspect that it's a *really* sheltered site with reliable insulating snow cover, too.)

Rain lily bulbs look like those of plump, single-nosed daffodils. Plant them as early as they're obtainable — in June, if possible. The rain lilies still may sulk and skip a year, and the first year that they do grow, they may merely wait until spring and then send up gray-green daffodil-like leaves.

An area with light shade is the best planting site, especially if it's at the edge of woodland. Soil with a good humus content — moist but not soggy — is ideal. Full sun is fine. Rain lily doesn't just like rain — it likes it wet. Constantly moist soil is ideal, but bulbs accept average conditions, too.

Flowering as it does without its leaves, the rain lily needs a foliage accompaniment that enhances the flowers and prevents you from digging around in summer when the bulbs are dormant. (Bulbs dislike disturbance and don't like to linger out of the soil. Plant them promptly and then be patient.) Hostas are one option; tall ferns are another.

Lycoris radiata is a stand-by in the mild climate of the southeastern United States. The hot humid summers, mild winters, and high rainfall probably remind bulbs of their native haunts in Japan.

Established *Lycoris radiata* bulbs pull themselves deeper and deeper into the soil, settle down, and make more of themselves. Over time, you end up with a thick clump of these beauties.

This rain lily sends up flowers in September and leaves in October. Because it doesn't wait until spring to send up leaves like other fall-flowering bulbs, this one is trickier in cold winter regions — the cold kills the leaves.

Another naked lady

Native to South Africa, this bulb *(A. belladonna)* makes itself at home in the similarly arid Mediterranean climate of Southern California. In August, tall gray-green stalks topped with large pink trumpet-like flowers rise from dried field grasses. Leaves appear later, in early autumn.

The bulbs are rather large and sometimes grow with their necks sticking out of the ground. That's two counts against their survival in cold winter regions — first the leaves freeze and then the bulbs. Sulky about moving, the naked lady is, however, very long-lived once it settles in.

Full sun, good drainage, and summer dry are the ideal conditions for naked ladies. (We were actually successful with naked ladies in a zone 6 garden, planting under a roof overhang and near a foundation wall, a situation that provided the dry, sheltered conditions necessary for this plant's survival.) Plant naked ladies promptly — just before leaves appear, if possible; that's the bulb's most active period. Otherwise, you may need to wait a year or two before even leaves make their seasonal appearance. Fleshy thong-like roots remain year-round — don't let them dry up.

Because their flowers can reach 2½-feet-tall, give naked ladies suitably sized companions. Ornamental grasses are a garden counterpart of field grasses. Aloes or smaller yuccas also make good neighbors.

Amaryllis x *Amarcrinum* (also called *Crinodona*) is a hybrid between *Amaryllis belladona* and *Crinum*. It's an excellent late summer-fall flowering bulb for the southeast United States.

Part IV
Special Bulbs for Special Places

The 5th Wave   By Rich Tennant

"That's the last time I buy a flowering bulb from a circus clown."

In this part . . .

All bulb books describe the virtues of tulips and the beauty of daffodils, but we humbly declare that this part makes our book special.

First, we offer information about some flavorful bulbs and tubers. That's right, we said *flavorful*. You can find information on growing potatoes, onions, garlic, and shallots, to name a few. These homegrown delights can boost the flavor of any meal.

Then we give you the scoop on growing bulbs in containers — so you can grow bulbs even if you don't have the time, space, or money to plant a garden or flower bed.

Chapter 17

The Kitchen Garden: Sensational Seasonings from Bulbs

*B*eyond a doubt, onions are *the* bulb that everybody — gardener or not — knows (even if only a slice on a hamburger). How bland would our food be without flavorful onions, garlic, and shallots? From the savory smells they emit while cooking to the palate-pleasing flavor we enjoy while eating them, these kitchen bulbs have it all.

Onions — Cold-Hardy and Versatile

Onions *(Allium cepa)* offer options. You can choose yellow, red, or white fleshed onions. You can raise onions from seeds or buy young plants (called transplants), or little bulbs (called sets). Do you want green scallions or bulb onions? They can both be grown from sets. Onions are so cold-hardy you can plant them while the weather is still frosty. And if you think that all onions are the same, you're in for a surprise.

Sets are easy to grow and can be planted very early in spring while the ground is still too wet and cold for seeds. However, bulb onions from sets don't store as well as those grown from seeds or transplants.

Onions generally available as sets are sometimes distributed just by color — yellow, red, or white. Named cultivars include 'White Ebenezer,' 'Red Wethersfield,' and 'Yellow Rock.'

Choosing the type of onion for your location

Where you live determines what type of onion you can grow.

All onions make bulbs in proportion to their tops — big tops make big bulbs, and small tops make small bulbs. A *photoperiod response* (a fancy way of saying a response based on the length of the day) tells the onion that it's time to stop making green tops and get busy making bulbs. Short-day onions start "bulbing up" in spring, long-day onions in late summer.

Short-day onions

Southern gardeners in climate zones 8 to 11 — and only Southern gardeners — can grow short-day onions.

Short-day onions are the really sweet onions you find in the supermarket. Look for 'Yellow Granex' or 'Granex 33' (stores sell these as "Vidalia"), 'White Granex,' and '1015Y Texas Supersweet.'

The seed of short-day onions is sown in autumn and grows over the winter. Plants start forming bulbs as the days begin to get longer in spring. (I know, that sounds confusing, but days are still shorter than they are later in the year.)

Intermediate-day onions

Gardeners in the Mid-Atlantic region, climate zones 5 to 7, do best with intermediate-day onions, from seed sown in spring. Or buy a bundle of transplants (about 50 to 75 in a bunch) or sets (which are sold by weight) for very early spring planting.

'Sweet Red' is a mild-flavored, large, somewhat flattened intermediate-day onion.

Long-day onions

Northern gardeners grow long-day varieties, which grow tops in summer and only start to form bulbs when summer days are getting shorter.

'White Sweet Sandwich' is a mild-flavored onion that stores well and even gets sweeter as it keeps. And if you want small, white, boiling onions, plant sets of a short-day white, really crowded together, in late April or early May.

Growing onions

A loose, open sandy loam, with lots of compost or well-rotted manure grows the best onions.

Onions are hungry plants — feed them well with 5-10-10 fertilizer. Dig it in before you plant — you want to push the baby plants along. After they start bulb formation, it's too late to fertilize them.

Ample water is important, too, in order to keep the green onion plants growing vigorously, making the big green tops that result in large bulbs.

The onion tops turning yellow is a sign that harvest-time is near. After about 75 percent of the growth is yellow, floppy, and fallen over, follow these steps:

1. **Use a rake to push over any green shoots still standing.**

2. **When the tops are all brown, you can dig the plants — they'll usually come out of the ground with just a steady tug on the old tops.**

3. **Let the bulb onions dry in the sun for three or four days, and then cut the tops close to the bulb neck.**

4. **Store in a well-aerated, cool, dry place.**

Onions can provide one harvest in spring and another later on. Plant sets close together in early spring. Pull some early to use green like you use scallions. Pulling some early thins the remaining plants, allowing them room to grow into bulbs for later use. If you want onions to store, grow from seed or transplants. Either way, it's fun to raise this culinary staple and bring it from garden to table.

Garlic: Odorific or Aromatic?

There's no getting around it; garlic is pungent! Eat it, and the whole world will know. However, the flavor it provides is indispensable to cuisine around the world.

Fresh garlic is great seasoning. And you can find many ways to enjoy it:

✔ Roast whole heads of garlic to spread on bread.

✔ Sliver cloves to poke into a leg of lamb before you roast it.

✔ Chop garlic fine and add to melted butter for lobster sauce or marinara sauce for pasta.

✔ Marinate peeled cloves in vinegar for salad dressing.

Just thinking about these dishes whets the appetite!

Choosing the ideal type of garlic

Why grow garlic when it is so widely available? Because you can find many interesting and flavorful kinds of garlic — far beyond the silver-skinned bulbs packed two to a box and obtainable at the supermarket. In the following sections are descriptions of hard-neck and soft-neck garlic cultivars that are worth trying.

Hard-neck type

The following are hard-neck types of garlic:

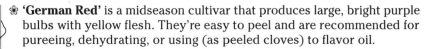

- ❀ **'German Red'** is a midseason cultivar that produces large, bright purple bulbs with yellow flesh. They're easy to peel and are recommended for pureeing, dehydrating, or using (as peeled cloves) to flavor oil.

- ❀ **'Korean Red'** is a unique selection — perfect if you like garlic with a hot taste. Plants reach 16 inches in height with wide, dark-green foliage that is good to eat. The midseason bulbs are best if you use them fresh. Each bulb typically has 6 to 11 cloves. It has a purple-striped bulb covering and sheath and is very easy to peel.

- ❀ **'Spanish Roja'** may just be the most popular hard-neck type. It's a midseason cultivar with what is said to be "true garlic" flavor. It's also an heirloom bulb, with culture dating from before 1900. You may find it referred to as "Greek garlic" in some areas.

Soft-neck type

Tasty varieties of soft-neck garlic include:

- ❀ **'Italian Late'** has excellent taste and pungent goodness. This cultivar certainly seems to have it all — good flavor and wonderful performance in cooking, as well as a long storage life (6 to 9 months). Reserve the largest of these cloves for planting.

- ❀ **'Silver Rose'** is a late cultivar with about the best storage capacity you can find — which makes it a good choice for braiding. The cloves' skins are striped pink to rose, and you can expect 7 to 10 larger outer cloves surrounding several smaller ones inside. Expect a sharp flavor from this one. Spring planting is successful just about everywhere.

Growing garlic

Plant hard-neck garlic in the fall. In regions with cold winters, plant 4 to 6 weeks before the ground freezes hard. In mild-winter areas, plant garlic right through winter but before February. If you live in the frozen north where fall-planted garlic dies, plant soft-neck garlic in spring.

Follow these steps for growing garlic:

1. **Unless your soil is naturally loose and light, add lots of organic matter in the form of compost, leaf mold, or well-aged manure.**

2. **Separate the garlic bulb into individual cloves (see Figure 17-1).**

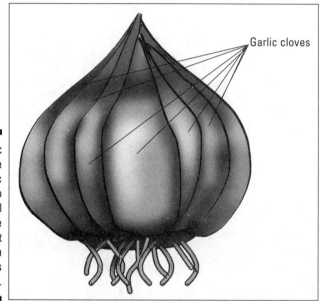

Garlic cloves

Figure 17-1:
Separate
the garlic
bulb into
individual
cloves; the
wider part
of each
clove is its
bottom.

3. **Plant each clove about an inch deep, with the slightly fatter end that was at the bottom of the bulb at the bottom of the hole.**

   The colder your winters, the deeper you may want to plant the cloves — as much as 2 to 4 inches deep.

4. **Space cloves 2 to 4 inches apart in the row, and rows should be 12 to 18 inches apart.**

   Or you can plant garlic in a block — rather than a row — spacing the cloves in a 4-inch by 8-inch grid. For even bigger bulbs, you can try spacing cloves on a 6-inch by 12-inch grid.

5. **Fertilize while plants are green and growing, and stop fertilizing after they begin to "bulb-up."**

   Late feeding keeps the garlic from going into dormancy, and the bulbs won't store well.

6. If rainfall is scanty, water while garlic plants are growing, just like you would any other green plant.

7. Garlic is ready to harvest when leaves turn brown, so start checking when five or six green leaves are left (pull a bulb to examine; see Figure 17-2).

Harvestable bulbs have a papery skin around each clove.

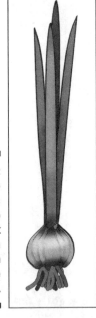

Figure 17-2:
Check to see if garlic is ready to harvest when only a few green leaves are left.

8. Garlic needs to cure before you store it; bundle eight to a dozen together by their leaves and hang in a dry place.

Or spread the cloves on an old window screen in a dark, dry, well-ventilated place. Curing takes from just under a month up to two months, depending on how dry and airy the place is.

Elephant Garlic

If you're one of those folks who finds garlic too pungent, with an after-taste that lingers, an alternative may be just the thing. Elephant garlic, *Allium ampeloprasum,* has a milder flavor. It's bigger, too, with a bulb six times larger and weighing as much as a pound.

Plant elephant garlic in late summer or early fall. You want some growth, just a few leaves, before the winter frost. If the plants make too much growth, they may die in winter or, come spring, they produce flowers rather than a good crop of cloves.

Like the ornamental onions we describe in Chapter 13, elephant garlic makes a large, showy flower. However, flowers are produced at the expense of bulbs, and the blooms reduce the bulb harvest.

Plant elephant garlic much the same way as regular garlic. Because the individual cloves are bigger than regular garlic, plant them deeper, about 4 to 6 inches, and space them 1 foot apart. After all, plants can grow 3 feet tall.

Typically, each clove grows into a large bulb made up of four to six large cloves. Sometimes, small cloves grow into an individual, onion-like round. If you want rounds, plant elephant garlic in late spring. They're great cooked like little white boiling onions, or you can replant them to make a typical head with several cloves the following season.

Harvest and store like regular garlic.

Shallots, the Soul of French Cuisine

Like garlic, shallots are a variation on an "onion" theme. As the French say, "Vive la difference!" This little multiplier onion makes a cluster of small bulbs with a delicate, aromatic flavor. They're easier to grow than any other onion — and, oh, what they'll do for a soup or stew.

Shallots can be grown from either seeds or sets — you may find sets easier and certainly quicker.

Choosing the best type of shallot

The shallot's subtle, aromatic flavor goes so well with delicate fish or chicken dishes, is fine for flavoring vegetables, and is super in a butter sauce for steak. Try these types of shallots:

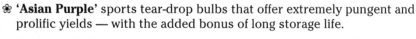

- ❀ **'Asian Purple'** sports tear-drop bulbs that offer extremely pungent and prolific yields — with the added bonus of long storage life.

- ❀ **'Brittany Red'** are plump, reddish-purple shallots, slightly oblong, and spicy with strong flavor. They're prolific at harvest, and the large size makes them easy to peal and chop. Plant one, and by the end of the growing season you may have as many as 15 bulbs.

❀ **'Dutch Yellow'** offers a gourmet treat from large — 1$\frac{1}{2}$ to 2 inches in diameter — bulbs with a sharp flavor and a yellow to cream interior and copper-red skin. They're among the best shallots for storing.

❀ **'Gray Shallots'** are often called "true shallots of France," and they are valued for their intense flavor that's ideal for many French recipes. The bulbs are dusky gray on the outside and creamy purple on the inside. Expect large yields with up to 25 bulbs per single shallot planted.

❀ **'Holland Red'** is a reliable producer with fat, round, coppery-red bulbs with reddish-purple flesh. Milder than Brittany, this cultivar offers fine flavor and superior storage ability. A single bulb often produces 10 new ones in a season.

Growing shallots

Although shallots can be planted in either spring or fall, fall planting yields the bigger harvest. Plant four to six weeks before cold weather comes to stay. You can grow shallots from either seeds or sets — you may find sets easier and certainly quicker.

Better soil means a better harvest, but shallots aren't as finicky as regular onions. They do okay in regular soil with adequate fertilizer in a sunny site. Just avoid low-lying soggy places or they rot. Follow these planting tips:

1. **Plant shallots 4 to 6 inches apart in rows 12 to 18 inches apart.**

   The bottom of the bulb goes down, and you want about an inch of soil over the bulb's tip.

2. **As bulbs mature and green leafy growth slows down, slow down on your watering.**

   Shallots mature best in dry soil.

3. **Harvest just like regular onions — when the tops are brown and fall over.**

4. **Handle gently to avoid bruising. Don't wash, just let the shallots dry and then gently brush away any loose dirt.**

5. **Air-dry for a couple of weeks, and then trim tops close to the neck (the top) of the bulbs.**

   Don't separate individual bulbs from the cluster until you're ready to use them.

6. **Store on an old window screen or in a mesh bag in a cool, dark, airy place.**

A high price at the store doesn't necessarily translate into difficult to grow. That's certainly the case for shallots. Grow them yourself, and you'll use them as lavishly as a French chef.

Chapter 18

The Kitchen Garden: Supporting Starches from Tubers

· ·

In This Chapter

▶ Potatoes: familiar and unique

▶ Sweet potatoes: a versatile alternative

▶ Jerusalem artichokes: an American delicacy

· ·

Some archaeologists theorize that agriculture started with bulbs. Imagine our ancient hunter-gathering ancestors digging up plump tasty bulbs and tubers to eat, tossing the little ones back in the dug over soil, and then moving on, only to come back the next year to find another harvest of nutritious, delicious bulbs and tubers. Small potatoes (not small change, actual golf-ball size potatoes) in the high Andes mountains of Peru, camassia bulbs in the Pacific Northwest, Jerusalem artichokes in the eastern half of North America, wild onions in Europe, and lily bulbs in Asia are just some of the bulbs and tubers first gathered from the wild.

Today, we enjoy lilies for their flowers, rather than their bulbs on the dinner plate. Sure, today, you buy potatoes at the store more conveniently than gathering them far afield from home. But fresh from the garden, potatoes taste *so* much better than those you buy in the grocery store, and you can enjoy some unique and yummy cultivars only if you grow them yourself. That's true of other familiar edible bulbs. Growing good-to-eat bulbs and tubers is easy and lots of fun. If you have children, growing your own is a great way to get them to eat their vegetables! All you need to begin is a sunny spot and some baby bulbs. You can even grow them in a container on your balcony or patio.

In this chapter, we discuss the easiest and tastiest bulbs to grow in your kitchen garden, starting with the familiar potato and sweet potato, and finishing up with Jerusalem artichokes, a tasty tuber not everyone is familiar with. You won't find turnips, carrots, parsnips, and other such vegetables because they're classified as roots rather than bulbs, corms, or tubers.

Everybody's Favorite: Spuds

Edible underground tubers are so important that the potato's Latin name of *Solanum tuberosum* emphasizes the plant's tuberous nature. The potato is a nourishing, essential food in many places around the world for a variety of reasons:

- ✔ Besides carbohydrates, potatoes provide high-quality protein.

- ✔ Potatoes mature faster than grains, producing small tubers just 7 weeks after planting, and, depending on the cultivar, reaching full size in 3 to 4 months.

- ✔ For the amount of space they occupy, potatoes have a much higher yield than other staple foods, such as wheat, corn, barley, and oats.

- ✔ Potatoes are adaptable. They are cultivated at sea level in cold climates. Near or on the equator, potatoes grow at high elevations in the mountains. Other staple food crops are not as versatile.

- ✔ Potatoes are versatile in how they're cooked: boiled, baked, mashed, or fried; you can even serve them cold in salads.

A mainstay of the fast-food industry, potatoes have been a basic culinary staple for centuries. The Peruvians first began cultivating potatoes 6,000 years ago. Over-age potatoes sort of taste that old, too. Well, not really, but if you want a dish to salivate about — a real gourmet's delight — try new little baby potatoes, freshly dug from your garden. Boil them and serve with a pat of butter.

In Europe, yellow-fleshed potatoes are more popular than white, perhaps because they look so buttery rich, but more likely because they taste *so* good. Surprise your family and dinner guests with blue potatoes. They taste the same as ordinary white potatoes, but have blue skin and flesh. Or try fingerlings, unusual and delicious potatoes you *may* find at a farmer's market, if you're lucky.

Potatoes used to be called Irish potatoes, because they were so important to that culture as a staple food. They were also called white potatoes, to clearly distinguish them from sweet potatoes. We guess that this label was before the blue and yellow kinds became popular.

Early maturing potatoes

Consider growing these early maturing types of potatoes:

 ❀ **'Bison'** is a terrific all-around red-skinned potato with yellow eyes and white flesh. It is less moist than many reds and so remains smooth and firm when cooked. Try it baked, boiled, and fried. It offers good resistance to late blight.

❀ **'Irish Cobbler'** is an heirloom favorite released in 1876, and it has been rewarding gardeners for, well, *years* with all white, oblong and flat potatoes with deep eyes. It has superior taste, and it's mealy texture makes it an excellent masher. Expect consistently fine early yields.

❀ **'Norgold'** offers white flesh and high yields. It's a variety with versatility — producing awesome flavor baked, boiled, or fried. It does not store well.

❀ **'Red Norland'** is a wonderful choice for summer harvests with lots of oval to oblong potatoes with smooth red skin and white flesh. Potatoes reach size rapidly if you give them space (plant 12 inches apart) or you'll have lots of smaller roasters if you plant them 6 to 8 inches apart.

❀ **'Red Pontiac'** delights with sweet white flesh, thin red skin, and shallow eyes. It's an adaptable sort, performing well even in heavy clay soils. It keeps well and offers fine flavor.

❀ **'Yukon Gold'** gives you everything you could ask for: yellow skin, rich yellow flesh, lots of flavor, good storage ability, and high yields. It's a popular potato that browns wonderfully fried and is great boiled or baked.

Midseason potatoes

Check out these midseason varieties of potatoes:

❀ **'All Blue'** delivers anything but the blues as you'll find when you harvest this unusual but perhaps best-known blue potato. It has indigo skin and white-streaked blue flesh that turns a soft purple-blue when cooked. Expect a nutty flavor and fluffy texture that is guaranteed to garner attention. Great baked, fried, and in salads.

❀ **'Chieftain'** is a popular white-fleshed cultivar with excellent flavor and high yield. It does fine in heavy soils and has a spreading habit with attractive blossoms. The depth and size of eyes varies.

❀ **'Kennebec'** wins points for all-around excellence. It has smooth skin and texture, white flesh, shallow eyes, and resistance to late blight. This one has great taste and high productivity.

❀ **'Russet Burbank'** takes the prize as perhaps the most widely-grown and successful potato ever. Excellent in every category, this one boasts flavor, firm white flesh and golden brown skin, large size, resistance to disease, keeping qualities and, well, what else is there?

❀ **'Yellow Finn'** is your choice if you're after rich yellow color and a potato that simply does not need added help from butter because it looks and tastes like you've already buttered it. Firm, sweet, moist, well-textured, and easy to keep — you can't go wrong here.

Late-season potatoes

Here are a couple of late-season potatoes:

- ❀ **'Butte,'** as an excellent keeper, is a wonderful choice for winter eating. It is high yielding with a good, thick skin and offers unbeatable flavor from a fine dry interior. Choose this one when you want a potato with high vitamin content.

- ❀ **'Green Mountain'** was developed in Vermont in 1885, so this light tan heirloom selection has a long and favorable track record. Why? It's productive, distinctly flavored, long keeping, and successful in many soil types and under many conditions.

Fingerling potatoes

The following are types of fingerling potatoes:

- ❀ **'Butterfinger,'** also known as Swedish Peanut, is an outstanding crescent teardrop with nutty-tasting yellow flesh and light russet skin. It stays very firm when cooked, giving it high marks steamed or boiled.

- ❀ **'French Fingerling'** stars with bright red skin and delivers an unusual look from red marbled flesh rich enough in flavor that this potato is another one that you don't need to drench in butter. Try this one pan-fried or mashed.

- ❀ **'Rose Finn Apple'** will delight you with rosy pinkish-bronze skin and yellow flesh with a waxy texture and fine taste. It matures midseason, stores well and is scab resistant, too.

- ❀ **'Russian Banana'** offers things other fingerlings only dream about: pale golden firm flesh from large and smooth tubers with high disease resistance. All this plus superb taste, high cooking quality, and very long keeping time make this cultivar a standout.

Growing potatoes

Potatoes are easy to grow, given the right conditions. They do best with a loose, fertile, sandy loam with a pH of 6 to 7, cultivated at least 8 inches deep.

Measuring soil pH

pH is a measurement of how acid or alkaline soil is. Neutral is 7.0, and most vegetables, including potatoes, grow best in neutral to somewhat acid soil. If you think that your soil may be too acid or too alkaline, you can check pH yourself with a simple kit available at most garden centers.

Start with certified "seed potatoes" bought at a garden center or through a mail-order catalog.

Seed potatoes aren't *really* seeds. They are small potatoes raised especially for planting, or pieces of potato, each with an *eye* or growing point, again for planting rather than eating (see Figure 18-1).

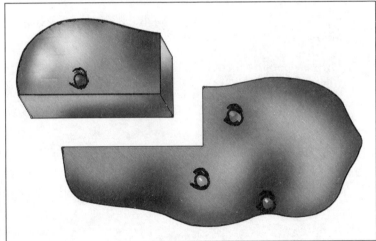

Figure 18-1: Look to the eyes when growing potatoes.

Follow these guidelines for planting potatoes:

1. **About three weeks before the last spring frost, dig the soil and add 5-10-10 fertilizer.**

2. **Wait 2 to 3 days and then plant potatoes in rows 2 feet apart.**

   The potatoes should be 1 foot apart, in a trench 8 inches deep.

3. **Cover the seed potatoes with 3 or 4 inches of soil.**

   Shoots sprout up in 10 days to 2 weeks.

Plant only certified seed potatoes

Thick potato peelings in a compost heap can sometimes grow harvestable potatoes. Supermarket potatoes sometimes sprout in vegetable bins. It may be tempting to plant these in your garden, but don't do it. Supermarket potatoes are fine to eat but are not necessarily free of potato scab disease. Certified seed potatoes are free of scab disease, and produce a bigger crop of unblemished potatoes.

4. **When the potato vines are 8 inches high, cover about half the growth with soil raked in from the side of the row.**

   This process is called *hilling up.*

5. **At the same time, side dress with more 5-10-10 fertilizer.**

   To side dress, just add a little fertilizer along the side of the row and cultivate lightly to mix it with the soil.

6. **Wait 2 to 3 weeks and hill up again with an inch or two of soil; hill up a third time 2 weeks after that, but don't add fertilizer.**

   The new potato tubers form between the original seed piece and the soil surface (see Figure 18-2). Potatoes don't need a lot of water if you keep them hilled up, well weeded, and properly spaced. In fact, they usually taste better, too.

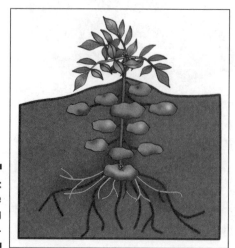

Figure 18-2:
The humble
beginning
of a potato.

This is very important: If potatoes are exposed to sunlight for any length of time — while they are growing, after you dig them from the garden, or when you bring them home from the store — they turn green. And that green part of the potato is poisonous.

7. **When you see the first flowers, about 7 to 8 weeks after planting the early cultivars, you can harvest a few baby potatoes.**

   Gently push a few fingers around the base of the plant to find out what's doing. If the little potatoes are forming and are about an inch and a half in diameter (smaller potatoes are too small to bother harvesting), you can pull up a whole plant (pulling the plant at the end of the row is less disruptive than pulling one in the middle) and take them all. That approach is usually easier than trying to snitch a potato or two from each plant without disturbing the potatoes you leave behind and reducing the final yield.

Your main harvest of potatoes will come 3 to 4 months after planting, when the leaves and stems start to turn yellow and wilt. Expect to harvest 9 or 10 pounds of potatoes for each 10-foot row.

Gardeners in the northern tier of states and those in the northeastern United States have it made, at least as far as potatoes go. Potatoes thrive in colder regions. (Just think of Maine or Idaho potatoes!) But you don't want to freeze the tops. The plants will sprout again and again. But each time the young shoots get frozen back, your final harvest not only gets delayed, but it gets smaller. Plant 10 days to 2 weeks before the last frost date for your region.

If you have heavy clay soil, or not much soil at all, grow potatoes under a mulch of clean straw, seed-free hay, or dried leaves. Do prepare the soil you have as thoroughly as possible. Instead of using a trench, plant the seed potatoes just below the soil surface or right on top. Cover the pieces with 6 to 10 inches of mulch right away and add more mulch as the plants grow.

Growing potatoes down south

Potatoes like cool weather, so gardeners south of the Mason-Dixon line need a few tricks to successfully grow potatoes. If frost comes late and autumn lasts a long time, try planting between mid-July and late August. Keep the soil mulched for a couple of weeks before planting to keep it cooler. If you live in really warm climates (Alabama, Mississippi, and other Deep South states), plant in late fall.

But you need to pretreat the potatoes. Chill the seed potatoes in the refrigerator for four to six weeks. Then put them in a paper bag with apples or bananas (just what you don't do with tulip bulbs!) and keep them at normal room temperature until they begin to sprout; then plant the just-sprouted spuds in the garden, from October through November.

Growing in containers: Patio potatoes

You can use individual containers if you want to grow just a few potatoes on a patio. Each container (for example, a flower pot, wooden box, or tire planter) should be at least 18 inches across, and 2 to 2¹/₂ feet tall.

Attach a cylinder of chicken wire (the same diameter as your container) to add the necessary height. Push the bottom couple of inches of the wire cylinder into the soil and use three or four wooden stakes to support it.

Fill the container with 8 inches of good rich soil, plant one seed potato, and cover lightly with 4 more inches of soil. As the vine grows, add more soil, mulch, or compost, but never cover more than a third of the new growth. Potatoes grown caged like this need more water.

One advantage is that container potatoes often out-produce those growing in the ground. Choose one of the fingerling potatoes, a 'Yellow Finn,' or a 'Red Pontiac' for container cultivation.

Keeping your potato plants disease-free

You can keep your potatoes disease-free by starting with certified, healthy seed potatoes and growing in the right place: Avoid raw, uncomposted animal manure, wet soggy soil, and high pH alkaline soils. Choosing the right site takes care of scab disease. You can avoid wilts and blights by growing potatoes in different parts of the garden so that they're never in the same place more often than one year in three.

Remember, potatoes are related to tomatoes, eggplants, and peppers. Don't grow potatoes where these plant relatives grew the year before. Planting potatoes right after tomatoes (or eggplants, or peppers) has the same effect as growing potatoes in the same place two years in a row. *Rotating crops* (growing the same plant in a different part of the vegetable garden the next year) reduces the build-up of wilt and blight diseases in the soil, and keeps populations of insect pests from building up, too.

Protecting your potato plants from pests

Colorado potato beetles can be controlled in a small garden by handpicking the striped adults and smashing 'em. Look under the leaves for clusters of small yellow eggs and mash them, too. You can kill the larvae before they turn into egg-laying adults by using *Bacillis thuringienses* variety san diego (BT var. san diego). It has no effect on adult beetles, only the larvae. You need to spray every 10 days to 2 weeks as soon as the plants are up. This product poses no risk for people, in fact this bacteria is similar to those that turn milk into yogurt. If squashing adult beetles makes you squeamish, use a rotenone or pyrethrin spray, two organic, insect-pest controls that kill the adult beetles.

Flea beetles make tiny pinholes in the potato leaves and if a lot of flea beetles are making lots of holes, the potato plants grow poorly, which means fewer potatoes at harvest time. Rotenone and pyrethrin control infestations of flea beetles, too.

Something Special: The Sweet Potato

Sweet potatoes are really a relative of the morning glory vine and have nothing to do with potatoes. Maybe you grew a sweet potato when you were a child. If one started to sprout, we'd stick three toothpicks in to support it on the mouth of a water-filled jar. Long vines with pretty, heart-shaped green leaves would sprawl over a windowsill. Nowadays, sweet potatoes you buy in the store are treated to prevent sprouting (for better storage). If you want to grow a windowsill sweet potato, you'd better buy one at the health food store. And if you want to grow sweet potatoes in the garden, you're better off buying little started plants called "slips" from a specialty supplier. They're ready to grow and, just as with seed potatoes, slips are disease-free.

Deciding which type of sweet potato to grow

You can choose from several cultivars of sweet potatoes:

❀ **'Beauregard'** is a highly productive, vine-type sweet potato developed for growing conditions in the Deep South. Some say it is the highest producer of all sweet potatoes. It has light rose skin and moderately deep orange flesh with uniform shape — it does not crack open — and above average taste.

❀ **'Centennial'** and **'Georgia Jets,'** vine types, are better for mid-Atlantic gardens with a shorter growing season because tubers are ready to harvest earlier than Beauregard. 'Centennial,' sometimes tagged as America's most popular, is good for short-season areas and can be dug as tender "baby bakers" in 90 to 100 days. It offers moist texture and is orange through and through. 'Georgia Jets' is another quick and heavy producer offering large, moist, orange-fleshed, red-skinned potatoes in 90 days.

❀ **'Porto Rico'** is a good choice for containers because it is a bush type, and all the sweet 'taters grow close to the center of the plant. Expect truly delicious results from this potato with copper skin and moist, reddish-orange flesh. It's excellent for baking.

Growing sweet potatoes

Sweet potatoes love sun and heat. (After all, they originated in tropical Central and South America.) They need at least $3\frac{1}{2}$ months of hot weather from the time you plant the slips to harvest.

If you want to heat things up, use black plastic mulch to warm the soil. Use a floating *row cover* — a sheet of thin, spun-bonded white fabric (Remay is one brand name) held above a row of plants on support hoops. No other vegetable grown in the United States tolerates more heat than sweet potatoes!

Even though they are related to morning glory vine, don't think that sweet potatoes need support to grow. Vines can sprawl on the ground or, if your garden is small or you are growing a few in containers, you can find bushy, short-vine types.

Sweet potatoes need a light, loose, open soil. If the soil is too heavy, roots are long and skinny. Don't fertilize heavily, or plants grow vines and leaves rather than a good crop of tubers. Use 5-10-10 fertilizer, a little less than half a pound per 10 feet of row. Dig it into the soil a couple of days before planting. Make ridge-mounds (which we describe shortly) on top of the fertilized soil.

To avoid diseases, plant sweet potatoes in a different part of the garden each year.

Plant slips after the weather is warm and settled, at least two weeks after the last frost. Create *ridge-mounds* by planting in row-long mounds of soil 1-foot wide and 10 inches higher than the ground. Ridges should be 3 to 4 feet apart. Set slips about 1 foot or 18 inches apart in the ridged mounds (closer for more even-sized roots, further apart for larger ones).

You can expect to harvest 9 or 10 pounds of sweet potatoes for every 10-foot row.

Set slips 3 to 4 inches deep and really soak 'em when planting. If you have only a few to plant and want to take the time, make a hole the size of a 19-ounce soup can. Fill the hole with water and let it drain. Set the slip in the hole and slowly fill with fine soil. As the soil turns to mud from all the water, the roots make good contact with the muddy slurry.

If you want to grow a sweet potato or two "just for fun," use a box or tub about 15 inches square and at least 1 foot deep, filled with a light, porous soil mix, for each slip.

Keep plants watered in summer if natural rainfall is scanty. At the end of the growing season, 3 weeks or so before harvest, plants don't need much water.

At harvest time, cut off vines to get them out of the way. Dig roots carefully to avoid any cuts or scrapes. Leave the soil on 'em; don't wash! Sweet potatoes must be cured — air dried — if you want to keep them for longer than a couple of weeks. Keep them indoors at about 75 to 80 degrees Fahrenheit, and high humidity of 90 percent. Keep air circulating with a small fan. After curing for a couple of weeks, store in a cool (at least 58 degrees Fahrenheit but under 65 degrees Fahrenheit) and dry place.

Sweet potatoes offer a variety of menu possibilities: sweet potato pie, candied sweet potatoes, or sweet potatoes on the Thanksgiving table. Try tempura sweet potatoes, batter-dipped and deep-fried for a delicious addition to your menu. French-fried is good, too, as are potato chips made from sweet potatoes.

A North American Treat: The Jerusalem Artichoke

With a common name of Jerusalem artichoke, you may think that this is a plant from the Middle East with the flavor and/or looks of an artichoke. Far from it, this is an American plant cultivated by Native Americans. Its Latin name, *Helianthus tuberosus,* is more accurate, emphasizing the importance of its fat tuberous roots (see Figure 18-3). Another common name is sunchoke.

Jerusalem artichokes are better than potatoes as a starchy vegetable for people who have diabetes, because the tubers contain inulin. The knobby roots, when eaten raw in a salad, taste like water chestnuts. They're great cooked or pickled, too — just be sure to cook them until just done (other-wise they turn to mush).

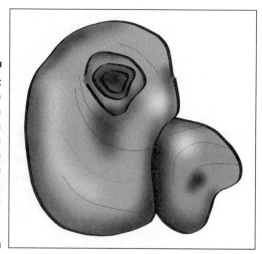

Figure 18-3:
The Jerusalem artichoke looks more like a potato than an artichoke, and tastes more like one, too.

Selecting a Jerusalem artichoke

Jerusalem artichokes grow wild along the roadside in many places. The tubers on the wild plants are just as tasty, but small when compared to commercial kinds. If you have trouble finding a commercial source for tubers for planting (look in Appendix A), you can plant the tubers you buy at the produce section of the grocery store.

'Stampede' is a tender cultivar of Jerusalem artichoke that has a sweet, nutty flavor you can enjoy raw or cooked. It has large, white tubers that often reach a half pound each. This perennial sunflower also serves up masses of yellow 4-inch daisy-like flowers on robust 6- to 8-foot plants. And it can be used as an attractive windbreak. Other cultivars you might enjoy are 'Fuseau' and 'Red Fuseau.'

Growing Jerusalem artichokes

Jerusalem artichokes are sun-loving, quick-spreading plants. You can plant them as a decorative hedge at the edge of the garden — one that's productive as well as pretty; their delicate yellow flowers are dainty beauties.

Jerusalem artichokes are vigorous, often invasively spreading plants. Do *not* plant them in a flower garden.

Loose open soil — similar to a site where you'd grow potatoes — produces the best harvest of the biggest tubers.

Plant in spring, as early as the ground can be dug over.

Plant small tubers whole, or cut big ones into pieces weighing 2 or 3 ounces. Plant tubers 4 inches deep, spacing them 18 inches apart in rows 3 feet apart.

Jerusalem artichoke plants grow 8 or 9 feet tall, sometimes as much as 12 feet! Hilling up, just like gardeners do with potatoes, helps support the tall stems against the wind. Hill up when plants are 3 feet tall, and again when they are 6 feet tall.

Don't plant Jerusalem artichokes where they'll shade the rest of the garden.

When small, cheery, yellow sunflowers open on the tops of the plants — in late summer — you can cut them for a bouquet at the same time you begin harvesting tubers.

Tubers don't store too well out of the ground. Dig them as you need them. Frost won't harm them, and you can keep digging after the tops die back. If you do need to dig them all up, store in a plastic bag in the crisper drawer of your refrigerator.

Eating Jerusalem artichokes

Jerusalem artichokes aren't just for curiosity or historical interest, or as wild-gathered, natural foods — they're tasty! Try Jerusalem artichokes raw — slivered and added to a green salad, or sliced and added as a garnish to a clear soup. Cooked, they're great lightly boiled and served like potato salad, or try them steamed or sauteed. Tubers cook quickly, so be careful not to overcook, especially the first few times you try them.

Chapter 19

Growing Bulbs in Containers

*I*f we have you hooked on flower bulbs, wait till you see what you can do with them in containers. Consider dazzling displays of brilliant golden daffodils and pots brimming over with sturdy tulips in a rainbow of colors, or maybe a simple dish filled with fragrant, cool, elegant hyacinths. With proper bulb selection and some TLC (tender loving care), you can find satisfaction and success.

The Up Side to Growing Bulbs in Containers

Growing bulbs in containers can be easy and rewarding. Here are some of the best reasons to choose this gardening method:

✔ Blooming bulbs in pots give you an up-close and intense mass of color. You get lots of enjoyment from a few bulbs — whether you plant lots of one kind for impact, or choose different bulbs for a more varied, longer show.

   Container culture is the ideal way to fully enjoy small flowering bulbs or fragrant cultivars. Crocuses, hyacinths, and freesias are charming in a bowl on your patio table or front door step.

✔ Portable containers are easy to show off during peak bloom, and easy to give a quick exit stage left before the buds form and later after the blooms wither.

✔ Protecting potted bulbs from temperature extremes is easy. Simply move pots indoors on frosty nights, or out of the intense summer sun.

- ✔ Growing bulbs in containers allows you to overcome poor growing conditions such as soggy soil or too much or too little sun. You control the environment — exposure, soil, drainage, water, and fertilizer — as needed so plants thrive.

- ✔ With successive plantings, you can enjoy colorful displays for weeks, or months on end. Start your plantings early and pot new bulbs every few weeks for a non stop flower show. Within one pot, for example, you can plant a layer of tulips below a layer of hyacinths and have an impressive, long show.

The Down Side to Container Gardening

In case you're thinking that growing bulbs in containers is, well, a bed of roses, so to speak, consider the following few little things on the drawback side (but hey, how many things in life come with ups and no downs):

- ✔ Don't be fooled into thinking that potted bulbs need less attention than those in the garden. Pots dry out more quickly and roots can't simply stretch out for more moisture or nutrients. Fertilizer and water are up to you to provide.

   You may need to schedule daily waterings — especially for thirsty summer plants. All this watering may leach out nutrients, so giving your plants an occasional boost of liquid fertilizer is a good idea.

- ✔ Growing bulbs in containers may not be a long-term investment because some bulbs don't do well in containers after the first year. Typically, tulips and daffodils fall into this category, but after the first season you can plant them in the ground and they very well may rebound (or maybe not). Just be patient.

- ✔ Because some containers — especially small ones — offer very little insulation, you must monitor the weather and move pots inside or under protection during adverse weather.

When, Where, and How to Plant Bulbs

Although many bulbs are adaptable and agreeable little fellows, they need the right conditions to provide you with the best show. Knowing what types to plant and when is a start. General planting times are the same for container bulbs as for those in the garden. Selecting the best container for your particular bulbs is also a key to success, and you have lots of choices. As for the bulbs themselves, the general rule is that shorter, more compact cultivars do best in containers. That rule is easy to understand because those bulbs have restricted root growth.

Planning ahead — when to plant spring and summer bulbs

Plant spring-flowering bulbs in the fall. If you have bulbs that need chilling, and your area doesn't offer chilly weather, buy either pre-chilled bulbs or refrigerate them before you plant. If you're ordering bulbs through the mail, be sure to include some container choices along with your regular fall and spring planting lists. For a longer show, include cultivars that are early, mid-season, and late-season bloomers. You'll get less impact because the flowers won't all open at the same time, but you'll have a longer period of bloom.

Excellent spring bulbs for containers include anemone, crocus, cyclamen, freesia, hyacinth, grape hyacinth, daffodil, tulip, ranunculus, and striped squill *(Puschkinia)*. But don't think that this list is it. Many other bulbs will work, too. Just ask your nursery pro if you're in doubt.

Plant summer bloomers in spring. Make successive plantings and enjoy flowers all summer.

Ideal choices for summer color are tuberous begonia, smaller decorative or patio dahlia, dwarf canna, calla, shorter or dwarf lily, freesia, shamrock, rain lily *(Zephyranthes)*, and caladium.

If for some reason you miss the planting period, all is not lost. You can find many bulbs for sale potted and already blooming or about to bloom in nurseries, home improvement centers, and even supermarkets. Be sure to choose plants with lots of buds — not open flowers — so you can enjoy each flower during its entire bloom.

Deciding which containers to use

When you choose containers, you're limited by a few requirements and then only by your imagination. The range of good containers is as varied as the kinds of bulbs you can grow in them. Go large with tubs, half barrels, window boxes, urns, or planter boxes. Go traditional with bulb pans (10 inches or more across and at least 5 inches deep); terra cotta, ceramic, or concrete pots; or hanging baskets. Go small with dishes or deep saucers, or go wild and whimsical with an old wheel barrow, recycled antique coal scuttle, wooden crate, or a hollowed-out tree stump.

All containers need drainage so bulbs don't sit in soggy soil. Drill several half-inch holes as necessary to ensure that excess water drains away.

Depth is important. Although container bulbs don't have to be planted as deeply as those grown in the ground, they need at least 2 inches of soil underneath for optimal rooting. Bulbs that will continue to live — such as lilies and small dahlias — require a container as least 12 inches deep.

Planting basics

Planting is easy if you pay attention to a few key elements — namely the soil mix and spacing. Don't worry if the bulbs are crowded; in pots they do okay with this high-density living. As the weeks go by, watch closely for signs of life, and the welcome green sprouts will signal that you're in the flower business. Follow these planting tips:

1. **Choose a potting mix that drains well but holds adequate moisture.**

   What? Can that happen? Yes, if you use a high-quality commercial potting mix with moisture-retaining ingredients such as perlite or vermiculite already mixed in.

2. **For nourishment, add some compost and fertilizer according to package directions (Bulb Booster is good, and so are the slow-release granules).**

3. **Place a layer of stones or pot shards over the drain hole and add a couple of inches of your soil mix to the bottom of the pot.**

4. **Next come the bulbs, and your first task is to decide which end of the bulb is up — usually the pointy part.**

   You may be able to find little pieces of dried roots indicating the bottom.

5. **Plant the largest bulbs first (daffodils and tulips) placing them a half inch or so apart and about an inch below the pot rim — unless you are planting in layers, in which case you need to plant them a couple of inches deeper.**

6. **In a layered planting, cover the large bulbs with an inch or so of soil, and then plant the smaller bulbs no more than an inch apart.**

   You're better off planting large bulbs (such as lilies or amaryllises) one cultivar per pot. A 6-inch pot is fine for large bulbs or a trio of miniatures.

7. **Barely cover the tops of the bulbs with more potting soil.**

8. **At this point, you can add an inch or two of organic mulch on top of the soil.**

9. **Water gently but thoroughly with a watering can or trickle from the hose until you see water drain away.**

10. **Store your container in a protected but cool spot.**

    If you live where severe frosts are the norm, put pots in the basement or garage. **Remember:** They have less resistance than bulbs in the garden. Check on things every couple of weeks and *only* water if the soil feels dry.

11. **In 6 to 8 weeks, you should see shoots poking up and you can remove the top layer of organic mulch and give the containers a protected spot outside — under a tree or trellis where filtered light will reach the little plants.**

12. **When buds appear, move the container to its place of honor and water it as needed to keep the soil moist but not soggy.**

Care and Feeding of Your Bulbs

Besides just basking in the rave reviews your container creations garner, you must attend to a few routine chores (but don't worry, you can tackle them without too much work):

✔ Check the soil moisture weekly or, in summer, daily — especially small containers or hanging baskets that dry out quickly. Water to keep the soil moist, wetting the soil and not the leaves.

✔ You can add a boost of liquid fertilizer every month or so to keep the foliage and buds going strong. Make sure to dilute the fertilizer as directions recommend. You can keep up these feedings even after flowers fade, while the foliage continues. This food helps the bulb build energy for the future. Stop fertilizing when the foliage begins to turn brown.

✔ Staking may be a necessity for some bulbs. Taller varieties of tulips, daffodils, and lilies may become top-heavy as may the long-blooming stems on freesias. Try to anticipate this requirement and place your support (natural twigs blend best) early when you plant so you don't damage the bulb.

✔ Cut flowers after they fade or, with fragrant selections, take stems as buds begin to open to enjoy the blossoms indoors.

✔ When the last flowers bloom, move the containers offstage again, so they can finish their natural cycle as the foliage slowly dies back.

✔ When everything is dry and finished blooming, upend the pot or dig down and pull out the bulbs. Remove any dead foliage and dust the bulb off. Store it in a dry place and next year give it a new home in the garden, however. . . .

> ✔ Some bulbs will do fine left in their containers. Lily, freesia, cyclamen, and amaryllis are examples of bulbs that can remain in their pots to wait out the off-season. Wait until normal planting dates to plant these bulbs, and begin watering to start the cycle again.

When you're designing container gardens, consider planting annuals with the bulbs. They're great companion plants and add continuous color, which is nice if some bulbs are finished and others are in bud. But be careful with size here; plants that want too much elbow room will crowd out your bulbs. In spring, consider violas and pansies, primroses, Dahlberg daisies, dwarf calendulas, toadflaxes (linarias), dianthuses, or sweet alyssums. In summer, try lobelias, impatiens, sweet alyssums, classic zinnias, sanvitalias, or cascading or multiflora petunias. See *Gardening For Dummies* (from IDG Books Worldwide, Inc.) for more information about annuals.

Sizzling Selections

Shoot for the stars with specialty bulbs that adapt well to life in containers. Some of the bulbs in this section will be familiar names to you, but others — tuberous begonias, callas, rain lilies, ranunculuses, and striped squills, for example — may be new characters for you to consider. In general terms, the best choices tend to be short-stemmed, low-growing, compact cultivars that don't need to occupy tons of space or to send up tall stems with top-heavy blossoms. Larger plants such as lilies, cannas, or even ornamental onions do well planted one to three per large pot.

Spring-blooming bulbs

In this section, we start with the big three spring blooming bulbs — tulips, daffodils, and hyacinths — all of which offer many attractive cultivars ideal for containers.

Tulips

Tulips deliver classy, impressive color, and you can have fine results with many types. The fragrant selections are a special treat. Medium height to shorter varieties are the easiest to manage.

Plant so that the bulbs almost touch and the tips are just below the soil. Remember to buy pre-chilled bulbs or cool the bulbs yourself if you live in a mild-winter area. Try unusual and eye-catching Rembrandt, fosteraiana (emperor), parrot, and viridiflora hybrids or greigii cultivars. Consider species tulips, too, because you can find many unusual flowers that make wonderful container accents on compact 6- to 8-inch plants. Move bulbs into the garden in subsequent years. (For more details, see Chapter 24.)

Daffodils

Daffodils make reliable and outstanding choices for bold, bright color that salutes the arrival of spring with style. Go for the more compact plants in smaller containers or try the larger varieties in tubs, barrels, or your largest pots. Cyclamineus (with flaired flowers) or triandrus (with multiple fragrant blossoms) cultivars offer excellent results. Plants do best in the garden after a year in a container. (See Chapter 24 for more information on forcing bulbs.)

Hyacinths

Hyacinths are container specialists — especially effective for forced indoor bloom (see Chapters 7 and 24). They're also a delight in patio pots and window boxes where you can enjoy their perfumed beauty up close. Be sure to apply a complete fertilizer to bloomed-out plants so they gain strength for the following year, and lift and store bulbs when all is said and done. Transplant bulbs to the garden after their first year in containers.

Other spring-blooming bulbs

Here's a quick rundown of a few other spring bloomers to consider:

- Crocuses offer welcome early color and put on quite a show when massed in dishes and shallow pots. Move bulbs to the garden after the first year.

- Cyclamens combine delicate, long-lasting flowers and attractive heart-shaped variegated foliage on plants that will re-bloom if left in the pots.

- Freesias are also adaptable little dudes who will live on for a year or more in pots and produce charming arching stems loaded with fragrant, bright flowers in a wide range of colors. Dutch hybrids produce the largest flowers. Try as many as a dozen corms in an 8-inch pot.

- Grape hyacinths are cool, spiky affairs with clusters of early small blue or white flowers and grassy foliage. Plant the small bulbs close together or use them as great fillers between larger bulbs.

- Ranunculuses really do the rainbow thing with fully double fluffy flowers in lots of extra-bright colors. Plant these in fall in mild climates, but wait until spring in frosty regions. Soak the tubers before you plant, and then set them an inch deep with the pointed fingers down. They need big pots at least 12 inches deep.

- Striped squills *(Puschkinia libanotica)* send up sturdy stalks, 4 to 6 inches high with loose clusters of pale blue star-shaped flowers. These are perfect for tucking in among tulips and hyacinths.

Summer-blooming bulbs

There you are, sitting on your deck, lounging and drinking a cool one as you gaze upon baskets and pots brimming with color and fragrance from an array of blooming bulbs that have friends and family in awe. Why? Because weeks back, in early spring, you potted tuberous begonias, lilies, dahlias, rain lilies, calla lilies, and for fabulous foliage, caladiums and dwarf cannas.

Tuberous begonias

If you were on a desert island and could only have one blooming summer bulb in a container, tuberous begonias would be a strong contender for the honor. Dazzling flowers, in single or double forms, come in an impressive array of colors from soft pastels to brilliant white, red, yellow, pink, orange, and crimson or stunning bicolors. Cascading forms flow over pot or hanging basket rims with dozens of flowers (see Figure 19-1), and upright cultivars are nearly covered in blossoms. Expect lots of flowers from summer into fall. Each stem produces large 4- to 6-inch blossoms (the male flowers) and smaller single female flowers.

Figure 19-1:
A hanging begonia makes a bountiful show.

Plant tuberous begonias outside when frosty nights are history, setting the large tuber-corms concave side up about an inch deep, one per 6-inch pot.

Be patient. From planting to full bloom may take three months, but the wait will be worth it when you see the vivid flowers opening week after week. Follow these tips for growing tuberous begonias:

1. To get a jump on the growing season, start the tuber-corms indoors in January or February in flats or shallow containers, setting them an inch apart with the tops showing.

2. Keep the soil moist, but not wet.

3. When sprouts appear, cover them with about a half inch of soil mix and move the container to a warm, bright location.

4. When the sprouts reach 2 inches, transfer each little guy to a pot or hanging container (wooden ones work well as do moss-lined wire baskets) and move them outdoors after frosts.

   In hanging baskets, space the tubers 6 inches apart or use three in small baskets and four in larger ones.

   Original plants are native to high altitudes in the Andes, so hybrid tuberous begonias prefer partial shade with moderate temperatures. Morning and late afternoon sun are fine, making window boxes on the northeast side of your house excellent sites.

5. Water regularly to keep the soil moist but avoid overhead spraying, which can cause powdery mildew.

6. Feed with a complete liquid fertilizer during active growth and blooming — until the leaves start to yellow.

7. Let the cycle finish and dig and store corms in mesh bags in a cool, dry spot.

Here's a rundown of popular tuberous begonia categories, which explains about growth habits and flower forms, and offers a look at outstanding container-grown cultivars.

❀ **Camellia-flowered begonias** show off with large, fully double flowers in vivid colors. They're great in window boxes, planters, and pots. Some catalogs call these "double begonias." Bloom time begins in July with 6-inch flowers. Plants grow 12 to 15 inches tall and tolerate shade well. For the largest blooms, pinch off smaller side buds as they form. Consider these cultivars:

- **'Bright Scarlet Red'** shows off perfect form and rich color from deep red flowers with just a hint of rosy pink.

- **'Buttery Orange'** pretty much says it all in the name. Try this one when you want a special look.

- **'Sunny Yellow'** is stunning with soft flowers offering exceptionally bright color.

❀ **Non-stop begonias** offer continuous color from fluffy, fully double 3- to 4-inch flowers. Plants are the most compact of all begonias, reaching 6 to 10 inches and have good heat resistance.

- • **'Non-Stop Copper'** generates large flowers in vivid coppery orange.

- • **'Non-Stop Pink'** sends out a cavalcade of rose-pink blossoms on vigorous plants.

- • **'Non-Stop White'** shines with glowing, snow-white flowers that light up any shady spot with elegance.

❀ **Picotee begonias** produce large flowers in unusual and rewarding two-toned color combinations. Plants reach 8 to 12 inches.

- • **'Picotee White, Pink Edge'** is simply stunning with each ivory petal artistically outlined in rosy pink, giving exquisite detail to the double-flower form. This variety is especially effective with double white or double pink cultivars.

- • **'Picotee Yellow, Orange Edge'** offers warm sunset-like color from golden petals edged in bright orange.

❀ **Cascade begonias** are the ideal choice for hanging baskets, tubs, or window boxes. They offer long-term bloom and graceful pendulous stems with bright, double flowers up to 3 inches across. Look for 'White,' 'Red,' 'Yellow,' and 'Pink' cultivars.

❀ **Lace begonias** display large, double flowers with wavy, fringed petals edged in white. You can find cultivars in white, pink, apricot, red, and salmon.

Calla lilies

Famous for familiar cupped white trumpets, calla lilies are excellent performers in containers and as cut flowers.

They grow 15 to 18 inches tall and a single bulb may produce a dozen 5-inch tall, 2- to 3-inch-wide blossoms under ideal conditions in a 12-inch pot. Plant the rhizomes 2 inches deep, one per 6-inch pot.

Blooms come in yellow, pink, orange, lavender, and rose to name a few shades. As an added bonus, callas have attractive dark green, sword-like foliage with white freckles. Check out these cultivars and species:

❀ **'Elliottiana'** has rich golden-yellow flowers that simply glow above the dark foliage.

❀ **'Flame'** offers an arresting collection of golden flowers flushed with varying degrees of red.

❀ **'Rehmanni Superba'** stands out with soft pink flowers flushed with deep rose in the center and along the edges. This one is an abundant bloomer with as many as 12 flowers from one $2^1/_2$-inch bulb.

❀ **'Rudylite Rose'** sends up almost translucent, smooth, hot pink flowers with a satiny texture.

The best of the rest

Ready for a few more summer-blooming bulbs? Try a handful or a dozen of the selections that follow.

Lilies

Lilies often get double takes when they're blooming with stately beauty on your patio or terrace. If you stick to lower-growing cultivars or special "dwarf" or "pot collections," you can have excellent results. Plant a single bulb in a 7-inch pot, three per 12-inch pot, or five in a 16-inch container. Use deep 12-inch+ containers, and the plants will grow happily undisturbed for several years. Consider these cultivars:

❀ **'Cote d'Azur'** is deep pink and grows to 18 inches.

❀ **'Elfin Sun'** is golden-yellow and grows to between 15 and 18 inches.

❀ **'Enchantment'** is a radiant orange-red Asiatic hybrid and grows to 48 inches.

❀ **'Reinesse'** is pure white and grows to between 15 and 18 inches.

Cannas

Cannas go with the shorter varieties in the 2-foot range. Plant them 2 to 4 inches deep in large containers — at least 12 inches wide and 14 to 15 inches deep. Check out these varieties:

❀ **'Opera La Boheme,'** a dwarf canna hybrid sports dynamic hot pink flowers.

❀ **'Picasso'** is spectacular with yellow and orange spotted flowers on compact plants.

Dahlias

Dahlias are familiar favorites that are ideal in containers if you choose compact cultivars such as those in the following categories: border decorative, small decorative, anemone-flowering, mignon patio, window box, pompon, and dahlietta.

In spring, plant tuberous roots 3 to 5 inches deep, one per 10- to 12-inch pot, three per 14- to 16-inch pot.

Try these cultivars:

- ❀ **'Bluesette'** offers a border decorative with purple-pink 15-inch flowers.
- ❀ **'Kochelsee'** is a pompon dahlia with 2- to 3-inch ruby-red globe-like blossoms on 24- to 30-inch plants.
- ❀ **'Murillo'** is a mignon patio in dark and light pink with 20-inch plants that produce up to 40 flowers.
- ❀ **'Royal Betty'** is a dahlietta that grows to 8 inches and produces dozens of 3-inch pink flowers with a hint of blue.
- ❀ **'Royal Lenny'** — another dahlietta — reaches 8 inches; this cultivar offers bright white blossoms in great numbers.
- ❀ **'Stolze von Berlin'** is another pompon to 30 inches with soft pink flowers that make ideal cut flowers.
- ❀ **'Sneezy'** — here's another mignon patio dahlia — grows to 20 inches and produces pure white flowers with bright golden centers.

Ornamental onions

Ornamental onions really get the reviews when these sensational, tall plants send up their arresting globe-like flowers. Plants are adaptable but need large, deep containers because many bulbs need to be 6 inches deep. For the utmost drama, try giant allium *(Allium giganteum)*.

Rain lilies

Rain lilies *(Zephyranthes)* — also known as Mini-Amaryllis — is a wonderful late-summer bloomer with 2- to 3-inch pink flowers in amaryllis style with star-shaped flowers. Plants reach 5 to 6 inches tall.

Caladiums

Caladiums make striking additions with dramatic heart-shaped leaves in green, pink, rose, red, and white tones. These plants are well-suited to pots, which you can enjoy indoors or out. Imagine a few of these as a backdrop to radiant pink, white, or crimson begonias. Hmmm. You'd have quite a show.

It's About Choice

Bulbs in containers offer lots of choices. The great thing is that you can pot as many or as few as you want to, and enjoy both the anticipation and the actual act, when things begin growing.

Part V
Getting Down to the Nitty-Gritty

The 5th Wave   By Rich Tennant

If it's all the same to you, I'd just as soon you'd hand me my bulbs for planting.

In this part . . .

In this part, we get down in the dirt — so to speak. If you want to know how to buy bulbs, plant bulbs, nurture bulbs, and protect bulbs (from creepy critters and deadly diseases), turn to this part and start reading.

Chapter 20
Buying Bulbs

. . . .

In This Chapter

▶ How to recognize good bulbs from bad bulbs

▶ Where and when to buy bulbs

▶ How to store bulbs

▶ What bulb to plant when

. . . .

*A*lthough buying a bag of bulbs on impulse while you're waiting at the check-out lane is okay, we're usually happier with the results if we first think about which bulbs we want for different parts of our gardens. So step one in buying bulbs is to decide what you want (see Chapter 2).

Perhaps you select daffodils and want the large yellow ones that are sold as cut flowers in the spring. 'Dutch Master' is an excellent choice.

Where you purchase bulbs and when you plant them is just as important as what you plant. The best bulbs in the world can be disappointing if you don't handle them correctly and don't plant them in a timely manner.

How a bulb has been handled before you buy it affects how it performs. And how you care for bulbs after you take them home also affects their blooming performance.

With just a little attention on your part, buying, storing, and planting bulbs is easy. Bulbs are so much more forgiving than perennials with stringy roots.

Choosing Healthy Bulbs

Have you ever bought an onion at the grocery store? Good — you already have an idea of which bulbs are good and which ones are not.

A good, healthy bulb is plump and firm. Reject any bulbs that are soft and mushy, or shriveled up. And make sure that no moldy patches are growing on them.

If the bulb is supposed to have a tunic, make sure that the tunic is still on the bulb. Tulips that have been roughly handled, for example, easily lose their thin brown tunics. These bulbs dry out more quickly and bruise more easily than tulip bulbs that keep their tunics.

In Chapter 1 we talk about what's a true bulb, what's a corm, and what's a tuber. All corms and some true bulbs have a papery covering called a tunic. Other true bulbs, all tubers, and tuberous roots do not.

Size is relative when you're comparing different types of bulbs — for example, you'll never see a crocus's corm as big as a gladiolus's. But within a category, bigger is better. A large double-nose trumpet daffodil will have more flowers than a single nosed "round" of the same cultivar (see Chapter 5). It's something to consider if you have a choice of sizes.

Basically, you want to look for plump, clean, healthy bulbs, heavy for their size — which means that they haven't begun to dry up. Of course, this approach works only if you're buying bulbs from a local vendor. When you're buying through a catalog, you must rely on a reputable dealer to send you high-quality bulbs. We talk about where to buy bulbs in the next section.

Where to Buy Bulbs

It's pretty obvious — you need to acquire bulbs before you can plant them. And the most obvious way to acquire them is to buy them. You can purchase bulbs from a home improvement store, nursery, grocery store, garden center, or a mail-order catalog.

In addition, don't forget that, just like other plants, bulbs can be propagated — from seed, by division, or some other means — so you can grow your own. We discuss propagating bulbs in Chapter 21.

In this section, we discuss bulbs that you buy.

Buying from a store

In the fall, you can hardly avoid spring-flowering bulb displays in nurseries and garden centers. You often see huge yellow banners announcing "Holland Bulbs Are Here!" If you decide to buy your bulbs at a garden center or

Leftover bulbs are no bargain

Buying leftover spring-flowering bulbs in the middle of winter just because they're cheap is a waste of money. Generally, all that bargain bulbs have going for them is a cheap price. Go for quality instead. Digging a hole for poor bulbs takes just as much effort as digging a hole for good ones, and the results are discouraging. Buy the best bulbs because they produce the best display.

nursery, you'll have access to knowledgeable gardeners who can help answer your questions. Grocery stores, on the other hand, don't hire a staff with gardening expertise, so don't expect to receive any help. Home improvement centers may or may not have qualified staff people, depending on the individual store.

Some nurseries display their bulbs loose in bins, allowing you to carefully examine each bulb that you intend to buy. However, small children may mix bulbs up. Although you can easily spot a tulip that falls into a bin of daffodils, recognizing a white flowering tulip from one with red flowers is difficult in the bulb stage.

Your local grocery store offers packages and net bags of bulbs, as do home improvement chain stores. Prepackaged bulbs are not always available in the numbers that you need — a box may include 10 bulbs when you want 15. Examining packaged bulbs to make sure that they're in good shape can be difficult, even if they're packaged in a mesh bag rather than a box.

Don't buy bulbs from any display set up near a heat vent or in a sunny window where it gets hot. Keep bulbs cool (50 to 65 degrees Fahrenheit) and usually well ventilated before planting them.

Coming home with bags of bulbs gives us a powerful sense of anticipation. The plain brown wrappers give no inkling of the colorful flowers that are waiting for spring. Planting bulbs requires some work and a long wait before spring, but you have many dreams between now and then.

Buying from a catalog

You've probably been receiving bulb catalogs in your mailbox since summer. Some catalogs provide pictures, and some don't. Some promise fabulous displays from a preselected assortment of bulbs, others leave the choosing up to you.

A specialty nursery can offer a wider selection of particular bulbs by mail than local nurseries can afford to stock. But because you're buying the bulbs sight unseen, you'll have to trust the dealer to be reputable and send you quality bulbs. On the downside, some (but not all) mail-order sources require you to pay for bulbs at the time that you place the order. Appendix A lists specialty bulb suppliers.

A good bulb catalog gives you lots of useful information — more than just when a bulb flowers, its color, and its size. For example, The Daffodil Mart's catalog describes 'Dutch Master' as an early to midseason trumpet daffodil with large, showy, medium-yellow flowers, growing 18 to 20 inches tall, and useful for forcing (but you'd need a huge pot). This general information on trumpet daffodils tells you where they grow best, their general garden use, the number of bulbs to plant per square foot, and bulb size — you have your choice of bedding or landscape.

If prices in one catalog are significantly lower than in other catalogs or local sources, smaller bulb sizes may explain the difference. Undersized bulbs are less expensive, but their flowering display is correspondingly small. Also, be cautious about the truth of claims of fabulous displays that grow anywhere and everywhere. If the company's claim sounds too good to be true, it probably is.

When to Buy Bulbs

An obvious fact is that you can't buy bulbs until they're available. And availability has a lot to do with when bulbs flower and go dormant. You wouldn't expect to buy daffodil bulbs in June or dahlias in September — at that time, those bulbs are busy storing up nutrients before their resting season, so they can grow and flower again.

Spring-flowering bulbs

Nurseries get the bulk of their spring-flowering bulbs around Labor Day. Buy early, and buy everything you intend to get. If supplies of something popular sell out, the nursery may not replenish them. Judy remembers one year when an article in *Martha Stewart Living* caused a run on ornamental onions. (See Chapter 13 for more on ornamental onions.) The bulbs sold out quickly, and that was that until next year.

Catalogs come out *months* before planting time, allowing you the opportunity to buy early. If some bulbs are in limited supply, an early order reserves them for you.

Catalog orders are often shipped in rotation — early order, early shipping; later order, later shipping — so, specify a shipping date. Most if not all mail-order sources promise to ship "at the appropriate time." We should know when our orders are coming so we can schedule our planting time. Also, if some bulbs in the order should be planted earlier than others, those bulbs won't have to wait with the rest of the order in case of a later delivery.

Summer-flowering bulbs

How better to beat the winter blues than dream of summer and order bulbs to beautify your garden. Nurseries, home improvement stores, and super-markets often have their supplies of tender-to-frost summer blooming bulbs while it's still winter. You should start to see catalogs for summer bulbs in your mailbox soon after New Year's.

As with spring-flowering bulbs, buy dormant summer-blooming bulbs when you see them. If you go back later, they may be gone.

You can pot bulbs for summer interest a month or more early — before frost-free weather arrives — if you have the appropriate indoor space to grow them. Early planting gives you a jump start on the season.

After the weather becomes mild and settled, some tender bulbs may be available as potted growing plants — dahlias, cannas, and caladiums in particular. Although potted plants are more expensive, you can buy, plant, and enjoy all on the same day.

How to Store Bulbs

Buying bulbs, rushing home, and planting them all the same day is unusual. Generally you have some time in between buying and planting. We tell you about appropriate storage times for specific bulbs in their individual chapters; in this section, we provide some simple rules to guide you in knowing which bulbs can wait better than others.

For bulbs, staying underground is natural — they are geophytes. Although bulbs can tolerate the digging, shipping, and hanging around in stores, some tolerate the horticultural stresses better than others.

Spring-flowering bulbs

Ideally, you want to plant spring-flowering blooming bulbs as soon as possible. But when immediate planting isn't feasible, keep the bulbs in suspended animation.

Cool and on the dry side is the best environment for storing most spring-blooming bulbs. Putting bulbs in the freezer is a bad idea — the freezing temperature will turn them into mush. However, after a bulb's planted and rooted in the ground, it can survive freezing under those conditions. Heat is also bad because it can harm the embryo flower bud inside true bulbs, such as tulips. A cool garage or tool shed is okay. A refrigerator temperature of 38 to 42 degrees Fahrenheit is excellent.

If you have room to refrigerate your bulbs before planting them, keep them away from apples and other fruit. Apples give off ethylene gas, which damages the flower buds within the bulbs.

Store most spring-blooming bulbs in open trays or paper bags, but not plastic bags. Even though the bulbs are sleeping, they are metabolizing at a very low rate and producing a little moisture. If the moisture collects in a plastic bag, the bulbs can get moldy.

Spring-blooming bulbs that dry out really easily — dogtooth violets and guinea hen flowers, for example — store better if you pack them in wood shavings like you use in a guinea pig or hamster cage.

Summer-flowering bulbs

Because summer-flowering bulbs are warm-weather plants, you need to treat them a little differently than other bulbs. Comfortably cool room temperatures for the holding period are best. If the temperature is too warm, the bulbs may awaken into growth before it's time to plant them outdoors. If the temperature is too cold, the bulbs can be damaged.

Newly purchased dahlia tubers are sometimes coated with paraffin to keep them from shriveling up. If they aren't, pack them in dry peat moss or wood shavings. Holding dormant canna tubers in some packing material is also a good idea. Dormant gladiolus or peacock lily bulbs (they're really corms) are okay in a paper bag.

When to Plant Your Spring-Growing Bulbs

Climate has a role to play with fall-planted, spring-blooming bulbs. Wait to plant these bulbs until the soil begins to cool off a bit. After the bulbs are in the ground for a full cycle of growth, they adapt to the seasons. But the first year that you plant them, planting too early can upset their natural pattern. This is especially true for tulips — be sure that you wait until the soil cools down, otherwise tulips push up leaves right away and will freeze in the winter.

Deciding what to plant first

Fall-flowering bulbs — colchicums and fall crocuses, for example — move to the head of the autumn planting list simply because of their growth habits. They flower in autumn, and they're better off in the ground, with roots, when they do so.

Smaller spring-blooming bulbs tend to dry out more quickly than bigger bulbs. So, plant crocuses and snowdrops before hyacinths. And any bulb without a tunic dries out more quickly than something that has that protection. So guinea hen flowers and wood hyacinths, for example, get priority planting over tulips and daffodils.

Some bulbs just don't like to wait — snowdrops have a tunic but are better off with as short an interval out of the ground as you can provide. Fritillaries all lack tunics and have an urge to grow roots right away. Plant all fritillaries — the big crown imperials and Persian fritillaries just as much as the little guinea hen flower — ahead of other kinds of bulbs.

Tubers become really shriveled up in storage. Winter aconites and Grecian windflowers get double preference — they're both tubers and small. Table 20-1 gives a brief overview of planting order.

Table 20-1	Bulb Planting Order
Type of Bulb	*Bulb Name*
Fall-flowering bulbs	colchicums, fall crocuses, nerines
Tubers	winter aconites, Grecian windflowers
Tuber-corms	cyclamens
Little bulbs without tunics	guinea hen flowers
Little bulbs with tunics	crocuses and snowdrops
Fritillaries	Persians, crown imperials
Big bulbs without tunics	wood hyacinths
Big bulbs with tunics	tulips and daffodils

Rehydrating (plumping up the tubers with moisture) winter aconites and Grecian windflowers before planting is a good idea — just place them in a container of damp peat moss overnight.

Deciding when the time is right

Deciding when to plant spring-growing bulbs is really simple:

- ✔ If you live someplace that has very cold winters, you can plant everything in autumn (except tulips) as soon as you have the bulbs. (Wait until the soil begins to cool off to plant tulips.)

- ✔ If you live in an area that has mild winters, hold off on just about everything until the soil begins to cool off.

  Holding off also gives you time to precool tulips and daffodils in the refrigerator, if you didn't buy them already prepared.

Just remember to sequence your planting by the specific bulb's ability to wait, and store the bulbs in the most appropriate conditions.

When to Plant Your Summer-Growing Bulbs

In essence, timing the planting of your summer-growing bulbs is simple:

- ✔ If you live in a region with mild winters, you can plant summer-blooming bulbs when they're available in the stores, which is usually February. They'll remain in the ground year-round.

- ✔ If you live in an area with cold winters, wait until close to frost-free weather if you intend to plant directly in the ground.

  You can plant two weeks before the last frost in spring; the weather will be frost-free by the time the bulbs send leaves above ground. Basically, if the weather is safe to plant tomatoes, you can plant tender bulbs also.

Space and place permitting, you can pot dahlias and cannas a month or more ahead and then plant outdoors during active growth. Caladiums need a longer head start, about three months.

For hardy bulbs in autumn — plant the little bulbs first, ones without tunics ahead of those with protection, and a few odd-balls (such as autumn crocus, colchicum, and crown imperial) early because they insist on jumping the queue. For spring-planted summer-flowering bulbs, wait until the weather is mild and settled.

Chapter 21

Planting and Caring for Bulbs

. . . .

In This Chapter

▶ Deciding which bulbs to plant

▶ Digging deep enough

▶ Finding the upside of a bulb

▶ Fertilizing and amending the soil

▶ Managing after the bloom

▶ Storing tender bulbs in cold climates

▶ Fooling Mother Nature: hardy bulbs in mild climates

▶ Propagating: making more bulbs

. . . .

*Y*ou did it! You succumbed to those gorgeous, seductive, full-color pictures in catalogs and attached to boxes and bags at the store. You bought bulbs, and now what do you do? Plant them, and that's easy. How about having them come back next year, and the year after? For most bulbs, that's easy too.

This chapter provides the basics of bulb planting and bulb care and maintenance, which includes propagating — making more of what you have. We include specific planting instructions in each of this book's chapters that describe individual types of bulbs. In this chapter, you can find more detail on planting, discussion of the whys and wherefores of fertilization, and the growing cycle for various types of bulbs around the seasons.

Planning Your Planting

Life would be simple if only one kind of bulb were available. Here's a package of daffodils, so that's what you buy and plant.

But most of us go sort of crazy when faced with making a decision about which bulb(s) to buy. We tend to go overboard — get some of these, a few of those, several of the others . . . and before we know it, we have an assortment of round brown, white, or even blue objects of various sizes waiting to go into the ground.

How do you decide which bulbs go in first? The following sections contain guidelines for determining which bulbs to plant first, presented in the ideal order of planting.

Fall planting for spring-flowering bulbs

The decision about what to plant when is especially critical in autumn, when you're doing fall planting for spring blooms. The bulbs must get well rooted before winter arrives.

- **Plant autumn-flowering bulbs first.** Some bulbs planted in autumn also flower in autumn. That's right; you can find more about these bulbs — which are suitable for folks with short attention spans who appreciate instant gratification, and those of us who enjoy pushing the envelope of the gardening season — in Chapter 16.

  Clearly, any bulb that plans on flowering in September or October would be better off in the ground as promptly as possible. So if you purchase colchicums or fall-flowering crocuses (and I hope you do), they go to the head of the queue.

- **Give little bulbs priority over big ones.** While bulbs are waiting around above ground, they lose moisture that can only be replaced when the bulbs grow roots. Little bulbs have proportionally more surface to their volume than larger ones do, so they tend to dry out more quickly.

  Plant snowdrops first, then crocuses before hyacinths, and species tulips and daffodils that have small bulbs before their larger-sized hybrid relatives.

- **Plant bulbs without tunics ahead of tunicate bulbs.** Many bulbs — daffodils, tulips, hyacinths, and onions among them — have a papery covering called a tunic. Others — lilies, crown imperials, and wood hyacinths — do not have this protective skin.

  Plant any bulbs that lack a tunic ahead of those that have a tunic.

- **Plant tubers ahead of bulbs and corms.** Some bulbs aren't really bulbs. Botanists have all sorts of definitions for what's a bulb — lilies, daffodils, hyacinths; what's a corm — crocuses, glads; and what's a tuber — winter aconites, Grecian windflowers. We explain the details in Chapter 1. Tubers dry out more rapidly than bulbs and corms do, and they can desiccate (dry out) too much to ever grow again.

  To avoid drying out your tubers, give them a jump start by planting them first, ahead of bulbs and corms.

To summarize: Plant little ones before big ones, tubers ahead of bulbs and corms, those that lack a tunic ahead of those that have one, and any bulb that flowers in the fall ahead of those that wait for spring to bloom.

Spring planting equals summer-flowering bulbs

Not all bulbs are planted in autumn. You plant most summer-flowering bulbs in spring, in both cold winter and mild winter climates.

If you live in a region with cold winters, you must wait to plant tender summer bulbs such as dahlias, cannas, glads, caladiums, and so on until the weather is frost-free at night — tomato-planting time for you vegetable gardeners. Waiting for frost-free weather is especially important if the bulbs have already started to grow and have above-ground, leafy growth.

If the tender summer bulbs (see Chapter 14) are dormant, you can plant them approximately two weeks before tomato-planting time. By the time they send up leaves, the weather should be frost-free.

If you want to give these tender summer bulbs a head start, pot them four or more weeks ahead of your local frost-free date and start them growing indoors. (This is the time when we park our cars outside and fill the garage bays with pots of cannas and dahlias.)

Lilies, which are hardy bulbs often planted in spring, are the major exception to the "wait till it's warm" rule. Plant lilies as soon as you can find them in the stores. Lilies have fleshy bulbs, permanent roots, and no tunic — holding them out of the ground any longer than you must between purchase and planting will harm them. If you need to wait more than a few days but less than a week, keep the bulbs in barely damp peat moss in a cool place. Lilies will wait until the correct time to come up, and light frosts won't harm them.

Digging Holes: How Deep Is Deep Enough?

Before you dig, let us ask: What are you going to dig with? A trowel?

Trowels are fine for individual bulbs in good soil — that almost mythical "high organic, moist but well-drained loam" that books recommend. If you have ten crocuses or ten tulips and good soil, using a trowel may be okay. But if you have ten lilies, using a trowel is out of the question. A shovel moves more dirt than a trowel and requires less effort on your part.

If you prepare the entire planting area for that bag of daffodils, planting them will be a pleasure. But if you make individual spot holes, not only will planting be a chore, but the bulbs may not grow as well either. And if you have the sort of heavy clay soil laced with rocks that Judy does, a *mattock* — sort of like a pick, with one broad end and a pointy end on the digging head — works really well.

If you have lots of bulbs to plant in a wooded area, look for the naturalizer tool, which looks sort of like a pogo stick without a spring. This tool has a T-handle, a shaft, a bar to step on near the bottom, and the working part is a V-shaped, fish-tailed piece of tool steel. Jab it into the ground, step on the lower bar to stab it further into the ground, wiggle it back and forth a bit, and you've made a nice hole in which to drop a bulb.

Avoid the silly things called bulb planters that look like an open-ended tin can on a shaft. They make a one-size-fits-all hole, but bulbs come in a variety of sizes. Unless you have perfect soil, they're difficult to get deep enough into the dirt for larger bulbs; either the soil stays in the columnar part in one solid chunk, or it all falls back into the hole as soon as you've made it — before you get the bulb in place.

The general rule is to plant bulbs twice as deep as their height from top to bottom. Suppose that you have a big trumpet daffodil bulb, 2 inches from base to tip. Dig a 6-inch-deep hole and set the bulb; you should have 4 inches of dirt above the bulb. (The basic rule is 5 inches to base for small bulbs and 8 inches to base for large bulbs.)

Follow these tips for planting in special circumstances:

- ✔ If your soil is light and sandy, plant a little deeper — 7 inches to base for small, and 10 inches to base for large.

- ✔ If your soil is heavy, such as a clay-loam, plant more shallowly — 3 inches to base for small, and 6 inches to base for large.

- ✔ When you plant rhizomes, such as cannas (which have a thick, horizontally organized rhizome), set them only a couple of inches deep.

One very important rule: Make sure that you place, or plant, the bulbs so that they make good contact with the soil at the bottom of the hole. If the bulbs are casually dropped into place and an air pocket exists below the bulb, roots can dry out.

Although you shouldn't just chuck bulbs around and scratch a little dirt over them, you needn't get uptight about planting correctly either. Bulbs move in the soil — they have to. If they didn't move around, how could bulb seeds fall to the ground and the growing plants eventually have their bulb end up below ground? Many bulbs have contractile roots that can pull the bulb deeper if needed. Bulbs are really rather smart that way.

Knowing Which Way Is Up

Planting bulbs right side up the first time gives your bulbs their best chance for healthy, hearty growth. Recognizing the upsides of bulbs and corms is easiest, because they have a vertical orientation (a definite up and down). If you look at them carefully, you see a flattened portion, called a *basal plate,* at the bottom. This is where roots emerge. When you plant, orient bulbs and corms so the basal plate is at the bottom of the hole (see Figure 21-1).

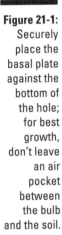

Figure 21-1: Securely place the basal plate against the bottom of the hole; for best growth, don't leave an air pocket between the bulb and the soil.

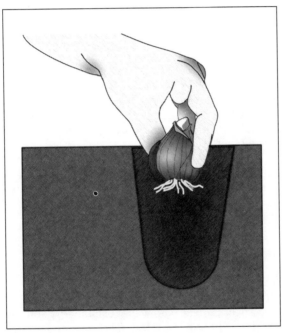

Some bulbs — such as lilies, crown imperials, naked ladies, and guinea hen flowers — have roots still attached to the basal plate when you buy them so you can't miss knowing which end is up. Guinea hen flowers have dried-up, wiry roots, but the others still have fleshy, functional roots that must be handled carefully when planting.

The tuber is the problem child. Tubers are dried-up, wizened, stick-like things, and even careful scrutiny may not be enough to reveal the top from the bottom. When in doubt, plant them sideways and let the plants figure it out.

Cannas have fleshy rhizomes. New growth is revealed as pointed, ivory-colored shoots. These shoots go up. If any roots are still attached, try and get them down. But the shoot growth orientation is more important.

Bulbs are so obliging. Even if you plant them upside down, they send their shoots up and their roots down. Sending up their shoots takes longer, and wastes some energy, but they manage. Eventually, the bulbs even reorient themselves in the ground. How about that!

Preparing the Soil: Fertilizing and Amending

Fertilizers provide food for plants, and soil amendments provide the roughage in their diets. Soil amendments — such as compost, leaf mold, and commercial dried manure, all of which may be available in bags at garden centers, supermarkets, and home improvement stores — are also very necessary for healthy plant growth.

Although bulbs store food very efficiently, you need to give them a good start at planting time for best results. After all, planting time is your only opportunity to get fertilizer down below the bulb. You need healthy soil in order for the bulbs to make use of available food.

Fertilizing the soil

Bulbs need some *nitrogen* in the soil for leaf growth. They also need *phosphorus* and *potash* for overall health, disease resistance, good root growth, and improved flowering. You find the relative proportions of these nutrients listed as the N-P-K ratios on the side of the fertilizer bag or bottle.

Fertilizers may be *inorganic* (chemically treated or laboratory created), or they may be *organic* (occurring from natural or once-living sources). Plants don't care, but gardeners have mixed opinions. Do remember that inorganic fertilizers tend to be more quickly available to plants, and, as chemical salts, they can burn roots, basal plate, or leaves if they come in direct contact. Organic fertilizers are generally richer in trace elements.

Don't over-do the fertilizing. If the label recommends 1 cupful per 100 square feet, don't increase the application: Adding more doesn't help; it harms.

Contrary to what some may think, modern-day bonemeal is *not* a good, complete fertilizer. Bonemeal used to be good back when bones were ground up fresh and had all sorts of little meat scraps and marrow attached. Now bones are steamed, cleaned, and then ground up, so the nutritive value is less. Additionally, gardeners in suburban and rural areas quickly learn that skunks dig up the bulbs, looking for the bones they think are there. They don't eat the bulbs, but you must make the additional effort of replanting the same bulb several times.

Amending the soil

Organic matter is useful for improving both low fertility, poor-water-holding sandy soils and generally fertile, poorly draining clay soils. The organic matter in the soil is used up and needs to be replenished regularly (every year) in a process known as *soil amendment*. It is easier to amend the soil when you are first preparing the area for planting. Dig the soil, layer on about 2 inches of organic matter, and then dig again, mixing the organic matter thoroughly with the existing soil.

In subsequent years, rather than amending the soil, apply organic matter as a mulch, cultivating it lightly into the surface layer of the planting area. If you notice poor growth and reduced flowering in later years, you need to reapply the soil amendments.

Applying fertilizer at planting time

Fertilizers come in either granular or liquid form. Granular fertilizers, comprised of tiny particles that don't dissolve quickly in water, remain in the soil longer than do liquid fertilizers — longer is better.

To apply fertilizer, first mix granular fertilizers, organic or inorganic, with the soil at the bottom of the planting holes. It's a good idea, especially with inorganic fertilizers, to add a thin layer of unamended soil (this is normal, ordinary soil — fresh from the ground, without any additives) to avoid any possibility of direct contact between the basal plate and fertilizer particles.

In subsequent years, when necessary because flowering is decreasing (not because bulbs are overcrowded), we fertilize spring-flowering, summer-dormant bulbs with a liquid fertilizer. This process provides a readily available, but short duration, source of nutrients. We use a fertilizer that's higher in phosphorus and potash, lower in nitrogen, and we apply it at half-strength when the bulb leaves are well out of the ground. We fertilize a second time after the bulbs have finished flowering. If we have the time, we give a third feeding, still at half-strength, two weeks after the second feeding. Just slosh it on with a watering can. Liquid fertilizers are absorbed through a plant's leaves as well as being taken up by their roots.

Half-strength is easy to figure out: Simply double the water *or* halve the amount of crystals. If the label suggests one tablespoon to a gallon of water, *either* use one tablespoon to two gallons of water *or* use one-half tablespoon to one gallon of water.

Fertilize summer flowering bulbs just as you would any other perennial in the summer garden. *Perennials For Dummies* by Marcia Tatroe and the Editors of the National Gardening Association (published by IDG Books Worldwide, Inc.) is a good resource if you need more information on perennial fertilization.

Some people find that it works best to fertilize monthly until the bulbs flower; then stop fertilizing.

Remember: Fertilizers are only available to plants when water is available to transport nutrients from the soil to the roots. If rainfall is lacking, you must water the bulbs as soon as they are planted. If the weather is dry, supplement rainfall during the growing season, too.

Keeping the Bloom in the Bulb

Bulbs usually flower well the first season after they've been planted. Getting them to come back year after year (perennialization) can be more challenging.

In Holland, the growers cut off the bulb flowers as soon as they're certain the bulbs are true to name (meaning that the flower has not mutated in some form or the wrong bulb got planted) and have been inspected for carry-over diseases. They want the energy to go into the bulb, not into flower or seed production. We gardeners want the flower show, however, so we're not that conservative. But unless you want bulb seeds for some reason, it's more efficient to cut off (or *deadhead*) the flowers as they fade (see Figure 21-2).

Make sure that you're removing the little green swelling behind the withering flower — that's where the seeds will form.

Be reasonable, however. Cutting off dead blooms makes sense for tulips, hyacinths, daffodils, lilies, and such, but you'd go nuts trying to deadhead crocus and snowdrops!

Figure 21-2:
Deadhead
the flowers
to avoid
having your
plants go
to seed.

When you cut lilies for bouquets, take as short a stem as is practical. The more leaves you remove, the less "factory" remains to manufacture food for the bulb to store for next year's display. That's why good gardeners keep bulb leaves green and growing as long as possible — the longer the leaves are greener, the more food the bulbs will store. And for the same reason, savvy gardeners do not fold, braid, bundle, or rubber-band bulb leaves — it's a poor technique if you want to grow good bulbs in subsequent years.

Storing in Winter: Tender Bulbs in Cold Climates

By providing tender bulbs with a winter vacation, you can easily carry them over from year to year.

Tender bulbs such as cannas and dahlias can only survive light frosts that don't last for weeks on end. Even so, the first time the temperature dips much below 30 degrees Fahrenheit, dahlia and canna leaves turn to black mush. That's your signal to take the following steps:

1. **Carefully dig the bulbs out of the garden.**

2. **Gently shake off loose dirt and clip back the mushy leaves.**

3. **For the next few days, leave the roots out in a dry area.**

    If you have a child's coaster wagon and a limited number of tender bulbs, you can easily wheel the bulbs in and out of the garage or garden shed as weather dictates.

4. **Shake off any additional crumbly dry dirt that comes off easily.**

5. **Pack the roots in a cardboard box lined with a perforated plastic bag and fill with dry peat moss, wood shavings, buckwheat hulls, vermiculite, or any other similar material.**

   Make sure that individual root clumps do not touch — keep them separated with packing material. That way, if one clump does start to rot, the rot won't spread to all the stored plants.

6. **Punch a few holes in the plastic so excess moisture can escape, but not so many holes that the stored roots will dry up.**

   Keep the box(es) in a cool, dry, place, for example, use the back wall of an attached, unheated garage, the one adjoining the house.

Check every couple of months to see that the material is not wet and that the roots are not shriveling from dryness. Along about early to mid-March or April, depending on your location, you can unpack the tubers and rhizomes to pot them up. (Sometimes they will have already begun to grow, sort of insisting that you pot them or lose them.) Otherwise, wait until two weeks before your frost-free date to plant dormant cannas and dahlias in the garden.

Gladiolus and related corms are handled differently. We give specific directions in Chapter 14.

Fooling Mother Nature: Hardy Bulbs in Mild Climates

We always want what we can't have. Just as cold-climate gardeners manipulate dahlias and cannas to keep them from year to year, mild-climate gardeners need to finesse daffodils and tulips that insist on having a winter in order to flower.

Hardy bulbs require several consecutive cold weeks (chilling) in order to send the correct signals to wake up the flower bud inside the bulb.

You could grow those cultivars of daffodils and tulips that are less demanding — tazetta and jonquilla daffodils (which we describe in Chapter 5), and *Tulipa clusiana* (which we describe in Chapter 6), are best suited for mild winter climates.

To have spring flowers in the winter house, use the same technique as when you pot these bulbs and chill them. See Chapter 19 for more about container planting.

Vendors in mild-winter regions sell *precooled bulbs*. While still dormant, these bulbs have been carefully held at low temperatures to fool them into thinking winter has come and gone. When you plant (using the same planting techniques you'd use anywhere), the bulbs will grow and bloom as though they had gone through the winter. The trick is what happens next:

 ✔ After the bulbs go dormant, it is up to you to dig and hold these bulbs through summer and then refrigerate for a couple of months before planting.

 ✔ Remember to keep stored, refrigerated bulbs away from fruit such as apples. The ethylene gas that the fruit gives off damages the flower bud within the bulb.

This process is a little trickier than storing tender bulbs in cold climates. You may want to handle these bulbs as annuals, discarding them after they flower and planting new bulbs each year.

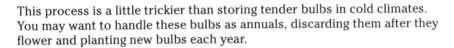

Making More of What You Have: Propagation

Buying bulbs is a sure way to get more bulbs. But conveniently, many bulbs make more of themselves, providing an easy, less expensive way to have more bulbs.

Growing by offsets

Daffodils are an example of bulbs that are excellent at multiplying themselves. The bulb you originally planted makes some *offsets* (daughter bulbs) at the edge of the basal plate. The original mother bulb nourishes them as they grow.

In due time (and it only takes a couple of years), the daughter bulbs become large enough to flower themselves. Then they start making daughter bulbs of their own. Eventually, the clump of bulbs becomes so crowded that heavy competition for nutrients can cause flowering to decline. At that point — or even sooner — you need to step in with a shovel and separate the bulbs.

The best time to separate bulbs is after the flower blooms have faded, but while the leaves are still green and growing vigorously.

It is much easier to find bulbs that still have leaves attached than search for leafless bulbs lurking incognito beneath the soil.

Offsets are actively growing plants and thus need different handling than do dormant bulbs in autumn; dig and divide a clump at a time to reduce the risk of roots drying out, and then follow these steps:

1. **If some bulbs are going into a new location, prepare the soil first.**

   Add organic matter — compost, leaf mold, or dry manure — and granular fertilizer. Have the same materials available to rejuvenate the original location.

2. **Dig the bulbs, one clump at a time.**

   Judy once dug two clumps of overcrowded daffodils and got about 50 bulbs from each clump. Dig only what you can handle at one go. Dividing snowdrops goes more rapidly than dividing daffodils.

3. **Have some wet burlap or wet newspaper to cover the bulbs as you work, and quickly but carefully separate the bulbs.**

   Just take a group and gently twist and rock the bulbs back and forth until they separate.

4. **Replant as many as you want at the appropriate depth.**

   You can choose to replant each and every division, down to the smallest, or only those big enough to flower in a year. It's your decision.

5. **Water regularly.**

   Watering is important because you want the roots to re-establish quickly and nourish the leaves, enabling the bulbs to store more food and flower sooner.

6. **Mulch.**

   Add a layer of shredded leaves or pine bark mulch to shade the soil, keep it cooler, and hold moisture better than if you do not mulch.

After you finish one clump, do another one. And another. And another, as long as your energy holds and you have overcrowded bulbs to divide.

Unlike daffodils that make offsets, glads make little *cormels,* or baby corms. After you dig at the end of the growing season and find these cormels, store them separately from the large, flowering-size corms. Before replanting the next spring, soak the cormels in lukewarm water for a couple of hours — they have a very hard tunic, and they can root more easily if the tunic is first softened by soaking. The new glads will probably flower the second year.

Reseeding

Offsets aren't the only means of propagation. A number of bulbs will reseed on their own, especially little ones such as scilla, chionodoxa, crocus, and winter aconite. Seedlings of the first three look like grass blades, and young winter aconites look like miniatures of the mature plants.

Disturbing these immature seedlings their first year is risky — the nascent bulb is so tiny that it is easily damaged. Wait until the plants are a couple of years old and then dig and move them *in the green,* as the English phrase it — while they are still green and growing.

Keeping Bulbs Growing

The process of growing bulbs is really very easy — bulbs are easy to plant and easy to care for. Pay a little attention to detail, and you'll be rewarded with the continuing pleasure of their blooms year after year.

Even when you don't see bulbs growing above ground, you can't assume that they're totally at rest. The spring blooming bulbs make autumn roots to help them get through winter. So when you plant tulips, daffodils, hyacinths, crocuses, and snowdrops, it is important to give them ample water at that time. This careful watering encourages healthy root growth and gets the plants off to a good start.

Remember, after bulbs have flowered, there's still work for bulbs to do as they prepare for the next year. Bulbs need their leaves to produce food to store as reserves in their underground structures. Chopping the leaves away right after the flowers fade is a lousy gardening technique. It halts food production right then and there, when the bulb is at its most depleted stage. Particularly common with daffodils (whose long strap-like leaves are more obvious than the small grassy leaves of crocuses), gardeners bent on "tidying up" cut, fold, or twist the leaves into haystack bundles. Such neatnik techniques actually harm the bulbs. Keep the leaves growing as long as they're green and healthy looking. Don't remove them until they begin to yellow.

Don't forget to feed your bulbs, especially those that grow when conditions are tougher. Bulbs that grow early in spring when the soil is cool and nutrients less available need a ready source of fertilizer. Liquid feeding that can be watered on the leaves as well as the ground is highly suitable for spring.

Consider taking a photograph of your garden so you know where the flowers are, and for later years' appreciation. Compare your gardens from year to year and marvel in nature's diversity. Above all, take time to appreciate your bulbs. Remember, the reason to grow bulbs is to enjoy them — from the cold-climate gardener's first snowdrops and winter aconites to spring's tulips and daffodils and summer's ornamental onions and lilies. Glads and cannas, dahlias and caladiums, even crocosmias enhance the summer garden nearly everywhere. And mild-climate gardeners have the luxury of exotic bulbs such as naked ladies, Peruvian daffodils, and amaryllises.

One thing's for sure: Wherever you garden, you can have a variety of wonderful bulbs to grow and enjoy.

Chapter 22

Minimizing Pests and Diseases

. . . .

In This Chapter

▶ Avoiding bulb diseases and pests: a pound of prevention

▶ Choosing your weapons against bugs: organic controls, beneficial insects, or chemicals

▶ Picking on pests

▶ Dealing with diseases

. . . .

*O*kay. There's great news, good news and, well, instead of calling it bad news let's call it *other* news — we cover that one last. The great news is that flower bulbs are tough plants and often provide years of outstanding garden service with truly a minimum of trouble from pests and diseases. The good news is that even if you do run into little problems, they're usually handled easily with a variety of methods. That *other* news is that the garden, being a garden, will sooner or later run into some sort of difficulty. So in this chapter, we give you some hints and tips for avoiding problems to begin with and ending them after they pop up.

All right. Here's what you can expect:

✔ **Pests:** You may deal with everything from the lowly snail or slug to formidable foes such as deer and raccoons. And of course, there's an in-between category that includes voles, mice, squirrels, and chipmunks.

✔ **Bugs:** You may find that bugs are a bother, too, when they burrow into your favorite bulbs, or eat the tender shoots emerging in spring, or munch on prized flowers. We look at how to battle such creatures as beetles, aphids, mites, thrips, and others (see the section, "Choose Your Weapon against Bugs").

✔ **Diseases:** Fortunately, few threaten bulbs. But just in case, we give you the lowdown on dealing with powdery mildew, botrytis, gray mold, and such lovely conditions as rots, viruses, and fungi — all of which sound worse than they actually are in most cases (see the section, "Down with Diseases").

Prevention: Your Best Medicine against Pests and Diseases

Before we get to the nitty-gritty of diagnosing and solving disease and pest problems, we take a look at how to *avoid* the trouble to begin with. Some of the following are specific tips about bulbs, and others you'll recognize as good gardening practices that benefit all the plants you grow:

- Start with high-quality, healthy bulbs. Inspect them carefully and choose firm, plump ones. Avoid those showing any signs of molds, soft rots, or insect damage. Plant bulbs as soon as possible and at the proper time.

- Store your bulbs properly. This can be an airy, dry, cool place; a warm dry one; or a cool moist one.

- Give bulbs the conditions they need: the proper drainage, soil, light, air circulation, and nutrition. Match the right bulb with the right conditions. Yes, this advice does mean that you must do your homework.

  Remember: The stronger your plants, the better their chances of fending off attacks from pests and diseases on their own.

- Water carefully to avoid wetting the leaves. Wet leaves may lead to mildew and other problems. Water early in the day or use a device such as a drip hose to wet the soil and not the foliage.

- Keep your garden ship-shape. A clean environment discourages pests and diseases. Remove dead leaves, faded flowers, and general debris, and you remove the potential for trouble.

- Be a detective. (The experts call this *scouting.*) By keeping an eye on your garden, you can spot and correct problems early, before they get bad. Look the leaves over — on both sides. Check stems and flowers, too. A bug here or there, a few chewed leaves, a faded flower or two are not worrisome, but if you see major discoloration, masses of insects, or deformed buds, you need to take action right away.

Choose Your Weapon against Bugs

Safety is a priority and maintaining ecological balance is a worthy goal, so pest prevention and nontoxic controls are your best bet. Sometimes, however, you may elect to protect your investments with chemical means. Use these methods as a last resort — sparingly, prudently, and carefully.

The good guys — bugs we like

Lots of garden critters that hang around are *just* the kind of guests we want to encourage because they actually prey upon the bad bugs (such as aphids) that harm plants. In a garden with a variety of plants and no pesticides, you can find some good bugs and some bad in a natural balance. If the bad guys get a bit out of hand, you can bring in these reinforcements:

- **Green lacewings:** Sounds like a dance troupe, we know, but actually these bugs in larval form and later as winged creatures eat up critters such as aphids, mites, and thrips.

- **Lady beetles or lady bugs:** These familiar red-and-black bugs feed on aphids, mites, and thrips (see the section, "Send Pests Packing," for details on these characters). You can buy mesh bags with hundreds of lady beetles and release them with the hope that they stick around. However, they are winged creatures.

- **Parasitic nematodes:** This term may bring to mind prehistoric monsters, but really they're microscopic worms that handle some soil pests, burrowing insects, and grubs.

- **Praying mantises:** These are the giants of the good bug army, and they'll do serious damage to aphids, caterpillars, leaf hoppers, and the like. You can buy a cocoon-like sack with praying mantis eggs inside, but you have no guarantee that the mantises will remain in your garden. And not all the baby mantises will survive; they are prey for larger insects and even each other. (**Note:** Watching them emerge is fun.)

The next step in bug control: Organics

If problems persist after prevention and signing on the good bug infantry, your next step is safe, organic, biodegradable controls. These methods include botanical insecticides (made from plants themselves), insecticidal soaps, and certain natural bacteria that are harmful only to the larvae of certain bugs:

- Try the Safer or Ringer product lines. These are sprays and soaps that handle a number of problems — including caterpillars, fungi, aphids, and mites — while remaining relatively safe for other garden creatures. Follow labels and warnings completely.

- Botanical insecticides derived from plants include:

  - **Neem:** Made from neem tree oil, and kills aphids, thrips, and whitefly, but repels Japanese beetles.

  - **Pyrethrins:** Made from a chrysanthemum and kills a wide range of insects, including some good ones, so use these with great caution.

  - **Rotenone:** Comes from legume roots and kills lots of creatures besides pests, including bees and other beneficial insects — so this should be one of your last resorts for big-time bug control.

A last ditch effort: Chemicals

If none of the previous methods work, your last line of defense is synthetic or chemical controls in the form of insecticides and fungicides. These kill fastest and have the most impact on the ecological balance in the garden. In all likelihood, you won't even need them. But if you do, follow the advice of a professional nursery staff person or agricultural extension agent to help you identify the problem and select the treatment. Follow instructions and safety precautions on product labels *exactly*.

Send Pests Packing

In this creature feature, we look at some specific common pests and what to do about them. This list includes insects, rodents, and other animals.

Irritating insects

Here are some insects that may do their dirty work on bulbs:

- **Aphids:** These tiny sucking pests hang out on tender new shoots, leaves, or flower buds. They can be black, green, or even purple, and they like lots of bulbs including crocuses, dahlias, tulips, daffodils, and glads. To control: Use ladybugs, insecticidal soap, or simply knock them off with a spray from the hose.

- **Beetles:** The Japanese variety and others seriously chew stems, leaves, and flowers. And the larvae in the soil can eat roots. To control: Physically pick them off and, well, do what you have to do. Or use neem, insecticidal soap, or pyrethrins.

- **Mites:** These microscopic dudes make web-like hideouts on leaf undersides and suck plant juices. They like crocus, cyclamen, begonia, hyacinth, lily, and freesia, among other bulbs. To control: Gently spray them away with the hose; hit them with insecticidal soap, or use a solution of soapy water made from 2 tablespoons dishwashing soap to a gallon of water.

- **Narcissus fly larvae:** These also have the delightful name of bulb maggots, and they bore in and eat bulb centers producing soft, mushy bulbs that do not grow well if at all. They go for daffodils, amaryllis, rain lily and others. Prevent problems by choosing firm, healthy bulbs. To control: Discard any infected bulbs.

✔ **Snails and slugs:** They leave their familiar trails and eat up soft tissue. To control: Hand pick (okay, wear gloves) at night or on gray, rainy mornings; set out saucers of beer; or go for poisonous baits — but use these with caution, especially around pets and children.

✔ **Thrips:** These nearly invisible sucking insects cause silvery streaks as they draw out plant juices. They may hit daffodils, lilies, irises, glads, and others. To control: Dust plants with Rotenone or tobacco dust.

Annoying animals

Tasty treats that they are, your favorite bulbs may turn otherwise law-abiding animals into serious criminals. Beware the mice, rabbits, voles, woodchucks, and deer that unearth and munch bulbs or crunch foliage and flowers. You need not stand idly by. Here's a tactic or two to try:

✔ Try planting poisonous bulbs such as daffodils, fritillarias, snowflakes, snowdrops, or colchicums. Not only will they be left alone, they may protect neighboring bulbs, too.

✔ To stop deer from eating bulbs, some people successfully use smelly stuff to repel them — placing bars of deodorant soap (but not cocoa-based soap) around the garden, or sprinkling baby powder. Commercial deer repellent sprays are available. You can try scare tactics — dogs, if contained, can bark them away, although neighbors may not appreciate the noise. Other methods include, of course, fencing them out with 8-foot deer fences, solid fences, or electric fences. Remember that deer don't seem to go in for calla lilies, daffodils, and irises.

✔ Rodents — including rats, mice, gophers, and voles — can be thwarted nicely by vigilant dogs and cats (although smaller breeds are easier on beds and borders). Some people go for traps, baits, or electronic controls, but you have to consider how much the method will cost (in dollars, trouble, and toxins) to win the war.

You can stop these irritating and often hungry creatures by planting your bulbs in a wire mesh cage (see Chapter 16). Line the planting hole (for a group of bulbs) with chicken wire. To hinder mice, use hardware cloth over the bed and remove it when shoots poke out of the ground.

✔ Woodchucks can be real bulb destroyers and are sometimes hard to combat. Try removing their favorite covers (weeds, woodpiles, and grass); planting a patch of clover or alfalfa to lure them away from the garden; or using repellent plants such as alliums, onions, or garlic. A 3- to 4-foot wire fence may do the trick, but don't secure it near the top (so that it's too flimsy for them to scale) and bury it 18 inches to stop burrowing. Employing the services of a dog may help keep these guys away, too.

The bonemeal blues

No doubt you've heard, at least at some point, that bonemeal and bulbs go together. Mix it in the planting hole and all that. Well, although it *is* a good organic fertilizer, it seems to be an even more valued appetizer by everything from the family dog to the resident raccoon or skunk. And these animals are serious. They'll definitely go digging if they smell this pungent treat. People have been known to find scores of bulbs unearthed and bitten into the very night after planting because bonemeal in each planting hole was too tempting for four-legged fiends. You have options. Try mixing a superphosphate or bulb booster fertilizer into the soil instead of bonemeal.

Down with Diseases

Your bulb-disease problems should be few because many bulbs seem to be naturally resistant to disease. But because we don't yet live in a perfect world, here's some help just in case:

- **Bulb rot:** Is just what it sounds like — mushy, soft bulbs that barely grow. The origin may be fungal or bacterial. To control: Choose healthy bulbs to start with and grow in well-drained soil, dust bulbs with a fungicide before planting, and use good storage practices.

- **Botrytis, also known as gray mold:** Shows up as brown spots on leaves and may turn black and finally gray. It's a fungus blight that thrives in warm, humid weather. To prevent this disease, space bulbs appropriately to avoid overcrowding and poor air circulation; water early in the day. To control: Remove infected leaves and destroy dead foliage, dig up and discard severely diseased bulbs, or as a last resort, spray with a fungicide.

- **Powdery mildew:** Is a wonderfully descriptive name that tells you what to look for: white or gray powdery areas on the leaves. This one can spread rapidly, so clean up and remove affected leaves, stems, and flowers on sight. Watering from below helps, too. To control badly damaged areas: Spray or dust with a fungicide.

- **Viruses:** Are toughies and show up as deformed, streaked, yellowed leaves or as streaked or blotched flowers. The bad news: No cure is available. Remove infected plants quickly before others are contaminated. Control aphids and other sucking insects, because they can spread various viruses. Prevent the problem by selecting good bulbs and growing healthy plants.

So there you have it. You'll most likely find that bulbs are hardy little soldiers that stand up well to problems. And if you do run into trouble, try these common-sense methods of reasonable control, which, when combined with good gardening habits, should get you back on the right track.

Part VI
The Part of Tens

The 5th Wave   By Rich Tennant

@RICHTENNANT

"Aside from a little beginner's confusion,
I've done very well with my bulbs."

In this part . . .

The bills need to be paid. The garden needs to be weeded. The dishes need to be washed. There just isn't enough time in the day. We understand, and in this part we give you short-and-sweet lists of ten suggestions — the ten best bulbs for forcing and cut flowers, the ten most fragrant bulbs, and ten heirloom bulbs (your great-great-great-great grandmother may have grown these).

Chapter 23

Ten Best Bulbs for Cut Flowers

In This Chapter

▶ Tips for cutting and keeping bouquets

▶ The best bulbs for cut-flower arrangements

*B*ulbs give us some of the most familiar — and reasonably priced — fresh cut flowers. Bulbs give us some of the most beautiful — and expensive — fresh cut flowers. And bulbs give us some of the longest lasting fresh cut flowers. Which statement is true? All of the above. From the first bunch of daffodils at the supermarket to the costly lilies priced per stem at an up-market boutique, bulbs are a "best buy" in the cut-flower trade. They're easy to grow, they ship well, and they last a long time in a vase. What more could you ask for? Well . . . maybe some types could be a little more reasonably priced. The principle is the same with bulbs as with houses: We call it "sweat equity." You provide some labor, and you can enjoy the final product at a lower cost than if someone else does all the work for you. If you grow the plants yourself, you can significantly reduce the expense of enjoying fresh cut flowers.

Ten Best Bulbs for Cut-Flower Bouquets

The following sections describe the ten best bulbs for creating beautiful, long-lasting, cut-flower bouquets.

Daffodils

Daffodils are probably one of the best bulbs for cut-flower use. The bulbs are relatively cheap. With a modicum of care, bulbs in the garden will flower year after year. Once cut, flowers open from bud ("Goose-Neck" stage) to bloom, and last for a reasonable period. Daffodils are best cut when the buds are very full and just showing some color. They continue to open indoors, lasting longer than flowers cut when they are already fully open. Not only are daffodils easy to grow, but you can bring them along into extra-early bloom.

One way to have daffodils to cut is just to go into the garden and pluck some posies from those already growing there. Take as long a stem with the flowers as you want, but leave the leaves. Even better than cutting flowers out of the garden is to have a cutting garden. Plan ahead and plant some bulbs in an out-of-the-way corner where you can cut flowers to your heart's content without weakening the garden display. See Chapter 3 for more about cutting gardens.

If you want flowers earlier than they'd bloom outdoors, daffodils will oblige. The majority of daffodils need a location with a temperature of about 40 degrees Fahrenheit for 14 to 16 weeks, and then they need somewhere cool but sunny for another 2 to 4 weeks or so to bring them along into bloom. This process can be complicated if you want more than a pot-full of flowers. See Chapter 24 for more details about forcing.

Paperwhites are a type of daffodil that are very easy to bring into early bloom. Basically, you just add water and wait. They need no chilling period, and they flower in six weeks or less from the time you plant the bulbs. Because they're not cold-winter hardy, you'll have no qualms about throwing them away after you cut the flowers. They're so depleted by forcing in water that they're no good for planting, even in mild-winter areas.

Remember: Cut daffodils give off a slimy substance from their stems. It blocks tulip stems, and they can't absorb water. So don't mix tulips and daffodils in the same vase.

Pussy willow branches are a traditional accompaniment to daffodils. Forsythia or branches of star magnolia are also nice.

Tulips

Tulips are great, what else can we say — a rainbow of colors and everything from a simple goblet shape of triumph hybrid tulips to the flora-dora snipped edges and flamboyant show of parrot tulips.

Remember: Cut tulips when they are in the tight, but well-colored (50 percent) bud stage. If you cut them when they are green, they won't open because it's too early. If you wait until the flowers have been open for a few days, they fall apart.

Tulips keep growing, even after they are cut. So don't be surprised if the stems elongate in the vase. Try and arrange them so that this continued growth won't upset the bouquet's appearance.

Tulips tend to nod their heads. You can reduce this tendency if you properly condition the flowers first. Follow these steps for success:

1. **If the flowers are not freshly cut, recut the bottom of the stems.**

2. **Fold sheets of newspaper or heavy tissue paper in half, and roll the flowers together in the paper.**

   Don't roll the flower heads one-by-one; roll the whole bunch, up to ten, together at once.

Hyacinths

Hyacinths are super as cut flowers, adding fragrance to their beautiful display. Their major flaw is a tendency to droop, even when freshly cut and kept cool in a clean vase with ample water. To prevent this problem, use a length of florists wire (available at craft shops) and insert it just below the tip of the flower stalk, through the hollow center, and out the bottom. Cut to length *after* you've tucked the wire into the stem. This technique not only stiffens the stem, but makes inserting the stem into floral foam easier.

Displaying hyacinths with the full bulb showing is currently in vogue. Pull 'em right from the ground, wash away the soil, and steady them in a clear glass vase to let it all hang out, roots and all. This presentation has a certain fascination, but remember, if you do display the full bulb, you can't replant and reuse it the next year.

Snowdrops

Small is beautiful. Snowdrops may be tiny but they really pack a punch as a nosegay. There is something so dainty and appealing about their fresh white flowers. Perhaps the appeal is that they bloom early, before other bulbs are flowering. Here are some tips for displaying snowdrops:

- ✔ Small flowers need an appropriate container. Choose something graceful for a nosegay that you'll enjoy close up on a desk.

- ✔ A mirror placed under a vase reflects the flowers, increasing their appeal.

- ✔ The delicate yellow flowers of witchhazel are open when the snowdrops are in bloom, and a small spray clipped from a shrub combines nicely with the dainty white flowers.

Lilies

Lilies are elegant as cut flowers — and usually at a regal price. Even just a couple of stems of lilies in a mixed bouquet creates a rich effect.

The following are some tips for using lilies in cut-flower arrangements:

✔ Some lilies are incredibly fragrant, so strongly perfumed that some folks find their scent overwhelming at close quarters. If that's true for you, choose Asiatic hybrid lilies for cut-flower use; they have no fragrance to speak of.

✔ Cutting lilies with long stems makes a great display but weakens the bulb for next year's flowers. Leave at least 50 percent of the leaves (more is better) still attached to stem and bulb.

✔ However long the stem, *always* strip off all the leaves that will be under water in the vase.

✔ Lily pollen has *incredible* staining power — clothes, table linens, and even skin. It won't wash off. The yellow or brown dust-like pollen is carried on six *anthers* inside the flower (those stalks that poke up from the center). Some folks use tweezers to remove the anthers before arranging lilies. Others think that removing the anthers is like "shaving off your eyebrows!" The choice is up to you.

Ornamental onions

Cut 'em now or cut 'em later; ornamental onions can be used as fresh or dried flowers. No tears either, because they have no onion odor.

Cut fresh flower-heads as the individual flowers in the cluster are beginning to open. Cut dried flower-heads after all the individual flowers have faded and turned brown. The stem is dry and stiff at this point.

Glads

Do you think that farm stands would sell so many glads if they weren't so easy to grow? In fact, we think that glads are better as cut flowers than they are as a landscape plant. Here are a couple of hints for effectively using glads:

✔ Cut a gladiolus when two to three flowers on the lower part of the stem have opened and the rest are still in bud.

✔ Plan ahead. By planting a sequence of gladiolus corms two weeks apart, you can have a succession of flowers to cut.

Dahlias

Dahlia are great because the more you cut, the more they'll flower. Cutting the blooms is like *deadheading* (removing faded flowers) but doing so before the flowers fade. This removal encourages the dahlia to bloom some more.

Some dahlias have flowers as large as a dinner plate. Finding a vase big enough, and tilt-proof, to hold them is difficult. Therefore, moderate-sized dahlias are easier to arrange.

Amaryllis

If you live where amaryllis *(Hippeastrum)* grow outdoors, consigning some to the cutting garden is certainly worth your while. But at five dollars or more per bulb, pot-grown plants are cherished as house plants. If, however, one becomes too leggy, or the cat tips it over, salvage the bloom by using it as a cut flower. Here are a couple of tips:

- ✔ Use green florist tape around the cut base of the stem to keep it from splitting.
- ✔ Use a thin wooden stake inside the hollow center of the amaryllis stem, both for support and to stabilize it in floral foam.

A single stem, cut just before the buds burst open, makes a splendid, long-lasting display.

Nerines

These funky South African bulbs like arid regions with mild winters. The spidery flowers in hot orange-red glitter appear as if they were powdered with diamond dust — pretty snazzy, especially when you can enjoy them at close range in a bouquet. Oh yes, they'll grow in pots, too. Here are some hints for presenting nerines in cut-flower arrangements:

- ✔ Cut in full, well-colored bud stage.
- ✔ Let them display on their own — even three stems makes a good show.
- ✔ If you must mix 'n' match, use an outrageous accompaniment such as fantail willow, with its flattened, contorted shape.

Tips for Creating Long-Lasting Bouquets

You can grow the bulbs for your cut flowers outdoors, just as you would other bulbs, or grow them indoors (either for earlier bloom or because they don't like winter weather). You must decide which approach is best for you. Suitable indoor space is one consideration, the location where you live is another. Cold climate gardeners cannot grow amaryllis as a year-round outdoor plant. Gardeners in mild climates can.

Here are some general points to remember:

- Keep your vases *clean*. Clean, clean, clean. Dirty vases shorten the display time.

- Forget about using pennies, aspirin, vodka — or whatever other folklore you may have heard — to prolong the life of your flowers. Concentrate on keeping your vases clean. That said, the specialized dissolvable crystals or liquid formulation of "flower extender" or "floral life" *do* help. They're made for this purpose.

- Add water. Remember to check the water level in your vase on a daily basis. Cut flowers are thirsty. As they drink, the water level goes down. When the water drops below stem level, the flowers wilt. Ideally, you should empty out the vase and add fresh water, but we often just add to the existing water.

- Cool is better. Why do you think that florists have those big glass-doored refrigerators? 'Cause the flowers last longer. So keep your arrangements away from heat registers; off the top of the TV; and out of sunny, south-facing windows. And if you are organized enough to put the arrangement into the refrigerator or in a cool hallway every evening before you go to bed — you won't see it while you're sleeping anyway — it will last even longer.

Really, many more than ten bulbs are good for cutting. Grape hyacinths are charming; crown imperials are impressive (if you can stand their stench); caladium leaves add a wonderful tropical accent to a simple bunch of white daisies. Bulbs are fine for outdoors, so why not enjoy them indoors as well?

Chapter 24

Ten (Or More) Best Bulbs for Forcing

. . . .

In This Chapter

▶ Getting the jump on spring: forcing tulips, hyacinths, and daffodils

▶ Forcing crocuses and grape hyacinths

. . . .

*W*hat would you say to a preview of spring while it is still winter outdoors? No, you don't need to travel to the tropics; it can happen right in your home. All you do is fool Mother Nature by condensing winter and bringing your bulbs to flower early. Forcing is fun, it's easy, and it helps impatient gardeners get through the February doldrums. This chapter tells you how.

Forcing Your Bulbs to Bloom Early

Spring flowering bulbs are primed to flower by a distinct number of cold weeks. Refrigerators, with a range of 38 to 42 degrees Fahrenheit, provide just the right temperature.

This required chilling prevents tulips and other spring-flowering bulbs from flowering too soon. However, just tossing the bulbs, still in their bag, into the 'fridge doesn't do it. The bulbs need to be potted. We've lined pots up along a garage wall. Inside, not outside. If you live in a city apartment, try an insulated picnic cooler on the balcony, with dry leaves or plastic packing chips filling in around the pots.

Remember to check the temperature. A minimum/maximum thermometer is best. This type has a little piece of metal that floats on the mercury to let you know how cold and how hot it has been since you last checked. Pots shouldn't freeze or get too warm.

Buying a refrigerator for your bulbs — nice but not necessary

If you really get into this business of winter avoidance through forcing bulbs, you may want to get a refrigerator dedicated to chilling pots of bulbs. If you have a choice, don't choose a frost-free refrigerator. The convenience of frost-free means that the air inside is dry (remember that mummified artichoke you found months after you purchased it?) and not as suitable for pots of bulbs as the old-fashioned kind. Twiddle with the temperature control so that the pots of bulbs spend their first six weeks at 42 to 48 degrees Fahrenheit, and then after bulbs are rooted turn it down to about 35 to 41 degrees Fahrenheit for the last six weeks. This adjustment produces even better root growth, but the warmer temperature is dangerous for food storage.

The chilling period lasts about ten weeks, which doesn't mean that all the pots come in at once. You can bring one or two (or a few if you prepared several) in every week or ten days for a staggered sequence of flowers.

Clearly, you need to think about this time interval in advance. In fact, buying some bulbs to force at the same time you purchase bulbs to plant in the garden is the best way to go about it.

Some vendors offer precooled bulbs that have been given a special treatment that makes them ready to grow. Gardeners in mild winter areas need to buy precooled tulips and daffodils for the garden because their local climate doesn't provide winter. Any gardener can use these precooled bulbs for forcing. These bulbs will start growing without the refrigerator treatment.

To pot bulbs in soil, you need a container with drainage holes. You have the option of keeping them going after blooming and to plant them in the garden come spring (except tulips — even tulips forced in soil should be discarded).

All pots are not alike, even in shape. A standard pot is as tall as it is wide (for example, 6 inches high and 6 inches wide). A bulb pan is half as high as it is wide (for example, 3 inches by 6 inches). There's a pot in between, called an azalea pot, which is two-thirds as high as it is wide (for example, 4 inches by 6 inches). This is the proportion we prefer for tulips and hyacinths. It gives good rooting room without being awkwardly tall on a table.

The earlier bulbs flower in the spring, the easier it is to condense their winter. The following sections suggest some bulbs that are easy to force with beautiful results.

Tulips

Look carefully at a tulip bulb. Hold it so the pointy part is up and look at the profile. One side looks flatter, the other rounded. The flat side of the bulb is the side where the first leaf on the stem will be. It doesn't pay to fuss about this in the garden, but considering bulb placement sure improves the appearance of a potful on the table!

Tulips potted the first week in October would come out of the refrigerator in mid-January. Tulips take anywhere from 14 to 17 weeks from potting to flowering, the variable being how early that particular cultivar flowers in spring.

Follow these tips for potting tulips:

1. **Cover the hole in the bottom of a pot with a piece of broken flower pot, window screening, or something else to keep soil in while letting water out.**

2. **Add a layer of potting soil, just enough to bring the tip of the bulb to the rim of the pot.**

   Check with a bulb to make sure that you have the amount right.

3. **Set the bulbs in the pot so there's a ring around the perimeter (with the flat side facing the rim) and one or more in the center.**

   This method gives a fuller appearance than if you leave the center empty.

   An important tip: Do *not* screw the bulbs firmly into the potting soil. Mashing them down makes it difficult for the roots to spread into the soil, so the bulb rises up out of the dirt on stilt-like roots. Scoop a little hollow with your fingers or a spoon, and set them gently into place.

4. **Cover with soil so the tips of the bulbs just peek out. Leave enough space to water.**

5. **Add a label with the date and type and cultivar of bulb.**

   If you pot some now and some next week, you'll know which were the earlier ones and bring them in first.

6. **Water thoroughly.**

7. **Set the pot(s) in a cool place. If you place them in the refrigerator, set them on a saucer or put them in a plastic bag (leaving the top open) to keep things clean.**

   An important tip: Always keep pots of bulbs away from apples and other fruit. In the close quarters of a refrigerator, the ethylene gas produced by the fruit aborts the flowers in their bud stage.

8. **Check periodically and water as necessary.**

9. **After 10 weeks, look at the drain hole to see if white roots are showing.**

   If they are, and if green shoots are showing above the soil, you can bring the first pot(s) indoors to more warmth and light. The room doesn't need to be hot, 55 to 65 degrees Fahrenheit is ideal. Warmer in daytime and cooler at night is best.

In a month or less, you'll have flowers!

Tulips good for forcing include any of the kaufmanniana and greigii hybrids, which naturally flower in early April. These varieties perform much better than the later, May-blooming triumph, lily-flowered, and parrot types of tulips. Single early tulips also do well, such as

 ❀ **'Apricot Beauty'** — salmon-rose, 14 to 16 inches

 ❀ **'Beauty Queen'** — peach, 10 to 14 inches

 ❀ **'Best Seller'** — orange, 10 to 14 inches

 ❀ **'Christmas Marvel'** — pink, 10 to 14 inches

 ❀ **'Kees Nelis'** — red and yellow, 12 to 16 inches

 ❀ **'Merry Christmas** — red, 10 to 15 inches

 ❀ **'Purple Prince'** — purple, 10 to 14 inches

 ❀ **'Silver Dollar'** — white, 12 to 15 inches.

Double early tulips are also a good choice. Try these varieties:

 ❀ **'Monsella'** — double red and yellow, 10 to 12 inches

 ❀ **'Monte Carlo'** — double yellow, 10 to 12 inches

 ❀ **'Stockholm'** — scarlet and yellow, 10 to 11 inches

Hyacinths

Hyacinths are relatively easy to coax into early bloom, and have the added bonus of fragrance. If you've ever bought a potful to cheer you from the winter doldrums and wondered why they cost more than the same number of bulbs, the reason is easy to explain. You're paying for someone else's time to pot the bulbs and care for them until they flower. Provide a little "sweat equity" of your own, and you can have a house full of flowers in the middle of winter. "Prepared" hyacinths will flower in about 10 weeks, maybe a little longer. Regular hyacinths potted the first week of October should be taken out of the refrigerator about the third week of January.

Hyacinths can also be forced in water. Use a special hyacinth forcing jar (available through mail-order catalogs and at garden centers) that has a cup at the top, a narrower neck, and a fat base. We urge you to select the shorter, squattier jars because the tall kinds have a tendency to fall over — hyacinth, water, and all — when top-heavy with a hyacinth in bloom. Fill the forcing jar with water to the narrow neck, perch the bulb on top, and there you have it. Set the container in a cool bright place to provide best growing conditions. Discard after the flowers bloom, just as you do with paperwhites (see the sidebar "Forcing paperwhite narcissus in pebbles and water," later in this chapter).

Hyacinths potted in soil are handled just like tulips, except that you needn't look for a flat side — hyacinths don't have one!

If after flowering you want to plant the hyacinths outside in spring, remember that you must keep the green leaves growing, water the plants, and add half-strength liquid fertilizer every other week or so. Finished pots of hyacinths can take up a fair amount of sunny space on your windowsills, so factor that consideration into your planning about how many pots to force.

Hyacinths for forcing include the following single blooms:

- ❀ **'Anna Liza'** — violet, 8 to 12 inches
- ❀ **'Anna Marie'** — pink, 8 to 12 inches
- ❀ **'Delft Blue'** and/or **Viking** — China blue, 12 to 15 inches
- ❀ **'Gipsey Princess'** — pale yellow, 8 to 12 inches
- ❀ **'Jan Bos'** — pinkish-red, 8 to 12 inches
- ❀ **'L'Innocence'** — white, 12 to 15 inches
- ❀ **'Ostera'** — purple-violet, 8 to 12 inches
- ❀ **'Pink Pearl'** — rose-pink, 8 to 12 inches

Double blooms for forcing include the following types:

- ❀ **'Chestnut'** — pink, 8 to 12 inches
- ❀ **'General Köhler'** — lavender, 8 to 12 inches

Daffodils

Daffodils are magical for forcing. Expect different cultivars to take anywhere from 12 to 16 weeks from potting to the time they flower. If you pot them the first week of October, you remove them from the refrigerator in mid-January. Follow these hints for potting lots of delightful daffodils:

1. **Use a standard pot (remember, that's one as high as it is wide), crock the bottom (place a piece of window screening or broken clay pot over the drainage hole), and fill one-third full of soil.**

2. **Set four daffodil bulbs equally distant from each other in the soil, say, north, south, east, and west for convenience in describing their placement.**

3. **Add another layer of soil and four more daffodil bulbs, setting them northeast, northwest, southeast, southwest.**

   If there is room, fit one more in the middle.

4. **Cover the bulbs with the remaining third of soil, leaving enough room for water.**

No fooling, all those daffodils will flower at the same time *and* at the same height. You will have a gloriously full pot of daffodils when they bloom.

Daffodils also need the same chilling and growing period as tulips and hyacinths do. Like hyacinths, you can also plant daffodils in the garden when spring arrives, but only if you've kept them growing until that time.

Smaller, earlier flowering daffodils are your best choice. Choose cyclamineus types such as

- ❀ **'Jack Snipe'** — white and yellow, 8 inches
- ❀ **'Peeping Tom'** — golden yellow, 10 inches
- ❀ **'Téte a Téte'** — deep yellow, 6 inches

We've also forced big trumpet daffodils this way, in a double layer. But you can just imagine the size of the pot needed for nine of those big double-nose bulbs — not for table-top display!

Trying Other Bulbs for Forcing

Tulips, daffodils, and hyacinths are the bulbs usually used for forcing. That's not to say that you can't pot other spring bulbs and coax them into early flowering. Because other bulbs tend to be smaller than tulips, daffodils, and hyacinths, the show will be more refined. And many of the little early bulbs don't last well indoors.

In the following sections, we discuss two of these other bulbs that you may want to consider forcing: crocuses and grape hyacinths.

Forcing paperwhite narcissus in pebbles and water

Paperwhite narcissus bulbs don't need a chilling period. They're raring to grow. In fact, they don't even need soil. Because these bulbs are flowers in a plain brown jacket, paperwhites will flower in a bowl of pebbles and water. Follow these tips:

1. **Choose plump heavy paperwhite bulbs.**

   Bigger is better, because large bulbs send up two or even three flowering stems while small bulbs produce only one.

2. **Select a watertight container.**

   It can be something pretty, such as a pottery bowl. We've also used a plain old plastic container, and then showcased it in a wicker basket or something attractive when the paperwhites are ready to flower.

3. **Add some clean pebbles.**

   They should be coarser than aquarium gravel, about marble size. In fact, we've seen paperwhites forced using marbles to support the bulbs. When we were children, we used crushed oyster shell but we haven't seen that for a while. Don't use gravel from your driveway — it has disgusting stuff on it that dripped from automobiles and is not good for plants.

4. **Set the bulbs so they're just about touching, as many as the container will hold.**

5. **Dribble some more gravel or stones around the bulbs, just about to their shoulders (where the bulb narrows).**

   Gravel holds them up when they have leaves and flowers.

6. **Add water, just enough to come to the bottom of the bulbs.**

7. **Set the bulb-filled container somewhere with cool room temperature conditions and bright light.**

In about 4 to 6 weeks, you'll have flowers! The closer you get to spring, the quicker they'll perform. Pot paperwhites around Thanksgiving and you'll have them flowering for Christmas. Start in January, and they'll flower in 2 to 3 weeks.

Hint: These bulbs make a nice gift, either in bloom or just a bowl. Give some bulbs, a bag of pebbles, and a little note explaining what to do.

After they flower, toss the bulbs away. They've exhausted the nutrients stored in the bulb and have no way to replace them. Besides, unless you live in a mild winter area, paperwhites are not hardy.

Crocuses

Crocuses are fairly easy, but unless kept quite cool while in flower their blossoms only last for a few days. Crocuses potted the first week in October come out of the refrigerator late in January. Expect crocuses to take 14 or 15 weeks from potting to flowering. Pot them the first week of October, and expect to remove them from the refrigerator about the third week of January.

You can buy teeny, tiny crocus forcing jars, like miniature hyacinth glasses. *Remember:* If you force crocuses in water, discard the corm afterward.

Crocus pots look like Swiss cheese — they have holes in the sides as well as a drainage hole in the bottom. The idea is to set crocus corms so their noses are pressed against the hole, filling in with potting soil behind them. Place a layer of corms on the top and then a final layer of soil (leaving room to water), and the container is ready for its chilly rooting period.

Grape hyacinths

Potted grape hyacinths are quite nice, with softer-colored flowers than they'd have in the garden. They'll grow and flower on about the same schedule as crocuses.

Because grape hyacinths have a small bulb, you can use a bulb pan (see the description in the section, "Forcing Your Bulbs to Bloom Early," earlier in this chapter). Choose a smaller pot than you would for tulips because grape hyacinths produce smaller blooms.

Pack bulbs tightly, almost touching. Cover with soil so their tips just peek out, but allow enough space to water without making a mess. Chill for 10 weeks minimum; then bring into light and warmer temperatures.

Chapter 25

Ten Most Fragrant Bulbs

. . . .

. . . .

*F*ragrance is a highly personal preference — not everybody's nose works quite the same way. Color is different — you may like or dislike hot pink, but at least everybody agrees about what color it is. So when it comes to fragrant bulbs, you may love the scent of paperwhite narcissus, or find it cloying and unpleasant. But at least everyone agrees that it has a scent!

Temperature influences fragrance. Warmer temperatures allow a flower to release more of its particular bouquet, and chilly weather reduces our perception of scent. In addition, an individual flower's age affects its level of perfume. Old flowers are generally not as fragrant as freshly opened ones. Time of day also plays a role; depending on what the flower intends to attract as a pollinator, the scent may be stronger in the morning than at mid-day, or vice versa. Folks with a cold have trouble smelling anything, and smokers are less sensitive to fragrance than those who don't smoke.

In this chapter, we discuss eight types of bulbs that produce sweet, appealing fragrances. We also warn you about two kinds of bulbs that produce beautiful blooms, but their odors aren't so pleasant.

Bulbs with Fragrant Flowers

These eight bulbs will fill your home or garden with sweet fragrance.

Hyacinths

We think everyone agrees that hyacinths smell great. All of them are fragrant. However, as Scott Kunst at Old House Gardens pointed out to us, they don't all smell the same. Some are muskier, others have fruity or spicy overtones, and some have a lighter, more floral fragrance. Grow a bunch of different ones and then have some friends over for a "tasting" of fragrances, just as you might host a wine tasting.

Daffodils

Daffodils allow us to generalize — *all* jonquilla daffodils, *all* tazetta daffodils, and *all* poeticus daffodils are fragrant. Jonquillas flower later than many other daffodils and have a sweet perfume that you can often detect before you even see the flowers. 'Pipit,' with two or three luminous yellow flowers per stem, and rich coppery yellow 'Quail,' with two to four flowers per stem, are two deliciously fragrant "modern" jonquilla cultivars.

The somewhat tender campernelles (choose a sheltered site in zone 6, and use caution in colder regions) come single or double, and both are fragrant. Glowing saffron- or goldenrod-yellow 'Orange Queen,' and dainty 6- to 10-inch tall double yellow 'Pencrebar' are fragrant heirloom cultivars.

Paperwhite narcissus are great for forcing (see Chapter 24). They have delicate to strong musky fragrance, more noticeable indoors than the same fragrance would be in a garden. 'Nony' ('Bethlehem') and 'Omri' ('Israel') are delicately scented, 'Galil' ('Galilee'), 'Sheles' ('Jerusalem'), and 'Yael' ('Nazareth') have a moderately musky perfume, and 'Ziva' is the most strongly scented.

Other deliciously perfumed daffodils include species: wild ones such as *Narcissus albus plenus odoratus,* with fragrant, gardenia-like, double, white flowers; *Narcissus canaliculatus* with four to seven sweetly fragrant gold and white flowers to each stem; late blooming, intensely fragrant *Narcissus gracilis* with three or four flowers on a stem, each with pale greenish-yellow petals around a darker yellow cup.

Tulips

On the whole, tulips are not fragrant. But remember that every rule has exceptions! 'Prince of Austria,' an orange-scarlet single early tulip introduced in 1860, is fragrant. So is 'Generaal de Wet,' an orange-flowered *sport* (a spontaneous variation) of 'Prince of Austria' dating from 1904. I find 'Prinses Irene' sweetly fragrant, a bonus addition to her orange flowers gently brushed with a tint of purple. 'Ballerina' is a sweetly scented lily-flowered tulip with showy flowers, marigold orange inside and lemon yellow outside, accented with blood red markings.

Among other fragrant tulips are the double-late, blush pink 'Angelique,' the yellow-to-soft apricot Darwin hybrid 'Daydream,' or the bright orange 'Oranjezon,' the early-double pink 'Peach Blossom,' and the lily-flowered, primrose-yellow 'Ellen Willmott.'

Oriental lilies

Oriental lilies were developed from *Lilium auratum, Lilium speciosum,* and other species. The auratum and speciosum species are fragrant, and so are their offspring. We describe a selection of oriental lilies and how to grow them in Chapter 12.

Trumpet lilies

"Regal" is an apt description for *Lilium regale,* one of the parents of the trumpet lilies. These tall midsummer beauties are elegant and smell good. Now, if only they were deer-proof! Look up trumpet lilies and their care in Chapter 12; deer-proofing tips are in Chapter 22.

Freesias

When Judy lived in Holland, her husband swore that he'd go broke from the cheap flowers she kept buying in the street market. They were inexpensive, but she just couldn't resist buying bunch after bunch of lemon-scented freesias.

These little freesia corms are in the iris family. Native to South Africa, they abhor cold winters outdoors. But they thrive in cool winter weather. If you live where the climate's Mediterranean — dry summers and rainy, almost frost-free winters — then freesias are a garden plant for you. Plant them in a partly shaded site in fall, and they'll flower 4 or 5 months later in spring. Several funnel-shaped flowers climb the stem, one to three stems per corm. Flower color varies from white to cream or yellow, pink, red, and violet, and are available as single or double-flowered types. It seems to us that the singles are more fragrant than the doubles, and the whites and yellows are more fragrant than other colors.

If you live where "snow" and "winter" seem like synonyms, then consider growing freesias in pots. Plant corms an inch or so deep, three to five corms to a pot filled with a light, airy peat moss, sand, and soil mix. Provide ample water and light while in growth. Flowers begin to form about 4 months after potting, and will last 3 or 4 weeks at living-room temperatures. Though most popular indoors as a winter-growing plant, planted in autumn, you can grow freesias in pots year-round, as long as corms are available. Outdoors, freesias are planted in spring.

Tuberose

Intensely fragrant, tuberose is popular as a garden plant in regions with warm climates, and as a cut flower. They need warm soil and a long season to flower. The sort of pear-shaped tubers are planted in loamy soil after frost-free weather has arrived, about 2 inches deep. Water heavily immediately after the tubers are planted, and then hold off until growth is visible. Water moderately while tubers are in active growth. The heavily perfumed white flowers open late, from September to November. If tuberose is grown where frost may come before the flowers, grow the tubers in a pot that can be brought indoors. *Polianthes tuberosa* 'The Pearl' is double-flowered; 'Mexican Single' is, what else, single-flowered. Tubers, especially if container-planted, are generally discarded after flowering.

Lilies-of-the-valley

The sweet fragrance of lily-of-the-valley is actually the base for a perfume, called *muget* after the plant's French name.

The plant is either incredibly easy or recalcitrantly difficult to grow, depending on your experience. Plants are suitable for garden use in cool temperate regions, and they do well in shade. Rambling white rhizomes are planted in a light to moderately shaded site with humus-rich, moist soil. A pair of oval green leaves clasp the stem, which has several dangling white bells.

If you want to gather flowers for a dainty bouquet, don't cut them. Hold the flower stem firmly near the base and gently tug it free from the base.

Remember! Lily-of-the-valley is poisonous, including the water in which flowers have been standing in the vase.

Lily-of-the-valley is easy to force, and specially prepared *pips* (as the dormant rootstocks are called) are available in winter and early spring.

Bulbs That Stink

Fragrant is sure not the right term for the two bulbs we introduce in this section.

Crown imperials

So you went to a museum and looked at those Dutch master paintings showing huge vases full of all sorts of flowers. And crown imperials, with their stately, good-sized orange bells and a top-knot tuft of pineapple-like leaves took your fancy. That's fine — if you grow them in the garden. But the powerful musky odor you perhaps will notice when you plant the bulb is also present in the leaves and flowers. And the scent is even more apparent if you cut the flowers and bring them indoors. Look up crown imperials in Chapter 11 and add them to your garden, but not an indoor bouquet.

Monarchs of the east

The word "stink" isn't strong enough to adequately describe the monarch of the east. "Stench" is probably more accurate. *Sauromatum guttatum* is one of those funky bulbs that flowers on a windowsill, no soil needed. The strange flower (it's also known as the "voodoo lily") is deep oxblood red with a dark, poker-like spadix sticking out. When we tell you that in its warm, subtropical native home flowers are fertilized by carrion beetles, you'll have some idea of the evil, rotting meat smell that pairs with the dead-meat color of the flowers that the plant uses to lure its pollinators. Hardy only in mild winter regions, monarch of the east needs a dry resting period as part of its annual cycle to remain healthy.

Chapter 26

Ten Bulbs Our Ancestors Grew

· ·

In This Chapter

▶ Reviewing a brief history of selected bulbs

▶ Cloning: Gardeners have been doing it for centuries

▶ Finding the perfect heirloom bulbs — history in your hand and in your garden

· ·

*I*n modern times, when planned obsolescence seems to be the rule, the idea of growing bulbs that were grown at the turn of the century or earlier seems absurd. But as far as these sturdy plants are concerned, modern times seem absurd. There are bulbs still available today that have been cultivated for centuries. In some instances, today's bulbs are genetically identical to those grown before the Christian era.

We are not the first to grow bulbs. People may have begun growing bulbs for food, but some bulbs found a place in gardens because of the charm of their flowers. Lilies are depicted in Minoan frescos at the palace at Knossos, dating from 1600 B.C., and the madonna lily, *Lilium candidum,* was cultivated by the Romans before Christians adopted it as a symbol of the Virgin Mary. The Greeks named gladiolus for *gladius,* a small sword, in recognition of the bulb's sword-like leaves. (Just think of gladiator, and you'll have another connection.)

Reasons for Choosing Heirloom Bulbs

So why grow an old type of bulb when you can have something new? Well, new doesn't automatically mean better. Tastes change, and contemporary fashions are different from those of the past — different, not better. And the bulbs grown centuries ago hold their own in beauty with today's new hybrid cultivars.

Consider these reasons for growing heirloom bulbs:

- ✔ Perhaps you like the idea of holding history in your hand and growing it in your garden.

- ✔ If you have an herb garden, you may want to grow bulbs that would have been contemporary in medieval or Elizabethan gardens.

- ✔ Maybe you've heard of the Englishman, John Parkinson, and his well-known book on herbs, *Paradisus in Sole Terrestris,* first published in 1629. Wouldn't it be a kick to grow the bulbs he mentioned?

- ✔ Do you have a colonial or Victorian house? It might be fun to grow some of the same bulbs that the original owners would have had in the garden.

We're sure that you can think of other reasons. But you don't really need a reason other than the fact that they're lovely enough to command the care that they've lovingly received from one generation to the next.

Facts about Heirloom Bulbs

On the whole, the older cultivars of bulbs are sturdy. After all, they've been growing in gardens for decades, if not centuries! However, the bulb that's grown today may not be the same as the bulb that first had that name. A case in point is the 'King Alfred' daffodil. It's a big yellow trumpet, very popular, and was first available to gardeners sometime before 1899. But the "King Alfred" (please note the double quotation marks) available today is not the same. As reputable catalogs will tell you, usually 'Dutch Master' is sold in its place. Why? Because 'Dutch Master' looks very much like 'King Alfred,' and it propagates faster. Most gardeners probably don't care about the name, but they should.

Single quote marks define cultivar name. When 'King Alfred' is actually 'Dutch Master,' the cultivar name is inaccurate; this should be reflected by use of double quote marks.

If you grow species bulbs, rather than cultivars, this variation doesn't matter. To make a wise planting decision, you need to understand the difference between species and cultivars:

- ✔ **Species** are allowed to be variable — within limits. Guinea hen flower, *Fritillaria meleagris,* can have nicely checkerboard-marked dark purple flowers, intermeidate hues, or white flowers. These variations will appear when you plant the species. If, however, you plant the cultivar 'Alba,' every last one will have white flowers.

✔ **Cultivars** are plants of garden origin. In order to remain *true* (a term used by botanists and taxonomists), meaning truly the cultivar first given that particular name, plants must be propagated *asexually*. This process can be as simple as division, which we discuss in Chapter 21. Any time you dig up a clump of overcrowded daffodils and separate the individual bulbs, they are genetically identical to one another. That's low-technology cloning.

Chipping is a process whereby growers chop a daffodil or hippeastrum bulb into pieces, creating two bits of scale attached to a fragment of basal plate (see Chapter 1 if you need an explanation of scale and basal plate terms). Chipping enables nurseries to produce zillions of identical daffodil bulbs for sale. And tissue culture, micro-propagation uses even smaller bits and pieces and requires sterile laboratory conditions to achieve the same results in even greater quantities. Division, chipping, and micro-propagation in a laboratory — all result in genetically identical bulbs. But as soon as daffodil bulbs are grown from seed, they lose that clonal, cultivar identity — genetic recombination scrambles their genes.

Selecting the Ideal Heirloom Bulbs for You

If you are content with species, then any reputable bulb source will do. If you prefer to grow particular cultivars, you need a particular, that is — a fussily precise — source. The best source of heirloom bulbs is Old House Gardens catalog is $2, run by Scott Kunst, located at 536 Third St., Ann Arbor, MI 48103; the phone and fax number is 313-995-1486; or e-mail at OHGBulbs@aol.com. Expect to pay more for these hard-to-find bulbs with limited availability than you would for modern cultivars available at discount stores and supermarkets.

The following sections describe some beautiful heirloom bulbs. We provide how-to-grow tips and techniques in the specific chapters devoted to each type of bulb.

Historical tulips: Cultivars

How about something that dates back practically to the time when tulips were introduced from Turkey to Holland?

❀ **Duc van Thol,** a red and yellow nearly identical to *Tulipa schrenkii* and the original wild species from which the following cultivars were developed, was introduced in 1620. The other Duc van tulips are "newer" (but that's relatively speaking) dating from the turn of that century, 1700. All offer early flowering from 4- to 8-inch plants.

- **Duc van Max Cramoisie** displays arresting crimson flowers.

- **Duc van Orange** offers glowing, vivid flowers in, yes, orange.

- **Duc van Rose** is a vibrant reddish-pink.

- **Duc van Violet** sends stems with rich amethyst blossoms.

❀ **'Lac van Rijn'** is a contemporary, also in cultivation since 1620, and it sports long, pointed petals in Byzantine purplish-red with broad white edges.

❀ **'Zomerschoon'** was first introduced into cultivation in 1620. It has an impressive, large, loose blossom with petals in a bright yellow to ivory accented with salmon-red flames.

❀ **'Couleur Cardinal'** is not quite as venerable, but very much easier to obtain and dates back to 1845. It produces long-lasting, fragrant flowers in deep scarlet with a plum blush, atop 12- to 14-inch dark stems.

Historical tulips: Species

Tulipa schrenkii, introduced in 1585, is the parent of the Duc van tulips we discuss in the preceding section.

The florentine tulip, *Tulipa sylvestris,* despite its woodland-sounding name is a sun-lover. Introduced in 1597, it is a charming bulb with rampageous tendencies — it prolifically produces offsets, spreading some distance from the mother bulb. Couple this tendency with its habit of diving deep into the soil, and you can appreciate that this tulip is hard to evict. So give it a place to stay and room to run, and enjoy this sturdy heirloom. It'll reward you with delightfully fragrant, golden-yellow nodding flowers.

Historical daffodils: Cultivars

Daffodils were and are popular in gardens, deservedly so for their ease of cultivation and sturdy character. Some old-time cultivars for your garden include the following:

❀ **Double Chinese Sacred Lily** was a daffodil carried to China along the ancient caravan routes from its origin in the Middle East. One of its cultivars, **'Constantinople'** is a very old tazetta daffodil dating from 1576. It only thrives outdoors where winter temperatures remain above 20 degrees Fahrenheit. Though pricey for a force-and-discard winter treat, it is ideal for gardeners with a Mediterranean climate.

❀ **'Van Sion,'** sometimes called 'Telamonius Plenus' (see, even the authorities can get confused!) is called the "Scrambled Egg" daffodil where Judy lives in New Jersey. If it wasn't introduced in 1597, then it was 1620 when it first was mentioned as growing in gardens. In any case, it produces early blossoms with a pale yellow trumpet and a greenish-yellow cup on 12- to 14-inch stems.

❀ **'Twin Sisters'** is a daffodil especially good in southern gardens where it is often known as "April Beauty" or "Cemetery Ladies." Introduced in 1597, probably even earlier, this is a daffodil for zones 6 to 8. With two blooms per stem, you get plenty of color from blossoms with white petals surrounding a delicate yellow cup. Plants perennialize quite well in southern gardens.

❀ **Chinese Sacred Lily,** *Narcissus tazetta var. orientalis,* is a "modern" paperwhite (a kind of daffodil) from the 1887 or earlier in that decade. Popular with the Victorians, it is easily brought into bloom to enhance a winter parlor. Quite tender, it could only be grown outdoors in mild winter and Mediterranean climates, where it naturally flowers from November to January. Blossoms feature a yellow cup and white petals on 16-inch stems.

Historical daffodils: Species

For heirloom daffodils, seek out the following:

❀ **Lent Lily,** *Narcissus pseudonarcissus,* is an absolutely charming miniature trumpet cultivated in gardens by 1570. They are tough and reliable, and among the earliest daffodils to flower each spring, sending up blossoms with long, yellow trumpets and pale yellow petals generally longer than the trumpet.

❀ **Tenby daffodil,** *Narcissus obvallaris,* is smaller than average, with deep yellow flowers.

❀ **Hoop Petticoat Daffodil,** *Narcissus bulbocodium var. bulbocodium,* is much sturdier than its diminutive size suggests. After all, if it has been around since 1629, it must be robust. Don't fuss with it, just provide a rocky site with turf, a sort of heath or short grass meadow setting. As a species, it is welcome to reseed, so don't bother deadheading; you'll enjoy the unusual flowers with wide, flaring golden-yellow trumpets season after season.

Hyacinths

You bet — hyacinths are big players in our bulb heritage. Even though all kinds and colors of hyacinths are available today, some of these older varieties from the late 1800s are equally as interesting and fragrant. In fact, almost all the double hyacinths are older cultivars.

Check out these double hyacinths:

- ❀ **'General Köhler'** from 1878 is stunning with 8-inch spikes completely covered with lavender florets lightly tinted with blue.

- ❀ **'Chestnut Flower'** from 1880 offers impressive double rows of pastel pink, very fragrant florets on 8-inch spikes.

- ❀ **'Madame Sophie'** from 1929 is elegant indoors or out with scented, pure white 8-inch spikes.

These single hyacinths are also worth consideration:

- ❀ **'Marie'** from 1860 is much like 'King of the Blues' with that same cool beauty, but she offers earlier flowers and slightly narrower spikes.

- ❀ **'Grand Monarque'** from about 1863 is a tried-and-true favorite for its prolific spikes covered in delicate light blue florets.

- ❀ **'King of the Blues'** from 1863 reigns supreme with large spikes of indigo-blue florets that offer a strong fragrance.

- ❀ **'L'Innocence'** from 1863 approaches perfumed perfection from glistening, pure white blossoms.

- ❀ **'Bismarck'** from 1875 is an all-time winner with solid purple florets with hints of deep blue. It also offers impressive fragrance.

- ❀ **'Distinction'** from 1880 earns its name from dark maroon, beet-red flowers on small spikes, half the size of most varieties.

Crocus

In cultivation since the early seventeenth century, crocuses are as popular today as when they were first introduced.

- ❀ **'Cloth of Silver'** crocus was popular with the Victorians. The type grown today, *Crocus versicolor* or 'Picturatus,' may be the same and has been in cultivation since 1574. If it's not the same thing, it's darn close and has been around since 1909. Expect this cultivar to produce plenty of dainty silver-white flowers accented with purple veins and an ivory-to-pale throat.

❀ **"Turkey crocus,"** also known as the "cloth of gold" crocus and *Crocus angustifolius,* was about the *only* crocus common in gardens before 1930 or thereabouts. It first showed up in English gardens, as early as 1587 or a bit earlier. Rich orange flowers with outer petals striped in mahagany highlight this prolific little selection.

❀ **"Mammoth Yellow,"** properly named 'Grote Gele,' has been in cultivation for the last three centuries. If you ever bought a mixed lot of "Dutch hybrid crocus" and had the yellow ones flower first, this is what appeared.

Lilies

Go back two and a half centuries, and U.S. plants were making their way to England, where they were exciting, new, rare introductions. One of the collectors was John Bartram, and among the plants he shipped back to Peter Collinson in 1738 was our turk's cap lily, *Lilium superbum,* which thrives in wet meadows from Massachusetts south to Alabama and westward to Indiana. This impressive native will grace your late summer to early autumn garden with dozens of nodding orange flowers with red accents and maroon spots.

Fritillaries

Crown imperial, *Fritillaria imperialis,* is a show-stopper plant, so stunning that John Parkinson placed it first in his herbal, and it was featured even earlier in Bessler's *Hortus Eystettensis* of 1618. These stately orange beauties with their unusual flowers have been cultivated since 1572.

❀ **'Lutea'** was described in 1665 as having dramatic dangling clear yellow flowers with faint purple markings.

❀ **'Aurora'** has been known since 1865 and has been revered for its dazzling orange-red flowers with purple veins set on 2- to 3-foot stems.

Guinea hen flower, *Fritillaria meleagris*, and its white flowering clone, 'Alba,' have both been in gardens since 1572. The guinea hen flower has charmed for centuries with its delightfully checkered 8-inch bell-shaped flowers in a range of purple and white shades. 'Alba' offers only pure white flowers, also 8 inches tall.

Snowdrops

Early, tough, and shade tolerant — what more could you ask for? *Galanthus nivalis* or the snowdrop has been in gardens since at least 1597, probably even earlier. Usually called "Common Snowdrop," this little one has nodding, white flowers with green tips on the inner petals, reaches 6 inches high, and naturalizes with ease.

Double snowdrop, *Galanthus nivalis* 'Flore Pleno,' is a relative latecomer, dating from 1731. It's a treat to get down low and look up into this flower that opens its pure white petals like a bird spreading its wings. At 6 inches, though, it'll be a stretch to find such a lowly, but worthy, perspective.

Snowflake

Somewhat later in bloom and more heat tolerant than the snowdrop we discuss in the preceding section, the summer snowflake, *Leucojum aestivum,* is called snowdrop by Southerners. Hardy from zone 5 south, the summer snowflake has been around in gardens just as long as snowdrops, since 1596. So you can imagine the number of people over time who have admired these fragrant bell-shaped flowers on 9- to 12-inch stems. Each flower petal is delicately dotted in green and matched by glistening, bright green foliage. Bulbs both naturalize and make fine cut flowers.

Wood hyacinth or English bluebell

Mentioned by Shakespeare, the bluebell of England has been shoved around by taxonomists through a plethora of name changes. No matter, the bulb knows who it is, even before it arrived in gardens by 1551. Nowadays, look for *Hyacinthoides non-scripta.* Be careful, for many firms ship Spanish bluebell, *Hyacinthoides hispanica,* in its place. Here are the differences:

✔ English bluebells *(Hyacinthoides non-scripta)* are more pendulous than Spanish bluebells.

✔ The fragrant English bluebells are dark blue to violet-blue, and Spanish bluebells are not perfumed, but do come in a range of colors from white to pink to light and dark blue.

Cannas

You better believe it; there are heirloom varieties of cannas, too — maybe not as old as some of the spring flowering bulbs, but still old enough to add a blast from the past to your garden. Consider these varieties:

❀ **'Florence Vaughn'** from 1893 is impressive with brilliant yellow flowers with a central orange blotch and generous spots. This leopard-like appearance set against very Victorian green leaves gives the 3- to 6-foot tall plants plenty of drama.

❀ **'Red King Humbert'** helped bring in the century, introduced as it was in 1902. And it did so with flair from scarlet flowers and dark leaves tinged with red on towering 4- to 8-foot plants.

❀ **'Wyoming,'** another bronze-leafed beauty, came along in 1906 offering an attractive contrast from tangerine flowers set against the dark foliage on 4- to 7-foot plants.

❀ **'City of Portland'** was in gardens by 1915 showing off large salmon-pink flowers and gray-green foliage on 3- to 4-foot plants.

Dahlias

A handful of dahlias are modern only by comparison to the cannas, dating from the 1920s and 1930s:

❀ **'Jersey Beauty'** is a few years older, dating from 1923. It sports large — up to 10-inch — formal decorative flowers in glowing pink on 5-foot stems.

❀ **'Bishop of Llandaff,'** 1927, is a striking plant, with simple cardinal red flowers that glow against the dark burgundy foliage on 3-foot stems.

❀ **'Thomas Edison,'** named for the wizard of Menlo Park, was introduced in 1929. This giant features perfectly formed 9- to 11-inch regal dark purple flowers on 40-inch stems.

Who knows if new bulb introductions will be the heirlooms in a century from now? But you can be sure that the old bulbs we mention here, and more, have stood the test of time. They're definitely worth growing in your garden along with new introductions.

Chapter 27

Ten Bulbs for Sunny, Dry, Mild Spots (Think California)

Granted, bulbs requiring dry summers and mild winters truly thrive only in relatively small corners of the planet. But what special "corners" they are. Several of the bulbs we describe in this chapter are native to the western half of South Africa, a region noted not only for its floral bounty but also for its Mediterranean climate. Taking its name from the dominant weather patterns throughout much of the Mediterranean region, this type of climate is noted for its rainy and mild winters (temperatures rarely fall below 25 degrees Fahrenheit), and dry and mild summers. Anywhere in the world that a similar climate prevails, such as southwestern Australia and much of California, these bulbs thrive.

A few of the bulbs we discuss in this chapter are premier florists' crops that just happen to be bulbs. Anemone, freesia, and ornithagalum are in this category. Gardeners all over the world know these plants, but unless you live where the climate is right (or have access to a greenhouse), they are difficult to grow.

All of the bulbs in this chapter are excellent "perennializers"; that is, they'll come back year after year, even increasing some each time. Although many other bulbs perennialize in a similar way, these varieties are the best if you happen to live in a mild winter, dry summer climate.

Amaryllis Belladonna — Naked Ladies

The name naked ladies (memorable isn't it?) comes from the fact that the tall, pink flowers appear when this plant is leafless. The effect is striking. In late summer, a tipped, half-inch-wide stalk emerges from the soil and soon opens to show the trumpet-shaped, six-petaled, and intensely pink fragrant flowers. After it dies (they're great to cut and bring indoors) and the rains begin in winter, the dark green, strap-shaped leaves return and grow through the winter, storing energy for another bloom season next summer.

Naked ladies originate in South Africa. They bloom in mid- to late summer for about three weeks. Flower color is usually pink, but hybrids of white and deeper shades of pink are available. Flowers grow 2 to 3 feet high; the mound of leaves in winter is about 1 foot high. Plant the large, 4-inch diameter bulbs about 8 inches deep to the base, or so the bulbs are covered by at least 2 inches of soil. Choose a location in full sun or light shade. You can let clumps of bulbs gradually expand unattended for years, or you can divide them in summer or fall when they are dormant.

Naked ladies are somewhat dormant when in full flower (they don't grow leaves until after they flower), making that moment a perfectly good time to dig them up to transplant, share with a friend, or otherwise mess with them. The bulbs are sound asleep and will never feel a thing.

Florists' Anemone

Florists' anemone, *Anemone coronaria,* shouldn't be confused with Grecian windflower, *Anemone blanda,* their more cold-hardy relative, which we describe in Chapter 4. The larger, showier florists' anemones come originally from the Mediterranean region.

The single-flowering De Caen bloom in spring and early summer in a range of colors:

- ❀ **'Bride'** is (what else) white.
- ❀ **'Hollandia'** has red petals with a white base, and a black center, very showy.
- ❀ **'Mr. Fokker'** produces blue-violet flowers.
- ❀ **'Sylphide'** has violet-pink flowers.

The St. Brigid strain has double flowers:

- ❀ **'Admiral'** is a strong, almost luminous violet.
- ❀ **'Governor'** is red.
- ❀ **'Lord Lieutenant'** produces deep blue flowers.
- ❀ **'Mt. Everest'** is white.

The 3- to 4-inch diameter flowers sit atop 12- to 15-inch stems. The lumpy looking tubers are only hardy in regions where the average minimum temperature in winter won't dip much below 25 degrees Fahrenheit, or stay there for very long when it does get cold. If you live where winter temperatures are that mild — basically the southern half (and much of the west) of the United States — you can plant them outdoors in fall. Otherwise, plant these bulbs in spring (as soon as soil is workable) for June flowering. Wherever you live, plant bulbs about 1 inch deep and 4 inches apart.

Florists' anemones are very easy to grow in pots if you live where winters are cold and you want to enjoy flowers indoors between mid-February and April. Pot in September or October, grow cool (50 to 60 degrees Fahrenheit) until mid-January, and then gradually bring the containers into warmer conditions.

Babiana — Baboon Flower

Babiana, baboon flower, earned its name honestly: Its corms are a favorite food of baboons and were eaten by the Dutch settlers who first arrived on South Africa's Cape. Wherever those furred cousins of ours aren't around to regularly feast on the bulbs, the bulbs will increase rapidly, even in dry and otherwise seemingly inhospitable gardens.

Although many kinds of baboon flower grow in Africa, the one most common in gardens is *Babiana stricta*. It blooms in spring with five or six cup-shaped flowers of blue, lavender, red, or white on 12-inch stems. Flowers of 'Tuberegen's Blue' are lighter in shade, and 'White King' is white with blue-colored anthers.

Baboon flower likes warm, temperate, subtropical conditions, and is not hardy where winter regularly brings freezing temperatures. In these places, the corms may be planted in autumn, setting them 2 to 3 inches deep and about an inch and a half apart. Where the corms are not hardy, you can plant them in spring for summer flowers.

Freesia

Have you ever grown a plant just for its fragrance? If not, you might consider trying freesia. Sensitivity to subtle odors varies by individual, but according to some people, this flower is the finest and sweetest scented of all. The old-fashioned, white cultivars normally produce the most fragrance. *(You can see one pictured in the color section.)*

Freesias are native to South Africa. They bloom in spring for several weeks in a wide range of colors: white, yellow, orange, lavender, red, and pink. The flower stalks are at least a foot long and sometimes so laden with flowers that they can't quite stand upright.

Plant the corms in fall if you live in a frost-free area. Or plant four in a 6-inch pot in early spring, and then bring them outdoors in spring after the last frost. (You can leave the bulbs in the pot for three or four years before they become too crowded.) Set bulbs under 2 to 4 inches of soil.

Homeria

Homeria is not planted often enough, even in those frost-free regions where it would grow happily. Their flowers are guaranteed to charm. The 6-petaled blooms are 2 inches in diameter and cup-shaped. Colors are either a soft apricot (*Homeria collina* 'Aurantiaca') or lemon yellow (*H. ochroleuca*). Each flowering stem produces many flowers that open in succession, each one lasting only a day. Altogether, you'll have blooming plants from late spring into summer for approximately 6 weeks.

Plant the corms in spring, in a location that receives full sun, setting them about 2 inches deep. Plants grow about 2 feet high. When conditions are right, they'll begin to spread with their own seeds.

Where bulbs are not hardy, grow them just as you would gladiolus.

Ixia — African Corn Lily

Ixia, the African corn lily, is one of those exotic flowers that florists love to add to bouquets, partly because it's unfamiliar enough to get attention, and partly because it's so long-lasting. But gardeners can grow them outdoors (where winter chill stays above about 20 degrees Fahrenheit), or indoors anywhere. The basic techniques are exactly as for glads. Plants may need some support, either stake them if you grow them in rows for cutting, or use a grid-filled peony hoop available from your garden center. The sword-like leaves are susceptible to fusarium wilt so try to avoid wetting them when watering — water the soil, not the plants. If you want to use ixia for bouquets, cut when the lowest two flowers on the stem show color.

Ixia blooms in spring over several weeks. Two-inch flowers are usually rose, red, orange, yellow, or cream. All have a dark center. Flowers come at the ends of long, wirey, 2-foot stems.

Early flowering cultivars include:

- ❀ **'Panorama'** is white with purplish-red markings.
- ❀ **'Rose Emperor'** produces soft pink flowers.
- ❀ **'Spotlight'** has yellow-red flowers.
- ❀ **'Titia'** has fuchsia-red blossoms.
- ❀ **'Venus'** flowers are magenta-red.

Later-flowering cultivars, also more suitable for marginal (that means spring-planted in cold-winter regions) areas, include:

- ❀ **'Castor'** is purple to reddish purple.
- ❀ **'Giant,'** with dark-centered flowers, offers petals with ivory-white tips.
- ❀ **'Hogarth'** is cream-colored and dark-centered.
- ❀ **'Marquette'** produces distinctive sulphur-yellow flowers with purple-black centers.
- ❀ **'Paradijsvogel'** ('Bird of Paradise') is yellow-red.
- ❀ **'Vulcan'** is orange-red.

Plant in fall and cover corms with 3 to 4 inches of soil.

Ornithogalum

Ornithogalums are a diverse group of South African and Mediterranean bulbs that includes some of the most resilient cut flowers in the world.

Flowers are usually white and 1 to 2 inches in diameter. They bloom in spring for several weeks atop 1- to 2-foot stems. In mild winter areas, plant bulbs in fall in a location that receives full sun or partial shade, and cover them with 2 inches of soil.

The bulbs in this section are not winter hardy, except for one variety. The only hardy ornithogalum, star of Bethlehem, *Ornithogalum umbellatum,* is a vigorous, freely multiplying thug that we suspect is capable of growing through asphalt. Hardy in regions where winter temperatures regularly dip to zero degrees Fahrenheit and below, it produces 1-inch-diameter white flowers on a 1 foot stem. It naturalizes like a champ, so much so that some gardeners consider it a weed. Also, its flowers close at night and reopen only in late morning, which makes it less desirable as a cut flower.

"Chincherinchee" is the common name of *Ornithogalum thyrsoides,* which is perhaps one of the all-star cut flowers of the world. Bulbs produce one, two, or even three stems with pyramid-shaped clusters of white flowers that remain attractive for up to three weeks after cutting. Suitable for warm, subtropical regions, the bulbs are not hardy in cold winter areas. Plant from mid-March to mid-May for summer bloom, and then lift them from the ground at the approach of frost. By the way, "Chincherinchee" is said to be the sound the flowers make when rustled by wind.

Ornithogalum saundersiae and *O. arabicum* have creamy white flowers in an umbel (the individual flower stems arise from a common point, like Queen Anne's lace). *O. arabicum* is further accented with a black ovary at the center of each flower. Bulbs should be planted 5 inches to base in a moisture-retentive soil, and located in a sunny site. By far the most tender is *Ornithogalum dubium.* It produces highly desirable orange or yellow flowers. New intergeneric hybrids, such as 'Chesapeake Blaze,' are becoming available that combine the best qualities of this species with chincherinchee and others.

For cut flower use, pick an *Ornithogalum* when the three lower flowers on the stem have colored.

Ranunculus

If you live where winters are cool and rainy and summers are dry, you must grow ranunculus *(Ranunculus asiaticus).* The brightly colored flowers — white, yellow, pink, gold, orange, and red — look like miniature double peonies. They make excellent cut flowers, lasting a week or more indoors in a vase.

The plant is native to Asia Minor, centering around Cyprus, Aleppo, and Damascus. It was first popularized by the Sultan of Constantinople, a man with an eye for the finer things of life, including garden plants. By the 1700s, plants were common in France and England.

The ranunculus is not winter hardy in cold regions; for best flowering, it prefers an extended spring with a long, cool growing season. Summer's heat ends flowering quickly. If you live in a frost-free area, plant tuberous roots (they look like a collection of little claws) in fall. Dutch growers raising them for cut-flower use soak the roots for a couple of hours before planting, to quicken their growth. But it is important to make sure that the site has well-drained soil, because the roots are prone to rot if kept constantly wet. Cover crowns with 1 to 2 inches of soil, and space the tubers about 3 inches apart. If you live where winters are too cold, plant one root per 4-inch pot indoors 2 months before the last frost.

Sparaxis — Harlequin Flower

Sparaxis, harlequin flower, is a hot-colored, showy little bulb that is ideally suited for naturalizing in frost-free winter, dry-summer regions. A native of South Africa, it is a resilient plant that happily competes with tree roots for space and nutrients. Multicolored, 1-inch diameter flowers of red, yellow, and black come on 1-foot stems in late spring, and they last several weeks.

Plant the $1/2$-inch-diameter corms in fall, about 5 inches deep to base and 2 inches apart, in well-drained soil. If winter rains are spare, be sure to water the plants while they are actively growing.

Check out these varieties:

- ❀ **'Alba Maxima'** has pure white flowers with a yellow center.
- ❀ **'Fire King'** produces orange-scarlet flowers with a yellow center accented with black.
- ❀ **'Horning'** is a vivid wine-purple with a large purple blotch at the base of each petal and a yellow center.
- ❀ **'Robert Schumann'** has white flowers striped red outside with dark blotches at the petals' base.

Zephyranthes — Rain Lily

Like the other bulbs listed in this chapter, zephyranthes, the rain lily, needs mild winter temperatures in order to thrive. But unlike all the others, it does very well with summer rains.

This diminutive charmer is native to the western hemisphere. In size and character, it is reminiscent of a crocus. White, yellow, pink, and rose flowers appear in summer and fall, often shortly after a summer shower (the reason for its common name). Flowers are 1 to 2 inches in diameter. They come one each atop 6-inch, wiry stems.

Plant rain lily in spring, spacing the tiny bulbs about 2 inches apart. Sometimes you can find plants growing and blooming in containers. You can plant these just as you would any container plant.

Zephyranthes grandiflora is often confused with *Habranthus robustus;* both have crocus-like rosy-pink flowers in summer. *Zephyranthes candida* is an autumn-flowering species with white flowers. And late summer-blooming *Zephyranthes citrina* has golden-yellow flowers. There's even a native North American species, the attractive summer-blooming, white-flowering atamasco lily, *Zephyranthes atamasco,* which grows wild in Virginia, Florida, Alabama, and Mississippi.

Part VII
Appendixes

The 5th Wave   By Rich Tennant

"The next time you order flowering bulbs, I suggest you have them express mailed."

In this part . . .

*L*ook both ways and step onto the information highway. In these appendixes, we give you resources to help you grow bulbs. We include a list of mail-order suppliers and, in case this book whetted your appetite for more, we give you a list of sources for more information on bulbs.

Appendix A
Where to Buy Bulbs

• •

*H*ere are mail-order companies where you're likely to find rare, obscure, and very special bulbs. If you want to know everything there is to know about one type of bulb or another, you can find the perfect jumping-off point in the catalogs listed here.

U.S. Bulb Suppliers — Specialists

A Thousand Alliums, 3915 S.W. Willow, Seattle, WA 98136; phone 206-935-7506. Catalog $2. Allium specialists offering over 30 species and cultivars.

Antonelli Brothers Begonia Gardens and Floral Design, 2545 Capitola Rd., Santa Cruz, CA 95062; phone 408-475-5222/888-423-4664, fax 408-475-7066; Web site www.infopoint.com/sc/market/antnelli. Begonias, ranunculus, dahlias, glads, lilies, and other summer-flowering bulbs.

B & D Lilies, P.O. Box 2007, 330 P St., Port Townsend, WA 98368; phone 360-385-1738, fax 360-385-9996. Catalog $3. Full assortment of species and hybrid lilies and daylilies.

Bonnie Brae Gardens, 1105 S.E. Christensen Dr., Corbett, OR 97019; phone 503-695-5190. For catalog send long self-addressed stamped envelope. Novelty daffodils and dwarf bulbs.

Cascade Daffodils, P.O. Box 10626, White Bear Lake, MN 55110; phone 612-426-9616; e-mail davekarn@aol.com. Catalog $2. A broad selection of novelty daffodils.

Grant Mitsch Novelty Daffodils, P.O. Box 218, Hubbard, OR 97032; phone 503-651-2742, fax 503-651-2792; Web site www.web-ster.com/havensr/mitsch/locate.htm, e-mail havensr@web-ster.com. Catalog $3. Rare hybrids of daffodils and other spring-blooming bulbs.

Jim Duggan Flower Nursery, 1452 Santa Fe Dr., Encinitas, CA 92024; phone 760-943-1658; Web site www.thebulbman.com, e-mail jimsflowers@thebulbman.com. Catalog $2. A specialist in dry garden and South African bulbs for warm climates, as well as dwarf, fall, spring, and summer bloomers.

Kelly's Plant World, 10266 E. Princeton, Sanger, CA 93657; phone 209-294-7676. Catalog $1. Tender summer blooming bulbs and rare, unusual bulbs from around the world.

Nancy Wilson Species & Miniature Narcissus, 6525 Briceland Thorn Rd., Garberville, CA 95542; phone 707-923-2407, fax 707-923-2407; e-mail nwilson@asis.com. Catalog $1. Dry garden bulbs, dwarf and species narcissus.

Neglected Bulbs, P.O. Box 2768, Berkeley, CA 94702; Web site members.aol.com/Nglctdblbs/index.html, e-mail nglctdblbs@aol.com. For catalog, send long self-addressed stamped envelope. Native California bulbs and dry garden bulbs.

Old House Gardens, 536 Third St., Ann Arbor, MI 48103; phone 313-995-1486, fax 313-995-1486; e-mail OHGBulbs@aol.com. Catalog $2. A choice of antique bulbs and heritage bulbs such as tulips, daffodils, and hyacinths, some from the 19th century.

Pleasant Valley Glads & Dahlias, P.O. Box 494, 87 Edward St., Agawam, MA 01001; phone 413-789-0307; Web site agawam.net/pvglads, e-mail webmaster@agawam.net. Catalog $1. Wide selection of glads and dahlias.

The Waushara Gardens, N5491 5th Dr., Plainfield, WI 54966; phone 715-335-4462, fax 715-335-4462. Catalog free. Selection of summer bloomers such as glads, dahlias, callas, and hybrid lilies.

Trans-Pacific Nursery, 16065 Oldsville Rd., McMinnville, OR 97128; fax 503-434-1505; Web site www.worldplants.com/tphome.htm, e-mail groe@wordplants.com. Catalog $2. South African bulbs.

U.S. Bulb Suppliers — Generalists

The following mail-order companies all offer a wide selection of flowering bulbs. Also note that many mail-order sources of vegetable and flower seeds, and perennials also offer bulbs in their catalogs.

Borbeleta Gardens, 15980 Canby Ave., Faribault, MN 55021; phone 507-334-2807, fax 507-334-0365; Web site www.deskmedia.com/~aerickso/borbeleta. Catalog $3. An assortment of flower bulbs.

Breck's, 6523 N. Galena Rd., Peoria, IL 61632; phone 800-722-9069, fax 800-991-2852; Web site www.gardensolutions.com/cgi-bin/WebObjects/GardenSolutions. Catalog free. Full selection of bulbs, offering an especially large number of spring-blooming bulbs.

Charles H. Mueller Co., 7091 N. River Rd., New Hope, PA 18938; phone 215-862-2033, fax 215-862-3696. Catalog $1. A broad selection of flower bulbs.

Dutch Gardens, P.O. Box 200, Adelphia, NJ 07710; phone 800-818-3861, fax 732-780-7720; Web site www.dutchgardens.nl, e-mail cs@dutchgardens.nl. Catalog free. A full assortment of high-quality spring and summer-blooming bulbs, and a full color catalog.

French's Bulb Importer, P.O. Box 565, Pittsfield, VT 05762; phone 802-746-8148/800-286-8198. Catalog free. A selection of fall-planted flower bulbs including hyacinths, freesias, tulips, daffodils, and ranunculus. Precooled bulbs for indoor forcing.

Holland Bulb Farms, P.O. Box 220, Tatamy, PA 18085; phone 800-283-5082; Web site www.hollandbulbs.com. Catalog free. A wide range of bulbs.

Jacques Amand, Bulb Specialists, P.O. Box 59001, Potomac, MD 20859; phone 800-452-5414, fax 800-452-5414; Web site www.bulbjam.com, e-mail Jamand@bulbjam.com. Catalog $2. A wonderful assortment of flowering bulbs.

John Scheepers, Inc., 23 Tulip Dr., Bantam, CT 06750; phone 860-567-0838, fax 860-567-5323; Web site www.johnscheepers.com. Catalog free. A good selection of spring- and summer-blooming bulbs.

Langeveld Bulb Company, Web site www.langeveld.com. Web site includes plant information, planting guide, gardening links, and retail sales locator.

McClure & Zimmerman, P.O. Box 368, 108 W. Winnebago, Friesland, WI 53935; phone 920-326-4220, fax 800-692-5864. A good source of uncommon as well as familiar bulbs, including species.

Schipper & Co., P.O. Box 7584, Greenwich, CT 06836; phone 888-847-8637/ 203-625-0638, fax 203-862-8909; e-mail schipper@colorblends.com, Web site www.colorblends.com. Catalog $1. "Colorblend" (bulb sets in complementary colors) collections of bulbs.

Spring Hill Nurseries Co., 6523 N. Galena Rd., Peoria, IL 61632; phone 800-544-0294; Web site www.gardensolutions.com/cgi-bin/WebObjects/ GardenSolutions. Catalog free. A wide assortment of bulbs.

The Bulb Crate, 2560 Deerfield Rd., Riverwoods, IL 60015; phone 847-317-1414, fax 847-317-1417; e-mail abulb@aol.com. Catalog $1. Offer fall, spring, and summer flowering bulbs.

The Daffodil Mart, 30 Irene St. Torrington, CT 06790; phone 800-255-2852, fax 800-420-2852. Catalog free. An impressive assortment of daffodils and other bulbs.

Van Bourgondien Bros., P.O. Box 1000, 245 Farmingdale Rd., Route 109, Babylon, NY 11702; phone 800-622-9997, fax 516-669-1228; e-mail blooms@dutchbulbs.com. Web site www.dutchbulbs.com. Catalog free. An excellent selection of most bulbs.

Van Dyck's Flower Farms, Inc., P.O. Box 430, Brightwaters, NY 11718; phone 800-248-2852, fax 516-669-3518; Web site www.vandycks.com, e-mail jan@vandycks.com. Catalog free. A full assortment of spring blooming bulbs (tulips, hyacinths, crocus, and so on).

Van Engelen, Inc., 23 Tulip Dr., Bantam, CT 06750; phone 860-567-8734, fax 860-567-5323; Web site www.vanengelen.com. Catalog free. Dutch bulbs in bulk quantities ($50 minimum order).

Veldheer Tulip Gardens, 12755 Quincy St., Holland, MI 49424; phone 616-399-1900, fax 616-399-1270; Web site www.veldheertulip.com. Catalog free. A full assortment of domestic and imported bulbs.

Wayside Gardens, 1 Garden Lane, Hodges, SC 29695; phone 800-845-1124, fax 800-457-9712; Web site www.waysidegardens.com, orders@waysidegardens.com e-mail info@woodenshoe.com. Catalog $1. A wide assortment of bulbs.

Wooden Shoe Bulb Company, 33814 S. Meridian Rd., Woodburn, OR 97071; phone 800-711-2006/503-634-2243, fax 503-634-2710; Web site www.woodenshoe.com, e-mail info@woodenshoe.com. Catalog free. Spring-flowering bulbs.

Canadian Bulb Suppliers

Aimers Seeds, Aimers Seeds, R.R.3, Ilderton, Ontario Canada N0M 2A0, phone 905-833-0282, Web site www.aimers.on.ca/first.html, e-mail bill.aimers@odyssey.on.ca. For catalog send long self-addressed stamped envelope. Features an assortment of bulbs.

Cruickshank Ltd., 780 Birchmont Rd., Unit 16, Scarborough, Ontario M1K 5H4; phone 416-750-9249, fax 416-750-8522. Catalog $2. A full range of flowering bulbs.

Fraser's Thimble Farm, 175 Arbutus Rd., Salt Spring Island, BC V8K 1A3; phone 250-537-5788, fax 250-537-5788; e-mail thimble@saltspring.com. Catalog $2. Dry garden and species bulbs, many Pacific Northwest natives.

Gardenimport, Inc., P.O. Box 760, Thornhill, Ontario L3T 4A5; phone 800-339-8314/905-731-1950, fax 905-881-3499; Web site www.gardenimport.com, e-mail flower@gardenimport.com, Catalog $5. A full assortment of flowering bulbs.

U.K. Bulb Suppliers

Avon Bulbs, Burnt House Farm, Mid-Lambrook, South Petherton, Somerset, England TA13 5HE. Catalog $5 (U.S.). Dwarf, species, fall- and summer-blooming bulbs.

Broadleigh Gardens, Bishop's Hull, Taunton, Somerset, England TA4 1AE. Specializes in dwarf bulbs: crocuses, fritillaria species, tulips, irises, hyacinths, and daffodils as well as other dwarf rarities.

Paul Christian Rare Plants, P.O. Box 468, Wrexham, United Kingdom LL13 9EP; phone 44 01978 366399, fax 44 01978 266466; Web site www.rareplants.co.uk, e-mail paul@rareplants.co.uk Catalog $5. Wonderful selection of rare bulbs, corms, tubers, dry garden bulbs, dwarf bulbs, South African, species, spring- and summer-blooming.

Monocot Nursery, Jacklands, Jacklands Bridge, Tickenham, Clevedon, Avon, England BS21 6SG. Catalog $3 (U.S.). A great selection of species bulbs as well as dwarf, South African, spring-, summer-, and fall-blooming bulbs.

Potterton & Martin, The Cottage Nursery, Moortown Rd., Nettleton, Caistor, Lincolnshire, England LN7 6HX; phone 01472 851714 Fax 01472 852580, International phone : 44 1472 851714, International fax 44 1472 852580; Web site www.users.globalnet.co.uk/~pottin01/index.html, e-mail pottin01@globalnet.co.uk. Catalog $6. Specializing in dwarf bulbs; species; and spring-, summer-, and fall-bloomers.

South African Bulb Suppliers

Rust-En-Vrede Nursery, P.O. Box 753, 7560 Brackenfell, South Africa; phone 021 981-4515, fax 021 981-0050. Catalog $2 (U.S.). Dry garden bulbs, dwarf, South African, spring- and summer-blooming, and tender bulbs for serious collectors.

Silverhill Seeds, P.O. Box 53108, Kenilworth, 7745 Cape Town, South Africa; phone 021 762-4245, fax 021 797-6609, International phone 27 21 762-4245, International fax 27 21 797-6609; Web site vvv.com/~amdigest/silvrhil.htm e-mail rachel@silverhillseeds.co.za. Catalog $2 (U.S.). Large selection of South African dwarf and dry garden bulbs.

Appendix B
Information Sources for Inquiring Gardeners

• •

*I*n case we have whetted your appetite for more information about bulbs, we provide in this appendix some suggestions for additional books to read. You can find recommendations for a few basic bulb books as well as some books about specific bulbs and related subjects.

General Bulb Books

Byran, John E. *Bulbs: Volume I, A-H, Volume II, I-Z*. Portland, Oregon: Timber Press, 1989. Expensive two-volume set of hardcover books for fanatic bulb fanciers.

Byran, John E. editor. *Bulbs*. New York: Hearst Books, 1992. Hardcover bulb book in the Hearst Garden Guide series.

Glattstein, Judy. *The American Gardener's World of Bulbs*. New York: Little, Brown and Company, 1994. Bulbs for all seasons for gardens across the United States (hardcover).

Mathew, Brian. *The Year-Round Bulb Garden*. London: Souvenir Press, 1986. British hardcover book on bulbs for all seasons.

Rix, Martyn and Roger Phillips. *The Bulb Book*. New York: Random House. Paperback book with photographs showing flowers and bulbs. No gardening information but a great way to compare different daffodils, tulips, and so on.

Scott, George Harmon. *Bulbs: How to Select, Grow and Enjoy*. Los Angeles: HP Books, a division of Price, Stern, Sloan, 1982. Paperback book offering basic information.

The Time-Life Gardener's Guide. *Bulbs*. Alexandria, Virginia: Time-Life Books. Hardcover book offering basic information.

Books on Specific Bulbs

Anderton, Eric and Ron Park. *Growing Gladioli*. Portland, Oregon: Timber Press, 1989. Hardcover book all about gladioli.

Blanchard, John W. *Narcissus, A Guide to Wild Daffodils*. Alpine Garden Society, 1990. Hardcover British book all about wild daffodils.

Damp, Philip. *Dahlias*. London: Century, 1987. Slim hardcover British book all about dahlias.

Davies, Dilys. *Alliums, The Ornamental Onions*. Portland, Oregon: Timber Press, 1992. Hardcover book with extensive information about ornamental onions (by a British author).

Doutt, Richard L. *Cape Bulbs*. Portland, Oregon: Timber Press, 1994. Hardcover book all about the tender (nonhardy) bulbs of the South African Cape.

Elliot, Jack. *Bulbs for the Rock Garden*. Portland, Oregon: Timber Press, 1997. Hardcover book by a British expert on bulbs for four seasons in the rock garden and cold greenhouse.

Grey-Wilson, Christopher. *The Genus Cyclamen*. Portland, Oregon: Timber Press, 1988. American edition of a hardcover, rather technical book on cyclamens by a British expert.

Heath, Brent and Becky Heath. *Daffodils for American Gardens*. Washington, D.C.: Elliott & Clark Publishing, Inc., 1995. Hardcover book by two experts and former owners of The Daffodil Mart bulb nursery — all about daffodils.

Jefferson-Brown, Michael and Harris Howland. *The Gardener's Guide to Growing Lilies*. Portland, Oregon: Timber Press, 1995. Hardcover book all about lilies (by a British expert).

Killingback, Stanley. *Tulips*. Secaucus, New Jersey: Chartwell Books, Inc., 1990. Slim hardcover book offering basic information about tulips (by a British author).

Mathews, Brian. *The Crocus*. Portland, Oregon: Timber Press, 1983. American edition of a hardcover, rather technical book all about crocuses (by a British expert).

Ogden, Scott. *Garden Bulbs for the South*. Dallas, Texas: Taylor Publishing Company, 1994. Hardcover book about bulb-growing in mild-winter areas.

Pratt, Kevin and Michael Jefferson-Brown. *The Gardener's Guide to Growing Fritillaries*. Portland, Oregon: Timber Press, 1997. American edition of gardener-friendly hardcover book about fritillaries (by a British expert).

Proctor, Rob. *The Indoor Potted Bulb* and *The Outdoor Potted Bulb*. New York: Simon & Schuster, 1993. Two pleasant little hardcover volumes on growing bulbs in pots, baskets, boxes, and more.

Trawling the World Wide Web

The Internet and the World Wide Web provide a wealth of information and images for gardening enthusiasts. You should enjoy the following sites. Be sure to check out links that provide good information for bulb enthusiasts:

`www.bulb.com` takes you to the Web site of the U.S. Netherlands Flower Bulb Information Center, the U.S. press office of the Dutch flower bulb industry. This site has lots of links to other neat bulb sites, and includes information on forcing bulbs, naturalizing, bulb guides, and frequently asked questions.

`www.bulbsociety.com` takes you to the Web site of the International Bulb Society, where you can find a trowel-ful of information, including bulb lore, book reviews, bulb and seed sources, and a gallery of bulbs.

You can reach the American Daffodil Society Web page at `www.mc.edu/~adswww`.

GardenNet, at `gardennet.com`, contains articles on gardening and a guide to gardens in the U.S.A.

You can join GardenEscape (for free) at `www.garden.com` and take advantage of customized shopping, a Virtual Garden Club, and lots of information.

The National Gardening Association site at `www.garden.org` includes an online version of *National Gardening* magazine along with information about educational outreach programs and research services.

The Garden Gate at `www.prairienet.org/ag/garden` has links to some of the Web's best gardening sites.

The Virtual Garden, Time Warner's Garden site at pathfinder.com/vg, has online magazines, a plant encyclopedia you can search, and lots more.

The GardenWeb at www.gardenweb.com has plant forums on anything you care to name, including a lively one on, what else!, bulbs. It also has a calendar of garden events, links to GardenWeb Europe and Australia, a merchant directory, and other useful information.

Index

fungicides, 258
'Fuseau', 216. *See also* Jerusalem
    artichokes
'Fusilier', 80. *See also* tulips
Futurity dwarf cannas, 162. *See also*
    cannas

• *G* •

Galanthus nivalis, 33, 289. *See also*
    snowdrops
garden centers, 234–235
Garden Gate Web site, 311
Garden Jargon icon, 6
garden planning, 19–21
GardenEscape Web site, 311
Gardening Tip icon, 6
GardenNet Web site, 311
GardenWeb Web site, 312
garlic, 199–200. *See also* elephant garlic
'General Köhler', 90, 273, 288. *See also*
    hyacinths
genus names, typography, 5
'George', 105. *See also* iris
'Georgette', 80. *See also* tulips
'Georgia Jets', 213. *See also* sweet
    potatoes
'Geranium', 63. *See also* daffodils
'Germa', 175. *See also* amaryllis
    (Hippeastrum)
'German Red', 200. *See also* garlic
'Giant'
  African corn lily, 297
  colchicum, 188
giant allium, 230. *See also* ornamental
    onions
giant snowdrop, 43. *See also* snowdrops
giant snowflake, 117. *See also* summer
    snowflakes
'Gipsey Princess', 273. *See also* hyacinths
'Gipsy Queen', 90. *See also* hyacinths
'Gladiator', 145. *See also* ornamental
    onions

gladiolus
  about, 149–150
  butterfly, 151–152
  choosing by color, 150–151
  companion plants, 154
  cormels, 252
  cut flowers, 153, 266
  dividing, 252
  growing tips, 152
  hardiness, 152–153
  peacock lily, 154, 238
  planting, 153
  storing, 154, 238
Gladiolus callianthus, 154. *See also*
    gladiolus
Gladiolus nanus, 152. *See also* gladiolus
'Globemaster', 145. *See also* ornamental
    onions
glory of the snow, 32, 98–100
'Gold Band', 138. *See also* lilies
'Golden Apeldoorn', 72. *See also* tulips
'Golden Harvest', 108. *See also* iris
'Golden Melody', 73. *See also* tulips
gophers, 259
'Governor', 295
gracilis amaryllis, 174–175. *See also*
    amaryllis *(Hippeastrum)*
grades of daffodils, 65
'Grand Paradiso', 134. *See also* lilies
'Grande Monarque', 288. *See also* heirloom
    bulbs
'Granex 33', 198. *See also* kitchen gardens
grape hyacinths. *See also* hyacinths
  choosing bulbs, 94–95
  companion plants, 95–96
  container gardens, 225
  cut flowers, 268
  forcing, 276
  multiplying, 93
  naturalistic gardens, 22
  planting, 95
'Gravetye Giant', 117. *See also* summer
    snowflakes
gray mold, 260

• S •

Notes